PERSON IN COSMOS

Metaphors of Meaning from Physics, Philosophy and Theology

Kevin O'Shea

FOREWORD by W. Norris Clarke, SJ
Fordham University

Wyndham Hall Press

PERSON IN COSMOS
Metaphors of Meaning from Physics, Philosophy and Theology

by Kevin O'Shea

Library of Congress Catalog Card Number

95-061960

International Standard Book Number

1-55605-264-2 (cloth)
1-55605-263-4 (paper)

Wyndham Hall Press
Bristol, IN   46507-9460

GENESIS

In the beginning God created the heavens and the earth.
Now the earth was a formless void,
there was darkness over the deep.
and God's spirit hovered over the water.
God said, 'Let there be light', and there was light.

Jerusalem Bible

In antiquity the Lord created the heavens and the earth.
Now the earth was desolate and empty
and darkness was on the face of the deep
and a wind from before the Lord was blowing on the surface of the water.
And the Lord said, 'Let there be light',
and there was light.

Targum Onkelos

From the beginning with wisdom the Son of the Lord
perfected the heavens and the earth.
And the earth was empty and without form,
and desolate
without a son of man or beast
and void of all cultivation of plants and trees.
And darkness was spread over the face of the abyss,
and a spirit of love from before the Lord was blowing
over the face of the waters.
And the Word of the Lord said: Let there be light,
and there was light according to the decree of his Word.

Targum Neofiti

At the beginning God created the heaven and the earth.
And the earth was waste and void,
desolate without the sons of men, and empty of animals.
And darkness was upon the face of the deep,
and the spirit of mercies from before God
blew upon the face of the waters.
And God said, 'Let there be light to lighten the world'.
And immediately there was light.

Targum Pseudo-Jonathan

PREFACE

Forty years ago, in the course of doctoral studies in systematic theology, I stumbled on the mystery of relationship.[1]

I have been stumbling on it ever since.

Above all, in teaching theology in Australia and elsewhere, especially to my fellow Redemptorists. Then in complementary studies in psychoanalytic philosophy, and in theoretical physics. And, recently, in an increasing conviction that 'person' was at the heart of relationship, and should be at the centre of theology.

I am grateful for thirty years of teaching opportunities in North America, especially at Fordham University, New York, (in the Graduate School of Religion and Religious Education), and more recently at the University of Notre Dame, Indiana, (in the Summer Institute of Retreats International).

From Redemptorist teachers I have learned the theological primacy of the paschal mystery and the divine missions. From Norris Clarke, at Fordham, I have learned how metaphysics and the study of the person can be the same thing. From the writings of David Burrell, of Notre Dame, I have learned to retrieve the thought of Aquinas and link it to contemporary discussion. To all of them, my thanks.

This book is a first contribution to a personalist theology in an interdisciplinary mode.

Kevin O'Shea
November 1994

NOTES

1. Published as *The Human Activity of the Word*, a study in the theandric act and the hypostatic union, Thomist Press, Washington DC, 1959.

FOREWORD

I am happy and privileged to introduce this remarkable book, not the least because it has made such creative use of my own philosophical explorations in "creative retrieval" of Thomistic metaphysics. *Person in Cosmos* takes on the daring project of bringing together for mutual illumination the world vision of modern science (in its larger lines, of course) and that of traditional Christian theology, mediated by a realistic, streamlined, Thomistically inspired philosophy. Except for a small number of creative Christian thinkers, Christian theology in the past has gone along its own way, with its won internal dialogue, quite independent of and unconcerned with the vast developments of modern science, in particular physics and biology.

But this is not a satisfactory situation, either for Christian theology--and its appropriate philosophies--or for the humanistic dimension of science itself. Our universe is *one* universe, created in its material and spiritual dimensions by one and the same Creator or Ultimate Source of being. In a participation universe like this it would be natural to expect various affinities resonating between the different levels of being, including the primary division between matter and spirit, and divine itself. To bring to light for reflection these large affinities, especially the veiled intimations of the higher in the lower, is precisely the work of this book. And despite the tentative and controversial character of many of its conclusions and suggestions, I think it carries out its task brilliantly.

It first sets the limits of each mode of discourse, with the ambiguities that spring up as each mode nears its own limits and tends to spill over into the next by the momentum of its own search. Then it searches for the large affinities of common laws at work on all or several levels. Thus one great common law of being as it unfolds itself on all levels, it seems, is the complementary law of diversification from an original unity, on the one hand, matched by the reverse movement toward convergence, on the other, tending toward integration of the diverse units into larger systems and wholes.

This holds true on all levels: (1) on the basic physical level from the original Big Bang in (almost) undifferentiated unity, where all physical laws are collapsed into one, to the gradual formation of increasingly complex galactic and planetary systems; (2) on the biological level from the primeval one-celled organism to the unimaginably complex system of the human brain and its body; (3) on the level of human persons, the first level of spiritual being, from their original beginning. Hidden so far for us in the mists of time, to the ever widening and more complex social organizations of humans tending toward global integration in political organizations like the UN, the World Bank, etc., spiritual ones such as international religions and Churches, as well as the more intimate relations between persons, such as love and friendship, in a word, the communion of persons in all its forms; (4) finally, even on the divine level, in the Christian theology of God as Triune in Persons, flowering out within the unity of the one Godhead.

The author then examines the light that each discipline can shed on fundamental questions like the beginning and possible ends of our universe, with the inherent ambiguities as each reaches the limits of its competence, leaving metaphor, he suggests, to bridge the gap. The author's hints here as to what might be the nature of a God who would create and work with such a universe are controversial indeed, but highly suggestive and stimulating.

The overall intention of the book, the author explains, is thus *informative*, for both sides of the discussion; *critical* as regards the language and tools used by each, with their limits; *constructive*, by illuminating one discipline through another; *synthetic*, "in the hope of demonstrating a convergence of ultimate reference in the various disciplines whole allowing them to retain their own distinctiveness and autonomy; and *imaginative*, in the use of suggestive metaphor to convey a hint of meaning, often half understood," to bridge the gaps between them.

The author has amazingly wide command of the large lines of both the sciences, on the one hand, and the tradition of Christian philosophy and theology--specifically the Thomistically inspired one--on the other. However much one may go along with the various conclusions and suggestions of the author, no one can sympathetically read such a book and not be enriched by it as by few others.

W. Norris Clarke, S.J.
Professor Emeritus of Philosophy
Fordham University

INTRODUCTION

Science is strangely becoming a collaborator with spiritual vision, to disclose a more complete picture of our place and destiny in the world. Physics is throwing light on the origin, the end, the history and the meaning of the universe. Many physicists are fascinated by the beauty and the mystery of the cosmos they are discovering, and, to make personal sense of it, are using language that can only be called spiritual. At times they seem disappointed that official religious institutions do not seem to share their experience of awe in the presence of ultimacy, and chide the theologians for lack of reverence.

Serious *theology* is experiencing a need for a new integrity in relation to the findings of the scientific community, a new willingness to dialogue with physicists and to learn their language, and a new sense of adventure in the attempt to say something pertinent both to the tradition of the past and the questions of the present.

On each side of the encounter, there are *real questions*. The *theologians*, and the religious community generally, tend to ask:

What *is* the 'New Physics'?

Does it make *religious claims*, or affect religious beliefs?

How does science describe the *beginnings* of the cosmos?

What is the *'Big Bang'*?

Does science claim that the cosmos *started itself*, so that there would be no need for a Creator?

How will, in scientific prognosis, the cosmos *end*?

Will it end?

If it doesn't, *what would it be like*?

What are things *made up of*?

How do things *work*?

What are the *basic forces* in nature?

Where do *humans* fit in?

Is there a kind of *contemplation* in nature itself?

How sure are we of our answers?

The *physicists*, and the scientific community generally, tend to ask:-

Do the principles of theology *touch reality*, or remain at an abstract level 'above' it?

Can theology *allow for* the persuasions of the New Physics?

What does *creation* really mean, theologically?

Does theology demand *a literal belief* in the end of the world, and, when it talks of resurrection, what sort of physical world does it assume for the bodies that rise?

Does *God leave the cosmos alone*, to operate on its own lines, or does God frequently *act 'from outside'* the cosmos to influence its history and development?

What sort of God does theology really talk about?

Is the scientific perspective of the new physics *compatible* with belief in that God?

In many ways, physics is asking questions that go beyond physics, while theology is asking questions that go beyond theology. To probe some common ground in this common interest, there is need to invoke the mediation of *philosophy*. It is philosophy's role to ask what ultimately the various disciplines of human thought are 'really' saying, and to weave from the results a larger vision. The particular philosophy which helps best, is called realism: it is interested in what is really real, and in how different disciplines speak of it. To do that, it has to be *critical*, both of claims that assert too much (because they get lost in idealist vision without testing it against the real) and of claims that assert too little (because they stop at the material description of phenomena without probing into their deeper reality). It functions as a *moderator* in its own domestic and intramural disputes, but only to bring out the full truth of all reality.

This philosophy of *critical moderate realism* is pre-eminently that of *St.Thomas Aquinas*. Our understanding of it has been progressively purified in the course of this century, which has undertaken a real *retrieval* of the historical position of the saint, and as a result has been *open* to the use of his thought in dialogue with other significant philosophies. Two of these, of particular relevance to the new cosmic physics, are philosophies of *participation* and philosophies of *process*. Participation is one way of conceiving things as different within a unity; process is one way of conceiving the underflow of things towards the fullness of their own reality.

The result has been a willingness, on the part of these philosophers, to think differently about the meaning of *relationship*. No focus could be more central to the interests of modern physics and cosmology. Profound work has been done on the relationships *between persons*, and on the relationship of the *cosmos with the Creator*. The insights of both are not far from the insights of physicists on the relationships that obtain *within the material cosmos* itself.

At Fordham University, New York, W.Norris Clarke has developed a philosophy of relationship between persons: *Person and Being*.[1] At the University of Notre Dame, Indiana, David B.Burrell has developed a philosophy of relationship between the cosmos and the Creator: *Freedom and Creation in Three Traditions*.[2] Many physicists who are attempting to integrate relativity, quantum, self-organisation, and field theories, are presenting an understanding of relationship within the material cosmos. Their common mood is exemplified in the proceedings of recent interdisciplinary *symposia at the Vatican Observatory*,[3] and of the *European Society for the Study of Science and Theology*.[4]

These trajectories do not quite meet. Clarke has worked more with person than with cosmos. Burrell has worked with the bond between creature and Creator, more than with the bond between creature and creature. The recent physicists either do not philosophise on their data, or use philosophies of participation (like Plato) or of process (like Whitehead), and have relatively little knowledge of the realist philosophies mentioned.

The *intention* of this study is to facilitate the dialogue between physics and theology, by presenting a philosophy that can hear both sides. It will try to do so by standing in the critical, moderate realist tradition of Aquinas, that is, of those who have retrieved his historical positions and as a result are open to new questions in contemporary culture, especially questions about participation, process, and relationship.[5] It will in particular stand in the footsteps of Norris Clarke and David Burrell. To enter into dialogue with the physicists, it will attempt to write a minor footnote to the metaphysical text they have given us.

The footnote is mainly about *metaphor*.

My suspicion has been that Clarke and Burrell, while rigorously sustaining the proper language of metaphysics, have opened the door to the *use of metaphor* to describe the mystery of being, which is the proper object of metaphysics. I would like to go through that door, and *find more metaphors*. I would like to look for them as implicit in the work of the physicists, harness them to the work of metaphysics, and then use them as mediators between physics, and theology.

I shall work with *five basic metaphors*: communion, music, emergence, presence, and joy.

Using these insights as instruments, I would then wish to retrieve some major themes of an older biblical-Patristic *theology*: the theology of death, the theology of the paschal mystery, the theology of covenant and communion, and the theology of the mission of the divine persons of the trinity.

My hope would be to make it clear that the *referent* of the metaphors implicit in the language of the physicists, and the *referent* of the metaphors implicit in the almost mystical language of the old theological tradition, can cohere.

This approach will allow us to perform a critical analysis of the inherent *ambiguity* of the *language* of the scientific community, and of the different *ambiguity* of the *language* of the religious community. The linguistic roots of apparent contradictions can then be understood, with sympathy.

Chapter 1 will introduce the general message of the physicists, and the general points at which it engages the principles of the realist philosophical tradition. It will then present a historical outline of theology's pondering of the cosmos, and put the present theological interest in it, in a larger context. It will spell out the limits of the language of all these disciplines, and suggest a path of *metaphor* as a way beyond their limits. The metaphor of *'communion'* will be introduced.

Chapter 2 will offer a conspectus of the thinking of physicists about the origin of the cosmos, and a critique of the ambiguity of their language. It will then present an overview of the history of the philosophy/theology of creation, suggesting that at its best moments, it has implicitly used *metaphors of relationship* to explain it. It will attempt to explicate and amplify this manoeuvre. It will do so by suggesting a significant difference between the Aristotelian *notion of relationship* and the notion of it that seems beneath the texts of Aquinas. It will also offer refinements to the notion of person and personal relationship, in that light.

Chapter 3 will look at the problem of the end of the cosmos, for physicists, for the language of eschatology and thanatology, and for a theology of the paschal mystery of Jesus Christ. It will criticise the present language of the scientists, as it will criticise the tendency to claim more knowledge of the eschata than a theology attentive to its own limits can have. It will suggest that the language of theology about the paschal mystery is at root a statement about the meaning of interpersonal relationship, and that the *mystery of the person*, not the end of the world, is its real agenda.

Chapter 4 will focus on the history, in between cosmic beginnings and cosmic endings. It will inspect the dynamics beneath the facts, rather than outline the factual details. These dynamics will be seen to be the *interplay of communion and differentiation*. As these could be taken as a summary of the dynamics of interpersonal relationship, an analogy is suggested between *personal and cosmic* relationships. We shall see how a realist philosophy, always at home with differentiation, has retrieved the more Platonic notion of communion, and delved into it for *metaphors of the real.* Theologically, we shall look at the dynamics of history, personal and cosmic together, as reflections and effects of the *mission of the divine persons* in the trinity. That mission is perhaps the ultimate language of all our understanding of history, and of reality itself.

Chapter 5 will allow the recent voices in physics to speak of self-organising systems, and the like, as images of nature. It will then see how a theology that makes use of the kind of realist philosophy we are suggesting, can become fascinated with this scientific vision. It will use the *metaphor of music* to unfold it all. Then it will, from a theological point of view, essay the idea that the cosmos itself is a paschal mystery, which is meant to find its climactic meaning in the person (of Christ).

Chapter 6 engages deep theoretical questions of physics, about time and fields. It tries to grasp the nature of 'flow'. As a result, philosophy itself is challenged to rethink its notion of the 'real', with the possibility that every distinct thing we call real is accompanied by a *background (music?)* of 'another' realness. Perhaps there is a truth that all is at one, while all flows along. If so, could theology look at the great *'moment'* of the paschal dying of Jesus, as actually accompanying the 'moments' of all our living and dying?

Chapter 7 asks direct questions about the kind of God that fits the kind of world we are talking about. We shall look at the present culture's avenues to come to a real God, at the biblical meaning of covenant, and its implications for an understanding of God, and at the images of a healthy, positive, outgoing, joyful God in current systematic theology.

Chapter 8 looks at information, experience, and the functioning of the human brain. It sees the evolution of information as the *spiritualisation* of information, and wonders whether the purpose and inner meaning of all information, and all knowing, is to be swept into the Divine Word, and to be given insight into it, person to person.

Chapter 9 is an appendix, asking what difference this vision of the cosmos could make to *social science*. It presents a kind of social grouping along the lines of the cosmos, as now understood, and looks for models of leadership that would reflect the kind of Creator that is the 'leader' of the cosmos.

The overall intention is to be informative (for theologians, about the new physics; and for physicists, about the humble but real limits of theology's claims). It is to be critical, especially of the character of the language in which the disciplines make their claims. It is to be constructive, above all of some philosophical horizons in which the positions of these disciplines can be located. It is to be synthetic, in the hope of demonstrating a convergence of ultimate reference in the various disciplines while allowing them to retain their own distinctiveness and autonomy, indeed, while insisting that they do. It is to be imaginative, in the use of suggestive metaphor to convey a hint of meaning, often half understood.

At the beginning, I would like to suggest some *criteria* for assessing the validity of this experiment in metaphor.

My aim in this book is twofold. First, I offer a synthetic outline of the vision of reality that comes from modern theoretical physics, and a sketch of the response to it made by philosophy and theology. Secondly, I suggest that both physics and philosophy-theology become silent at certain limit points of their disciplines, and that certain *metaphors* can be developed that enable us to speak in that silence.

Physicists usually make a strong distinction between 'phenomenological modelling' and 'proper physical theory'. When I suggest the development of some new metaphors, I am certainly proposing some new phenomeno-logising. I do so, however, not prior to and independently of true physical theories, but exactly at and after the moment at which they have made their contribution and fall silent in awareness of their limits. The test of the new metaphors will be their *congruence* with the physical theories themselves, and their capacity to *provoke* theorists into better theory.

Philosophers and theologians of a true metaphysical tradition usually make a strong distinction between the metaphysics of being, and attempts to describe, for example in metaphor, the character and quality of being. I am certainly proposing some new descriptive metaphors, but I do so at the limit point of metaphysics, and suggest that phenomenology may be harnessed by metaphysics precisely at that point.   The test of this procedure will be its *congruence* with metaphysics itself, and its capacity to *provoke* even further insight at that level.

My perspective is that of a *moderate critical realism* focussed on the centrality of the *person* in the cosmos, which is its home.

§ § §

NOTES

1. Marquette University Press, Aquinas Lecture 1992.

2. University of Notre Dame Press, 1993.

3. *Physics, Philosophy, and Theology*, a common quest for understanding, eds., R.Russell, W.Stoeger, G.Coyne, University of Notre Dame Press, 1988. *Quantum Cosmology and the Laws of Nature*, scientific perspectives on Divine Action, eds., R.Russell, N.Murphy, C.Isham, Vatican Observatory Publications, 1993.

4. Chapter 1, n.32.

5. S.Jaki has studied the position of Aquinas in relation to contemporary science, Thomas and the Universe, *Thomist*, 1989, 545-572. An ongoing correlation between the thought of Aquinas and present movements in science may be found in the chronicles and bulletins of philosophy of science, in *Revue des Sciences Philosophiques et Théologiques*, usually presented by J.Courcier, e.g. 1989, 281-313, and 1990, 259-292.

TABLE OF CONTENTS

CHAPTER 1
FINDING WORDS FOR THE BEYOND?
physics: relativity, quantum, complexity.
philosophy: realism, principles, being.
theology: traditions, metaphysics, anthropology, cosmology.
silence at the limits: boundaries, a direction through person, cosmos and communion.

CHAPTER 2
STARTING THE STORY
physics: Big Bang, interpretation through Relativity and Quantum, their combination.
philosophy and theology: affirmations, interpretation in Church Fathers, Aquinas, Process.
recovering a language: personalist interpretation, analysis of language, the core - relationship, participation, personhood.

CHAPTER 3
GUESSING THE END
physics: predictions, principles, and a language.
philosophy: eschatology - myth, rhetoric, ideology.
death and dying: thanatology - experience, psychology, personhood.
theology: claims, sense of Jesus, personal mission.
Ultimate Grace: the Benignity of Being.

CHAPTER 4
TELLING THE TALE

PHYSICS
general introduction
historical introduction
theoretical introduction
value-significant introduction
popular introduction

PHYSICS AND RELIGIOUS STUDIES
historical perspectives
speculative perspectives

COSMIC HISTORY
descriptive studies
theoretical studies

COSMOLOGY AND PHILOSOPHICAL THEOLOGY: Symposia

Vatican Observatory series
European series

THEORETICAL PHYSICS: **Attempts at Synthesis**
  overall horizons
  self-organisation theories

PHILOSOPHY: **Contemporary Realist Tradition**
  realism, **retrieved and expanded**
  philosophy in **dialogue** with theoretical physics.

THEOLOGICAL TENTATIVES
  various European authors

CULTURAL AND SPIRITUAL REFLECTIONS
  probings into consequences.

CHAPTER 1

FINDING WORDS FOR THE BEYOND?

Finding the meta-physical,
and the meta-metaphysical,
issues.....

I shall first review the world-vision of PHYSICS, of PHILOSOPHY, and of THEOLOGY. Then I shall attempt to pinpoint the reasons for silence, at the limits of all three.

PHYSICS

Let us look at ancient physics, Newtonian physics, and more particularly, at the physics of Special and General Relativity, and of the Quantum.[1]

Ancient physics was a very religious, and a very human, pursuit. It related directly to God, as creator and carer of the cosmos, and to human beings on planet earth, as the real centre of the cosmos. The real issue was the conviction that everything had a real *CENTRE* and that in a physical and logical sense we were that CENTRE. Copernicus (1473-1543), Galileo (1564-1642) and Kepler (1571-1630) created a major upheaval by suggesting that the sun was the true centre of the cosmos: but in effect they still believed in a centre, and that we were 'centrally' related to it.[2]

Newtonian physics (1642-1727) was less interested in centres than in movements. For Newton, space and time were infinitely extendable continua. *Motion* occurred, uniformly, through a limitless, absolute space, in a straight line, seeking inertia. Time was a code for calculating the predictability of this motion. A centre did not matter: unless it was the implied 'centre' or 'term' of every movement, a state of rest called 'inertia'. The vision was not without theological implications: all movement in a sense reflected the immutability of God, and God in his continuing activity in the cosmos was bringing everything to rest with God.

Einstein (1879-1955) was deeply indebted to Newton, and shared his interest in motion. Wave motion, and the extension of the idea of wave motion to light, had already been discovered. Einstein studied instances of such motion that appeared to be exceptions to Newton's laws, in that the motion did not seem to be uniform, and time could not be assumed to be a universal constant. He was considering motion in a flat space, where gravity was weak, and where the velocity approximated that of light (c). Relative to an observer travelling at the same velocity, the mass, length, and time-rate of the moving particle change significantly: the mass increases with velocity, the length decreases and the rate at which the clock carried by the particle ticks, appears slower with the increasing velocity. This is *Special Relativity*. In effect, mass-energy is conserved in a special relationship with the speed of light: time is estimated in relation to the speed of light and is made into a fourth dimension on a par with the three dimensions of space: the world is a mystery of *'spacetime'*, in which space is not space as hitherto understood, and time is not the clear and universal constant previously assumed; and *light* - not motion - is the greatest wonder.[3]

In his *General Relativity* theory, Einstein went on to realise that spacetime itself was far from flat. In fact, it was curved, or warped. The *curvature* was established by the distribution of matter and energy, that is, by the density of the particles and radiation in the cosmos. The curvature is not predetermined, but constructed in this way. This means that motion does not follow a straight line: the geodesics are curved. All reality is bent, and everything moves in curves.

Matter isn't really 'stuff' but maps that tell light, and everything moving at a velocity less than that of light, how to bend. Gravity is the curvature of spacetime. As light bends, it loses or gains energy. Mathematical symbols can be used to represent any of the dimensions of four-dimensional curved spacetime, but the geometry that enables them to be used meaningfully is not that of Euclid. Einstein had recourse to that of Riemann. He developed his *field-equations*, which show precisely how stress-energy determines the geometry. Our 'reality' is a light-cone of such curved four-dimensional spacetime.

This theory has been verified by observation in weak fields, through solar eclipses, quasars, gravitational redshifts, and the precession of the perihelion of Mercury.   In strong fields, it would predict the existence of black holes.

The upshot of this, is that the universe cannot be imagined as 'contained' in some kind of *'container space'* that is not the universe.   It has *no real 'centre'*, but rather, the observer creates a centre of observation at whatever point the observer is.   Motion is not the main thing, but is a manifestation of a *geometric beauty* that unfolds.   As our minds and imaginations are geared exclusively to centred, measured motions in straight lines, this whole picture is beyond our picturing: it is *counter-intuitive*, and cannot be visualised.

The principles of General Relativity would also indicate that spacetime was not infinitely extendable.   It predicts black holes and they imply 'singularities' where the dimensions appear to be infinite, and suggest that the theory has broken down and does not apply.

When we are dealing with motion at velocities much less than the speed of light, in 'ordinary' flat space with weak gravity, (such as that of cars, aircraft, planets in the solar system), pre-relativistic physics applies.   Are we living in practice in one kind of world while knowing that deeper down we are living in a different kind of world altogether?

We must come further, to the world of *Quantum Physics*[4], with Max Planck (1858-1947) and Niels Bohr (1885-1962).   Light is the starting point.   Light is invisible at ordinary temperatures, but at higher temperatures it glows red, yellow, and white.   Is there then a parallel between light waves and heat waves?   Heat comes from the motion of molecules, oscillating and vibrating.   What makes up the light waves?   The suggestion, from Planck, was that they are made up of micro discontinuous packets called *quanta*, or photons.   The further suggestion was that this 'discontinuity in small packets' applied to all micro levels of reality, and that everything micro was made up of quanta.   Nature was, radically, *'discrete'*.

The Rutherford model of the atom presented electrons circling (in perfect circles) around a solid nucleus of protons and neutrons.   Niels Bohr saw the atom as comprised of quanta or energy packets.   If a photon was absorbed into the atom, there would be a jump from a lower to a higher discrete orbit of energy; if a photon was emitted, there would be a fall from one level to another.   There was a *'leap'* of quanta (the 'lumps jumped'!).   "Orbits" were really discrete states of energy fields.   Their exact character could be stated mathematically, and chemistry for example could become not descriptive but mathematical.   But no one really knew *why* these particular mathematical numbers described the discontinuous states the micro world was made of.

This is only the beginning of a quantum mentality.   It had been assumed that reality was made up of particles and waves.   Quantum physicists noted that if an observation was set up to look for particles, particles presented themselves, while if one were set up to look for waves, waves resulted.   The observer, or measurement, was essential to the reality apprehended.   It depended on *observer participation*.   The observer was not in a privileged neutral position 'watching' reality: the observer was intrinsic to the whole system.   Reality was not one way or the other before observation but was determined to be one way or the other precisely by the observation.   Beforehand there is only a 'probability' of its self-presentation one way or the other, a *'probability'* of its collapsing all its complementary aspects into one upon observation, or measurement. The probability *'amplitude'* is expressed in a wave function through a *complex number*.   Such accuracy, almost unprecedented, has been verified by experiment, and has opened the way to many and various applications (lasers, superconductors, etc.).   Yet quantum theory is in itself enigmatic, paradoxical, whimsical, mystical.   "The Tao updated in a London fog": where space is a swarming in the eyes, and time a singing in the ears.   It reminds one of G.M.Hopkins' 'dearest freshness deepdown things'.

This means that really there are no fundamental states of space or time. Even the mathematics of it loses real meaningfulness at certain precise points: at the Planck time, of 10^{-43} of a second; at the Planck length, of 10^{-33} cm, etc.   To use numbers smaller than these, would be like speaking of 'one degree N of the N pole'.   The complex numbers break down at these points.   *Quantum smearing* has occurred.

This also means that when observation collapses the wave packet in one direction, it cuts off the possibility of knowing what reality would have been like in response to a different observation.   Thus, in *quantum uncertainty*, we can never know complementary aspects of reality, so that if we know the position of a quantum we cannot know its momentum, etc. Einstein's field equations have to be supplemented by quantum 'field' matrices to get in touch with the full reality available to us, and even then, we touch the limits of the knowable.

What is really real, then for quantum theory?   It depends on which interpretation of quantum theory we are using.   Some interpretations refuse to consider the question at all.   Others do.   Standard, or Copenhagen, interpretation (Bohr) would accept no real world independent of observer-measurement: there are only 'observables', not 'be-ables'. A qualification of Copenhagen theory would suggest that there could be an observer-independent physical reality, but that it is modified by consciousness, or even by the 'will' of quanta themselves, or that there is an infinite series of universes actually existing, only one of which is made real to us by the kind of observation we can do.   Other non-standard and non-Copenhagen interpretations (Einstein, Dirac) propose a world which may be deterministic, or stochastic, or which obeys a quantum logic which is not that of our conscious minds, or which corresponds to different solutions of field and matrix equations.   The Copenhagen interpretation is in general more ready to accept anomaly and paradox in the universe, even such anomalies as non-local influence and simultaneous happening, as well as real randomness and chance.

All the interpretations, however, concur in having recourse to some deeper, perhaps less than four dimensional, reality, 'behind' the world as it presents itself to our observation.   Something more than quantum appears needed to articulate it.

A word on *Complexity Physics*.   Beyond the specific range of quantum uncertainty, there is an uncertainty at large in many deterministic systems. In a deterministic system, you should be able to read the future by looking at its present state, since it is 'regular as clockwork'.   Complexity physics comes from the realisation that you can never know the *exact state* of any system.   One reason for this is that we can never measure it accurately without any micro error.   Another reason is that there are infinitesimal differences in the *'initial conditions'* originally inscribed into the system. This makes the system supersensitive 'downtrack', so that the differences tend to escalate.   That is, a small input 'error' can lead to a large 'output' error.   You do not have to think of roulette balls, or of insect populations, or of the weather: computer simulations, nervous systems, and even galactic systems are 'complex' in this sense. This is why you can predict long-term for the system as a whole, but not short-term; and you can predict short-term, but not long-term, for any dimension of the system.[5]

Let us *review* this brief conspectus of modern physics. We have come beyond centredness, contained space, and calculated time, into the pure geometric beauty of patterns where light plays. We have come further still into the discrete world of quanta whose leaps depend on observer participation within the system. The probabilities of any result can be expressed in complex numbers, but the numbers smear out, into uncertainty, and a hesitation about how much is objective and how much subjective in the 'really real'. And when we return to the macro world we discover supersensitive complexities whose implications are literally unpredictable.[6]

This is the world-view of physics from which I would begin the reflections of this book. The world-view has implications for philosophy.

PHILOSOPHY

I want to begin by outlining the philosophical tradition in which my thinking is situated, and then examine possible conflicts between it and the world view of physics today. Quentin Lauer has said:

> 'Philosophy is not so much a discipline or a mode of knowing as it is an attitude of inquiry which demands a willingness to see all issues against a background of ultimate meaning, the meaning of humanity's need to struggle for growth and enrichment.'[7]

He adds:
> 'It is a spiritual journey in which we appropriate by rethinking it what human genius reveals to us'.[8]

He further insists that such a journey cannot be made in the ivory tower of its own solitude - it must enter into real dialogue with all forms of thinking. The very word 'thinking' tells us that the endeavour is essentially *rational*: that there is an intelligibility, a rationally discernible comprehensibility in reality, and in the cosmos that is unified where it thus makes 'sense', and that is relatively autonomous as it stands in its own meaning. This philosophy distinguishes itself from all forms of mysticism in this way, and accepts its own commitment to the ethical implications of the 'reasoned life'.

The *'horizon of ultimate meaning'* is what distinguishes philosophy from science. It is natural and perhaps inevitable that scientists write of the 'ultimate meaning' of their discoveries, and to that extent they are philosophising; but the mental instrumentalities which scientists rightly use as scientists are intended to communicate a more *'proximate'* horizon of meaning than those of philosophy. This is why one tradition in science, and especially in physics, has for a long time been that of positivism: a philosophical stance, in which it is believed that all that can be said about reality is the statement (positing) and description of the phenomena as they appear to us and appear to be constructed and mutually connected. This is also why much of the more recent work in physics, and especially in the Copenhagen interpretation of quantum physics, has veered towards an *idealist philosophy*. Idealism believes that there are no intelligible structures of meaning embedded in reality itself prior to their imposition upon reality by human consciousness. The logic of positivism and the logic of idealism ultimately are akin. Both share the conviction that there is no 'reality' other than phenomena as they appear and mental constructs as they are imposed by us. There is often a mixture, in scientific writings, of scientific presentation in terms of proximate meaning, and of implicit philosophical presentation in terms of ultimate meaning, and in the latter, there is often an eclecticism that meanders from positivism to idealism to an unsophisticated realism.

The philosophical tradition in which this study stands is one of *critical moderate realism*. It is committed to realism in the relationship of consciousness to reality. It believes that human thought does appropriate a structure of meaning in reality that it does not impose upon reality. It is also committed to the position that science can describe this reality, but cannot, while remaining within science, engage its ultimate horizon. If there is to be any engagement between science and theology, such a realist philosophy is profoundly necessary.

Let us examine, concretely, some *key areas* where the essential world-view of such a philosophy might seem to contradict the world view of modern physics outlined above. My contention is that when both are understood, there is no contradiction. The areas are: *causality, change, relationship,* and *laws of nature.*[9]

In a philosophy of the real intelligibility of things, it is insisted that there be a *'sufficient reason'* for everything. As a consequence, the *'principle of causality'* demands that for every effect there be a true and proportionate cause. What is meant here is basically efficient causality: the causality that is the effective source of the coming into being of the effect. Note that the principle applies to effects as such: to all realities which are not themselves the source of their own coming to be.

The first problem which science has with such language, is that in many situations it cannot verify experimentally what is exercising an influence on what. As a result it tends in its own language to settle for what is perceived to be *antecedent* and what is perceived to be *consequent*, rather than what is claimed to be source or cause, and what is claimed to be effect. A second problem is that science has to work with *predictability* in estimating what is antecedent and what is consequent - predictability according to deterministic or statistical law. Now modern physics is precisely interested in what cannot be so predicted, either because of quantum uncertainty or because of complex unpredictability (e.g. chaos). Science is also very alive to the truth that we do *disturb data* by our observation and measurement. It therefore speaks of many things being unpredictable in principle, and is hesitant to use the language of antecedent and a fortiori of cause. In fact, it speaks of many such undeterminables as *'uncaused'*. I suggest that science is here using the word 'cause' in a very different way from the way in which a realist philosophy uses it, and that at root there is no conflict between a scientific statement that there is no cause, and an ontological statement that there must be one. The problem is complicated further by the difficult question of the meaning of *time*. The natural imaginative panorama that goes with a philosophy of cause, is that of an arrow of sequential time. The natural imaginative panorama that goes with a science of uncaused unpredictables (in the scientific sense) is one of simultaneity. The two panoramas conflict, but that does not mean that there is conflict in principles between the essential points made by the two disciplines.

With regard to *change*, a realist philosophy would demand, in the name of sufficient reason and causality, that there be a true inherent efficacy to explain all real becoming. Science seems to run counter with this, when it faces the issue of *evolution*.

The demands which philosophy must make in the arena of evolution are quite specific, and do not contradict what science must say in its own right. There are *two scenarios* open to philosophy: either that an *intervention* is needed from outside a non-self-explanatory system, to explain its 'next' evolutionary jump; or that a *latent active potency* is present in the system which makes the system adequate for the next evolutionary jump, without any outside intervention.   In either case, no principles of philosophy are violated.   The former explanation appeals to some philosophers, who regard the interventions as *intermittent*, and the latter to others, who regard them as going on *all the time*, while both types are inclined to regard the interventions as evidence of the constant collaboration of the creator with the creation.   The latter explanation appeals to those who are impressed by the *adequacy of systems* to deal with own future development, and who see a mysterious latent energy in things, and they tend to marvel at the original creative largesse of the Creator.   Some who hold this view, would make *an exception* for the origin of humankind - for this they would demand a special intervention.   Their reason is that evolutionary process is usually towards complexity, whereas the mystery of the human, as they see it, is rather one of simplicity than one of complexity.   But these variables are minor in philosophy, and the choice for one rather than the other is more one of *aesthetic intuition* than philosophical principle.   In all cases, the field is open for science, at its own level, to develop its own language for what it perceives to be taking place.   Philosophy is not in contradiction to evolution.

It is concerning the meaning of *relationship* that more real clarification is needed between philosophy and science.   Modern science is increasingly persuaded that all reality is interconnected, systematically interwoven in a *matrix* that is all-inclusive.   In that sense, it thinks both cosmically and relationally.   Realist philosophy, in its usual and standard approach, seems to have assumed that relationship is an *accidental* phenomenon, accessory to and secondary to 'the main thing' which is the solidity of separate and self-sufficient substances.   But realist philosophy has been listening to the scientific evidence (and to phenomenology) and has in the past few decades integrated a *more open idea* of relationship.   It too is now persuaded that all beings are related, not accidentally but essentially, to all other material beings.   That means that 'to be' is no longer taken to be a statement of exclusivity and separation.   'To be' is *'to be in a system'*, where 'system' is taken to be a set of relations forming a unified order: not a sum of individual added-connections, but a new irreducible category (a 'system' or *'whole'*) capable of attributes as a whole which are not predicable of its 'components'.   Indeed, philosophers are much more appreciative than they were of the change induced into a system of this kind, by any *observing-intervention* that would see its components as if they were not holistically integrated.   To be, is not simply to be in a system, but to be in many systems all at once, that is, to be in a universe of systems, or better, in a *universe-system*.   What appear to be substances are actually nodal centres of action and relationship in a complex web or map or network: that is, a substance is always a substance-in-a-system, and relationship is at the heart of the real, always, and not just something extra, added on.   Indeed, once philosophy realises that an isolate notion of substance removes it from its own real systemic being, and changes its functioning and status, philosophy has no difficulty in dropping such a notion, in the interests of the value to which philosophy is committed, namely, the realness of the real.   Further, such an advance opens the way to a new understanding of causality, less as exchange between separate entities, than as a *pulsing through* the entire 'space' of a system or 'force-field' of an energy that belongs primarily to the system itself.   Its 'localisation' in one point of space or time may be more our construction than the reality of nature.

What then are the *laws of physics*, or the *laws of nature*?[10]   Philosophy would today see them as real, but not as imposed by arbitrary will from outside, indeed rather as intrinsic to the natural systems involved. Further, they are understood both as descriptive of what happens, and prescriptive of what can happen, but with reservations.   It is increasingly realised that the further we get towards concrete detail, the less we can adequately either describe or prescribe what can and does happen.   There is a new sensitivity to the difference between basic principle and the articulation of how basic principle may work out in practice.   Science and philosophy are far from being in conflict here.

Science likes to speak of *'initial conditions'* as well as laws of physics, or nature.   The initial conditions would in effect determine the context in which the laws would work themselves out.   Philosophy has no problem here, but it suggests that the choice of such initial conditions is often more *aesthetical* than rigorously demanded either by philosophy or by science. There is no fundamental conflict between them.   It is clear then that philosophy wants to ponder reality in an ultimate horizon, and that science wants to ponder it in a more proximate one, but that both are *converging* towards a consensus.   A number of points can be made to describe that convergence.[11]

First, based on the notion of relationship sketched above, both philosophy and physics think *holistically*.   This - on the part of both - is not as rationalistic, or analytical, or positivistic, as it was once.   There is a new paradigm for both.

Secondly, this holistic thinking - for both - is *processive* and *historical*. Structures are giving way to processes, and the processes themselves, as dynamic influences, are expressions of relational wholes manifesting their full meaning.   The historicity of nature is being recovered.   In a general sense, an holistic-historic evolutionary point of view is common ground for science and philosophy.

Thirdly, one of the prime laws of method in both science and philosophy is *contextualisation* - placing anything in the context of holism and history. Uncontexted thought is bad thinking.

Fourthly, not just the content of these disciplines is changing: their manner of thinking is changing.   There is an *epistemic* difference: *participatory* knowledge is assumed to be the only viable form of knowing. The observer is observed as well.   We cannot be objective, without including our own subjectivity in the objectiveness as well.   The network is all inclusive.

Fifthly, there is a greater *humility* than before in both disciplines.   In the above perspective, formulas are never absolute: experimentation, language, and even theory at its best, is less than fully comprehensive of the real.

There is, finally, one arena in which the *differences* between the world-view of modern physics and that of a realist philosophy must be admitted and stated clearly.   Physics at root puts its faith in *mathematics*: its ultimate language is that of equations. From the perspective of a mathematical physicist, this is indeed 'all there *is*'.   There is really *fire* in those equations, because of the intrinsic nature of the equations - they *'are'* 'real'!   That is why there is a tendency among such scientists to think that they are touching not a proximate horizon of reality but the very *ultimate* one.   There is a tendency for them to think as though everything articulatable as possible in a mathematical equation is also by that very fact *actual and real*.   The mathematical objects are timeless and eternal, and if we do not see them fully, we see their traces and shadows in our world and history.   They are the *reasons for the real*.   They are self-justifying.   The phenomena that present themselves to us are simply their limited *instantiations* in our limited world.   It is quite easy for a science of this persuasion to come to a conviction that there is a world more real than our 'real' one, a world of almost *Platonic ideas* and forms and equations, which is the primary object of our interest and the primary place of our being.[12]

And yet, in most of these beautiful considerations, a realist philosophy does *not* concur.   Why?   Because of one word, the word *'being'*.   A realistic metaphysics is primarily concerned with being.   Being is not an accident, as if it were merely 'facticity', or the factual instantiation of a pre-conceived idea.   If it were, being would not be of any greater interest than the beautiful thoughts expressed above, indeed, it would be much less.   Being is not one more feature of reality, that also would ultimately be expressible in a mathematical equation.   Being is neither facticity nor a feature of the real; it is *the most intensive and positive act of be-ing real, by which all real things actually are*.   We get to an awareness of it in a moment of awakening to the mystery that there is an actual realness beyond the features of reality that are describable (even in mathematical equations), an actuality that is far from the happenstance of something just 'being around', that is the key to the ultimacy of all ultimate horizons because it is the *Fundamental Act* of all possible acts.   Every actual being participates in the Actuality of Being according to its own features, or essence, which delineates and thereby delimits its own particular being. If it is legitimate for a moment to use a metaphor, there is fire here that is not the fire that is in the equations of mathematics and physics: they are ultimately descriptive of the peculiar delineations and delimitations of being that take place in particular beings.   But being is more than that.

It is true that there are within this overall metaphysics *different approaches*. An older moderate realism put its confidence in an abstraction of the mystery of being from our grasp of material things.   Science has challenged the naivete of that grasp, and as a result has often left unexamined the mystery of being that seemed to depend on it.   More recent metaphysical work in the realist tradition does not depend on that but on more profound *intimations of transcendence and interpersonhood* that give us our anchorage in the real actuality of being together.   It is within these later traditions that the present study should be located. There is more room here to reach back to the world of science and appreciate its different yet convergent world-view.[13]

Let us *review* this brief conspectus of the world-view of critically realist metaphysics.   It tries to be rational in a horizon of ultimate meaning.   It neither stops at recording phenomena, nor indulges in imposing its subjective meaning on the real.   It takes from the real, the meaning of the real that is really there.   It insists that that meaning demands an adequate explanation of anything that happens, and changes.   It realises that this world of the real is less a world of separate and autonomous 'things' than a world of relatedness and interconnectedness of everything, holistically, cosmically, historically.   It senses that the laws of nature and of physics are limited expressions of the inherent dynamism of this all-embracing relationality itself.   There are ways in which this world-view almost coincides with that of modern physics, and ways it which it profoundly diverges.   The coincidence is in vision and method of approach: holistic, processive, historical, contextual, epistemically participative, humble. The divergence is chiefly about the difference between mathematics and metaphysics: about the difference between idealisations and being. And if there are questions about the source of any grasp of such a mystery of being, it does go back to the peculiar relationship called inter-personhood.

We are really faced with a dialogue between an authentic physics, and an authentic meta-physics.   What can *meta* mean here?

THEOLOGY

I shall begin with the great traditions of Abrahamitic faith, and their implications for an understanding of the real. Then I shall mention the myths that popular religion has given them. Then we can look at the beginnings of a realist theology in service of the faith-traditions, and see how its historical development has influenced its relationship with philosophy and science.

In the *three great traditions* of the book and of the word, Israel, Islam and Christianity, God is One, God is the One Who is, the One Who gives Torah, and lives in Sabbath. This God is a God of history (not of possible scenarios), of story (not theory), of real interaction (not possible connectedness). This God is the absolute originator of newness for us, in a free and gratuitous gesture of gift-giving and invitation. It is no wonder that these faith-traditions present this God as *Creator* of the entire cosmos. They are not interested, from the point of view of faith, in the how of the cosmos' origin: they are fascinated, in gratitude, with the why.[14]

Popular *myth* , usually of the unified order of the cosmos created by God, has surrounded these convictions. There has been a Hebrew myth that everything is made up, mystically, of sevens: seven days of creation and of the week; seven branches of the temple candlestick; seven planets and elements; seven sacraments; seven orders of ministry and classes of nobility; seven virtues and seven capital sins. There has been a Greek myth, shared and owned by Arabs and Christians, of nine spheres between the One (God) and the lunar sphere which governs all movements on our earth. In some of the great cathedral churches of Europe, there were astronomical clocks, to ensure God's will was done on earth, as it is in heaven.[15]

But this is not the stuff of *theology proper*. That begins with a critical analysis of previous patterns of myth and especially philosophy, to extend and amplify them, so that a faith tradition can reclaim its full voice. I would stress 'full' voice: theology is not simply a hermeneutical discipline unfolding what the tradition has meant, but a truly scientific vision of what reality really is in the light of that tradition.[16]

The inherited patterns at the time of the medieval doctors were mostly *Platonic*. We must remember that in thirteenth century Paris there was an extraordinary confluence of multiple streams of religious thought: from the Patristic church, from new translation/commentaries of/on Aristotle by leading Arab practitioners of *falasifa* and Jewish thinkers. Plato's patterns of understanding the cosmos came to Paris via the church fathers, and via Ibn Sina and Ibn Rushd. With assistance from Al Ghazali, Aquinas performed a *creative transformation* of these patterns when he broke from both Aristotle and Augustine and put his newly conceived philosophy of being at the service of his Christian (and ecumenical) faith. The result is a theology of the *Creative Act* and simultaneously of the appropriate autonomy of the *created cosmos*. It spelt out how being is the gift of Being. But it did not enter into the imaginative realm of how that gift was given, nor the technical realm of how its implications could be described in the creature. That would be the later work of a philosophy and a physics.

What Aquinas did was re-interpret the traditional theme that the divine Logos had implanted logoi or principles of intelligibility and meaningful action, dynamically into the cosmos. This made the cosmos a unified totality, with all the *phuses* (natures) in it. God worked in and through it. It was a theology of a Creator, *alive and intrinsic* to the cosmos, though distinct from it as Being from being, and unseparated from it as Being from being as well.

But by the end of the high middle ages *other approaches* prevailed possibly because they were closer to the mythic patterns of the popular religious imagination. God was conceived as more *exterior* to the cosmos: both as lawgiver, and as prime mover (from 'afar'). God's *power* became the focal point of reflection rather than God's Being. A distinction was made between God's *'ordinary'* power (in the exercise of which the cosmos was left with its own God-given autonomy), and God's *'extraordinary'* power (in the exercise of which God intervened in the cosmos). Faith and myth combined in some minds to incline them to accentuate one rather than the other. Leibniz is an example of the former, and Newton the latter. Eventually *'science'* understood in a restrictive sense assumes proprietorship of the former, while *'theology'* again in a restrictive sense domesticates the latter to itself. This is the beginning of a two-domain and two-language situation that many today would like to overcome. *Philosophy* in the course of time had to assume a mediating position by undertaking a hermeneusis of both of these streams of thought.[17]

At the end of the middle ages, a *'common' position* emerged in theology-faith-myth-philosophy which is not that of Aquinas nor that of present theologians.   It assumed God to be the creator of an ordered closed system maintained by God and intervened in by God.   The macrocosm reflected God's presence, and man the microcosm reflected both the cosmos and God.   In this sense man was (at) the *centre* of the universe, and the universe and everything in it existed to help man in his vocation. This vocation was supernatural, not natural, and man's first duty was to aspire to a state of grace in order to worship God in heaven and in the life to come.   Inquiry into the nature of the world and the causes of events was relatively unimportant.   It could have some support if it demonstrated the wonders of God's work and enhanced man's reverence.   All such inquiry had to respect divine revelation, church tradition, reason, and - as a poor fourth - observation, and it was subject in its conclusions to the judgment of the church.[18]

In fact, by this time, there was an *'established' theology* of this kind, integrated with a science of a sort.   When the heliocentrists eventually appeared, they were rejected by the church authority because they appeared to attack this integration.   It has taken until almost now for this position to be officially reversed.   The general theo-cosmological framework continued in schools of higher learning - for example, it was obligatory at the Sorbonne to present a thesis in cosmology as a require-ment before commencing postgraduate theological work.   The synthesis was supported by increasingly strong insistence on distinctions between nature and grace, natural and supernatural, creation and salvation, always with the accent on the second member of the couple.   But the old synthesis could not hold, and the advent of the Reformation, and then the German Enlightenment, led to the emergence of an *idealist philosophy* which paved the way for a new cosmology.[19]

What actually took place was not a cosmological turn, but an *anthropologi-cal* one.   It was a discovery of what it means to know, and what it means to be a transcendent personal subject of action and interaction.   For sure, idealism is the enemy of realism in that it radically reverses the relation-ship of knower and known.   But it also threw the emphasis so much on to interiority that it allowed the old cosmological viewpoint to recede from view, and it also paved the way for a new understanding of personhood that would eventually lead back to a new understanding of the cosmos. This anthropological turn also led to the development of new sciences of hermeneutics, which, when applied to biblical narratives of creation, liberated theologians from too literal an interpretation. But it was only with the eventual deconstruction of idealism that the doors were really opened towards a new cosmology.[20]

Meanwhile, the older cosmo-theology got into the myth system of the people. One can see it clearly in Baroque Catholicism. In fact, each religious tradition seems to have made its own particular adaptation of it.

The *Greek-Russian* tradition of the orthodox church relies on the anthropology of the Greek fathers, in two dimensions. Jesus Christ is the only authentic human being, in the image of God. For us, hominisation is Christification. Since the fall, we are ontologically different from the condition God had and has in mind for us, through Christ. The wisdom of the sciences is the study by fallen men of a fallen world, and needs to be supplemented by and counterpointed with a theology of transformation and transfiguration, in which a perichoresis of natures replaces their pretended autonomy, a perichoresis that is achieved by an increasing kenosis of nature to nature as history goes on. The cosmos is ever more an icon of the Holy.[21]

Protestant theology would often consider our actual nature and world to be in a kind of winter of creation, frozen and fixed there. It is degraded, in chaos, and condemned to cosmic death. Its only hope is redemption and reconciliation in Christ, and that will not take place without massive, dramatic conflicts and disorders and even extinctions, as - in a divine storm - the future of God breathes anew on the cemeteries of history. This theology is pessimistic and negative, defeatist and catastrophic. Its world is truly a fallen one. And its salvation is in a very apocalyptic parousia of the cosmic Christ.[22]

Anglican theology avoids both the transfigurative hope of the orthodox and the radically Germanic negativity of the Protestant tradition. It attempts to be moderate, and sees in studies of the universe both a reflection of

God's fidelity to creation, and a highlighting of the precariousness of the gift of freedom that is ours from God's love.[23]

Roman Catholic theology in its own way also interprets the cosmos in terms of anthropos.   Creation was always for the purpose of the emergence of a transcendent humanness.   Catholic theology has been more at pains to make use of models of creation in a less technical sense, as images of the evolution of human culture (in the first world), and of the liberation of the human (in the third world).   The great masters of modern catholic theology have contributed little to a direct study of the cosmos in itself.[24]

It has taken until now to see this anthropological turn itself turn around and become a *new quest for a cosmology*. The deconstruction of idealism, and of a Eurocentric vision of the human, have created a void, into which the new probings of the scientists have moved rapidly.   We stand at the very beginning of a new theological understanding of the world, and that understanding is much needed as a dialogue partner with present philosophy and present physics.[25]

In a keynote letter to a symposium held at the Vatican Observatory to mark the 300th anniversary of the publication of Newton's Principia, *Pope John Paul II* gave catholic theology a charter:

> "Turning to the relationship between religion and science, there has been a definite, though still fragile and provisional, movement towards a new and more nuanced interchange... It is crucial that this common search based on critical openness and interchange should not only continue but also grow and deepen in its quality and scope.

> "Contemporary physics furnishes a striking example. The quest for the unification of all four fundamental physical forces - gravitation, electromagnetism, the strong and weak nuclear interactions - has met with increasing success.   This unification may well combine discoveries from the subatomic and the cosmological domains and shed light both on the origin of the universe and eventu-

ally, on the origin of the laws and constants which govern its evolution... Is it not important for us to note that in a world of such detailed specialisation as contemporary physics there exists this drive towards convergence?

"Religion is not founded on science nor is science an extension of religion.   Each should possess its own principles, its pattern of procedures, its diversities of interpretation and its own conclusions.

"If the cosmologies of the ancient Near Eastern world could be purified and assimilated into the first chapters of Genesis, might not contemporary cosmology have something to offer to our reflections on creation?   Does an evolutionary perspective bring any light to bear upon theological anthropology the meaning of the human person as the imago Dei, the problem of Christology - and even upon the development of dogma itself?   What, if any, are the eschatological implications of contemporary cosmology, especially in the light of the vast future of our universe?   Can theological method fruitfully appropriate insights from scientific methodology and the philosophy of science?

"The matter is urgent.   Contemporary developments in science challenge theology far more deeply than did the introduction of Aristotle into Western Europe in the thirteenth century.   Yet these developments also offer to theology a potentially important resource.   Just as Aristotelian philosophy, through the ministry of such great scholars as St. Thomas Aquinas, ultimately came to shape some of the most profound expressions of theological doctrine, so can we not hope that the sciences of today, along with all forms of human knowing, may invigorate and inform those parts of the theological enterprise that bear on the relation of nature, humanity and God?

"Can science also benefit from this interchange?   It would seem that it should.   For science develops best

>when its concepts and conclusions are integrated into the
>broader human culture and its concerns for ultimate
>meaning and value.   Scientists cannot, therefore, hold
>themselves aloof entirely from the sorts of issues dealt
>with by philosophers and theologians...."[26]

This is surely a challenge to theologians, and others, to think in a way that
is different both from the anthropocentrism that has dominated since the
Enlightenment, and from the 'established' theological position, as I have
called it, that comes from the end of the medieval period.   It is also a
challenge to think in a way different from Aristotelian philosophy.   This
must mean a readiness to engage theologically with the world-views of
contemporary science and philosophy.

A *process* is already in place to structure such an encounter.   It consists
of *international symposia* at an interdisciplinary level, programmed over the
coming decade.   A beginning took place in 1984 in Cracow, on the
Galileo case.[27]   Again in Cracow, in 1987, a conference was held to
celebrate the 300 years of the publication of Newton's Principia.[28]   This
led to a conference at the Vatican Observatory in 1987, on Physics,
Philosophy, and Theology.[29]   In consequence, the *Vatican Observatory* is
sponsoring a series of five conferences spaced over the coming decade.
The overarching topic is "God's action in the world", and the specific fields
of study are, quantum cosmology, the origin and status of the laws of
nature; chaos, complexity and self-organisation; the mind-brain problem;
biological evolution; and quantum physics.[30]   The first of these symposia
was held in 1991, and is now published.[31]

Around the same time, the *European Society for the Study of Science and
Theology* was formed, and is holding a conference every two years.   It has
already studied evolution and creation; science and religion; the science
and theology of information; origins, time and complexity; and the nature
of nature.[32]

Similar interdisciplinary work is going on in North America, e.g. at
Princeton, Chicago, and Berkeley.

For the first time in the history of modern theology, philosophy and
physics, a process is in place to ensure that they do not develop at a

distance from each other, but rather in the kind of stimulative interchange desired by John Paul II.

SILENCE AT THE LIMITS

It has been necessary to introduce this study with an *overview* of the present directions of physics, philosophy, and theology.   On the basis of this presentation I suggest that each of these disciplines trembles at the edge of its capacity to speak more amply about the things which properly concern it.   My overall contention is that metaphor may be developed which allows further articulation of the mystery beyond.   This would be both meta-physics (beyond what physics says and believes it can say) and meta-metaphysics (beyond what metaphysics says and believes it can say).   This further articulation is in the service of a faith tradition, and so in a true sense is an essay in theology.

Let me introduce the task, first, by spelling out the various *kinds of silence at the various limits* of these disciplines, and secondly, by suggesting the *direction* in which we might move to surpass those limits.   Where is the silence at the limits of physics?

I suggest that there are *four kinds of limit*: the limit of language; the limit of non-explanation; the limit of cessation of intelligibility; and the limit of unverifiable speculation.

The *limit of language* occurs in physics when its practitioners rightly say that there is more to physics than metaphor.   They demand that we accept the intrinsic incapacity of metaphorical language to convey real insights in physics.   They are not opposed to the use of metaphor in a popular pedagogy of these things, but they do oppose it as a valid and adequate language for its real tenets.   They have recourse to mathematics, of various kinds.   A good example for this kind of limit, is the counter-intuitive, counter-visual mystery of four dimensional spacetime in relativity theory.

The *limit of non-explanation* occurs in physics within a physical theory, when the kind of understanding it advocates fails to explain coherently the data presented to be understood.   An example would be quantum theory's ability to use the Uncertainty Principle, but its inability to explain why there should be an uncertainty principle in operation.   The same would apply to quantum anomalies, like non-locality and simultaneity, and to the (at least) apparent presence of randomness and pure chance - in which the system 'plays dice'.   We could also mention the hypersensitivity of a deterministic system which results from delicate initial conditions - the consequences are explained but not the manner in which such initial conditions occurred.

The *limit of cessation of intelligibility* occurs in physics when the mathematics on which its theories rely fail to apply meaningfully beyond certain defined limits.   Thus there are statable limits beyond which Newton's laws do not apply.   There are singularities in the final predictions of relativity theory, and false infinities with them.   There is a quantum smearing of the complex numbers that define the magnitude of the quanta when the Planck wall is reached.   There is an inability to say why those precise complex numbers are the 'right' ones, even though they so manifestly 'work' correctly when applied.

The *limit of unverifiable speculation* occurs in physics when the discipline admits that in defined domains concepts have lost their accepted meaning and are endowed for the purposes of hypothesis with a meaning that cannot be verified, or indeed used intelligibly outside the theory concerned. A good example is the meaning given to time, and to space as well, in the relativity theory's use of 'spacetime'.   Another example is the speculation that perhaps there is more than one cosmos, on the grounds that mathematical equations could be written to describe cosmic proportions that are different from those belonging to our cosmos.   A further example is the merging of the meaning of the word 'possible' with the word 'actual' and the application of such a speculated combined meaning to mathematically coherent formulas.

We can note that when physics reaches these limit points at the edge of its discipline, it typically has recourse to *mathematics* first, then to *chance*, or to a *'docta ignorantia'*, and finally to the *imaginative creation of meaning* that does not necessarily follow from the principles and laws of physics. This last manoeuvre must remind a philosopher of a *Platonic* cast of mind, if not of actual speculations that have been articulated in a Platonic tradition.   To this extent, what physics does at its limit (when it is no longer formally doing physics) does present a conflict with the realist tradition of philosophy we have proposed.

Where is the silence at the limits of *philosophy*?

I speak of a realist philosophy or metaphysics of being, and I suggest that there are *two kinds of limit*: the limit of principles whose application cannot be empirically described; and the limit of the inability to articulate the character of 'being' in a descriptive way.

The *limit of principles whose application cannot be empirically described* comes from conviction that is known to be absolutely correct in principle, but which cannot be exemplified clearly, given the limiting contributions of contemporary physics.   The clearest example is the principle of causality which we have already outlined.   The result is the relegation of philosophy to a closed internal world and a conviction that it has nothing 'real' to say, even if the tautologies it mouths are intrasystematically coherent.

The *limit of the inability to articulate the character of 'being' in a descriptive way*, is the real limit of an authentic metaphysics.   Genuine metaphysicians would not only accept it but demand it.   You cannot 'describe' being: it is not directly categorisable, it is transcategorical.   To be 'being in act' is not a subset of 'possibility': it is an ab-original mystery of pure being, which is the only real word for it.   It is neither form nor feature. The result is that analogies which are attempted for being, but which are founded in motion (which is not the same thing as being) or in a style of relation (which is not the same thing as being) do not really convey being to us in its inner, hidden richness.

We can note that when metaphysics reaches these limit points at the edge of its discipline, it typically has recourse to glorying in the simultaneous achievement and limitation of the human mind before ultimacy.   But this internally congruent manoeuvre does not give it much communicable to say to the physicists and mathematicians who give up chance and ignorance and play with Plato because no one else is around!

What is the silence at the limits of *theology*?

Without the instrumentality of science and philosophy, theology in a critical sense has nothing to say: it degenerates into the uncritical narration of metaphors or the even more uncritical recourse to apophatic mysticism. This is why so much current theology in this field is fascinated with eastern religion or retells the biblical tale of creation.

What then?

We find that at the edge, all three disciplines, physics, philosophy, theology, reach their limits, and at that point *play with metaphor*, knowing it is not quite valid, but hoping that there might be some scintilla of reality in it. What is missing is a theory of *why* some kind of metaphorising here is both legitimate and necessary, and *how* it gets past some of the impasses all three disciplines experience. Because that is missing, there is to my mind *no critically developed set of actual metaphors* for what all three disciplines differently sense is going on in the heart of the real.

That is why the purpose of this book is to work in metaphor precisely where metaphor has been triply refused, in the name of mathematics, metaphysics, and mysticism. Is there *a direction* in which the task can be undertaken?

The basic direction is that given by *W. Norris Clarke* in his recent writings on *Person and Being*.[33] He presents his work as a creative retrieval and completion of the metaphysics of Aquinas. In the words of Gerald McCool,

> "In Clarke's metaphysics, grounded as it is on Thomas'
> dynamic act of existence, person is not considered a new
> perfection added to the perfection of existence. Per-
> sonal being is rather the form in which existence reaches
> the fullness of its own reality in its supreme spiritual
> instantiations: God's Infinite *Esse*, the *esse* of pure
> angelic spirits, and the *esse* of the lowest spiritual crea-
> ture, the incarnate spirit. In those higher instantiations,...
> the act of existence can unfold its own intrinsic plenitude
> in the knowledge and love of consciously self-possessing
> and self-transcending persons. To be a conscious, self-
> possessing person means simply *to be* most fully".[34]

What Clarke has done, is present 'person' as the active subject of the 'act' of that person. 'Act' in that interpersonal sense of relational communion, is the fullness of that other 'Act' which Thomists rightly call the fundamental act of all act, namely the act of being itself.   This means that an *analogy does hold up* between interpersonal act and the act of being.   In the dynamics of interpersonal act we have *a reservoir of metaphor* which may truly apply to the reality of being as we seek it.   Clarke has written:

> "the natural connection between being and its overflow into action:... to be, in the strong sense of to be real or actually existing, is seen to be ambiguous, incomplete, empty of evidential grounding, unless it includes, as natural corollary, *active presence*, that which *presents* itself positively to others through some mode of action.   To be is to be co-present to the community of existents".[35]

David Burrell calls this a *'metaphorical resonance'*, and comments:

> "So Aquinas' presentation of *existing* as an *act* introduces an analogical use of act which is at once grounded in a pattern of discourse whose meanings can legitimately be extended (Aristotle's scheme of potency/act) and offers illuminating metaphorical resonances as well."[36]

The value of this direction for our study is that it indicates a reservoir of philosophically valid metaphors that are not *exclusively anthropomorphic*, but metaphysically universal.   It could then be argued, as it will be in the following chapters, that resonances of these very metaphors occur in the domain of the micro and macro dimensions of the *cosmos* which is the proper study of physics.   Concretely, we may be able to get past the impasse at the edge of physics in a way analogous to the way we can get past the impasse at the edge of metaphysics: by discovering in both the mysterious *interrelationality of communion* that in its own way constitutes all being and supremely human beings.   We are then able both to remain within a tradition indebted to philosophical anthropology and to transcend that tradition.

We are able to honour with real congruence the kind of world-view that physics has offered us, and to do the same with the world-view of a realist philosophy. If there is a word for it, it may be the word *'COMMUNION'*, and that too is congruent with some of the better directions of contemporary theology.

It remains to see how a quest built on these foundations can lead us to metaphors for the beginnings, the endings, the middlings, the manner and the movement of the cosmos, as God-communing-with-us communes through us with it.

§ § §

NOTES

1.   A.Lightman and R.Brawer, *Origins: the lives and worlds of modern cosmologists,* Harvard University Press, 1991 P.Davies (ed.), *The New Physics*, Cambridge University Press, 1990.

2.   S.Toulmin, *The return to Cosmology: postmodern science and the theology of nature,* University of California Press, 1985 A.Peacocke, *Creation and the World of Science*, Clarendon Press, Oxford, 1979 J.Polkinghorne, *One World*, SPCK, 1986, *Science and Creation*, 1988, *Science and Providence*, 1989, *Reason and Reality*, 1991.

3.   G.Ellis and W.Stoeger, Introduction to General Relativity and Cosmology, in *Quantum Cosmology and the laws of Nature: scientific perspectives on divine action*, ed. R.Russell, N.Murphy, C.Isham, Vatican Observatory, 1993, pp.33-48.

4.   N.Herbert, *Quantum Reality: beyond the new physics - an incursion into metaphysics and the meaning of reality*, Doubleday, 1985 T.Hey, P.Walters, *The Quantum Universe*, Cambridge University Press, 1987 J.Polkinghorne, *The Quantum World*, Penguin, 1990 C.Isham, Quantum Theories of the Creation of the Universe, in Russell, Murphy, Isham, eds., op.cit., pp.49-90.

5.   M.Waldrop, *Complexity*, Doubleday, 1993.

6.   J.Briggs, F.Peat, *Science, Order and Creativity: a dramatic new look at the creative roots of science and life*, Bantam, 1987 F.Capra, D.Steindl-Rast, T.Matus, *Belonging to the Universe: new thinking about God and nature*, Penguin, 1992 R. Weber, *Dialogues with scientists and sages*, Penguin, 1986 D.O'Murchu, *Our World in Transition: making sense of a changing world*, Temple House Books, Sussex, 1992.

7.   *The Nature of Philosophical Inquiry*, Marquette University Press, 1989, p.104.

8.   Ibid, p.12

9.   In this section I am indebted to the course on Metaphysics, of W.Norris Clarke, Fordham University, pro MS.

10.   W.Stoeger, Contemporary Physics and the Ontological Status of the Laws of Nature, in Russell, Murphy, Isham, eds, op.cit., pp.209-234.

11.   I am indebted here to the reflections of W.Drees, summarising much of the work of the *European Conference on Science and Theology*, Freising/Munich,1994.The outline is parallel to that to be found in Capra, Steindl-Rast, Matus, op.cit., n.6.

12.   J.Courcier, Chronique de philosophie des sciences: la signification des mathématiques et des langages formels selon J.Dieudonné, J.Vuillemin, et D.Dubarle, in *Revue des sciences philosophiques et théologiques*, 73, 1989.

13.   G.McCool, The tradition of St.Thomas since Vatican II, *Theology Digest*, 40, 1993, 324-335.

14.   D.Burrell, *Freedom and Creation in Three Traditions*, University of Notre Dame Press, 1993 D.Burrell, B.McGinn, *God and Creation*, University of Notre Dame Press, 1990.

15.   K.Schmitz Moorman, Evolution in a Roman Catholic Perspective, in *Evolution and Creation: a European Perspective*, ed. S.Andersen, A.Peacocke, Aarhus University Press, 1987.

16. P.Clayton, *Explanation from Physics to Theology, an essay in rationality and religion*, Yale University Press, 1989.

17. C.Kaiser, *Creation and the History of Science*, London, Marshall Pickering, 1991.

18. J.Trusted, *Physics and Metaphysics*: *theories of space and time*, London, Routledge, 1991.

19. J.Brooke, *Science and Religion, some historical perspectives*, Cambridge University Press, 1991.

20. A.Arnould, R.Bergeret, J.Fantino, R.Klaine, J.M.Maldamé, D.Renouard, Bulletin de Théologie, théologie de la création, *Revue des sciences philosophiques et théologiques*, 78, 1994, 95-124.

21. P.Nellas, *Le vivant divinisé, anthropologie des peres de l'Eglise*, Paris, Cerf, 1989.

22. J.Moltmann, *Der Weg Jesu Christi, Christologie in messianischen Dimensionen*, Munchen, Kaiser Verlag, 1989.

23. J.Polkinghorne, op.cit. n.2.

24. J.M.Maldamé, *Le Christ et le Cosmos, incidence de la cosmologie moderne sur la théologie*, Paris, Désclee, 1993 P.Trigo, *Creation and Theology*, Tunbridge Wells, Burns Oates, 1992.

A.Gesché, J.Demaret, P.Gibert, R.Braque, P.Gisel, *Création et Salut*, Bruxelles, Facultés Universitaires St.Louis, 1989.

25. R.McKinney, Towards the resolution of paradigm conflicts: holism vs. postmodernism, *PHILOSOPHY TODAY*, 32, 1988, 299-311.

26. *Osservatore Romano*, n.46, November 1988, p.3-5.

27. G.Coyne, M.Heller, J.Zycinski, eds., *The Galileo Affair: A Meeting of Faith and Science*, Libreria Editrice Vaticana, 1985.

28.   G.Coyne, M.Heller, J.Zycinski, eds., *Newton and the new direction in science*, Libreria Editrice Vaticana, 1988.

29.   R.Russell, W.Stoeger, G.Coyne, eds., *PHYSICS, Philosophy and Theology, a common quest for understanding*, University of Notre Dame Press, 1988.

30.   R.Russell, Introduction, in *Quantum Cosmology and the Laws of Nature: scientific perspectives on Divine Action*, Vatican City/Berkeley, 1993, p.2-3.

31.   The volume cited in n.30 is the fruit of the first of these conferences, Specola Vaticana, Fall, 1991.

32.   The first of these conferences was held in 1986 in Loccum, Germany, and has been published as *Evolution and Creation, a European Perspective*, eds. S.Andersen, A.Peacocke, Aarhus University Press, 1987.The second was held in 1988 in Twente, Netherlands and has been published as *Science and Religion: One World - Changing Perspectives on Reality*, eds. J.Fennema, I.Paul, University of Twente Press, 1990.The third was held in 1990 in Geneva, Switzerland, and has been published as *The Science and Theology of Information*, eds. C.Wassermann, R.Kirby, B.Rordorf, Geneva, Labor et Fides, 1992.The fourth was held in 1992 in Rome, Italy, and has been published as *Origins, time and complexity*, eds. G.Coyne, K.Schmitz Moorman, C.Wassermann, Geneva, Labor et Fides, 1993-94.The fifth was held in 1994 in Freising and Munich on the theme *The concept of nature in science and theology*.The next conference is planned for 1996 in Cracow.

33.   W.Norris Clarke, *Person and Being*, Marquette University Press, 1993.

34.   G.McCool, review of Clarke, *Person and Being, International Philosophical Quarterly*, 1994, 121-123.

35.   Clarke, op.cit., p.65.

36.   D.Burrell, *Freedom and Creation in Three Traditions*, pp.32-33.

CHAPTER 2

STARTING THE STORY

A phenomenology for
an incomparable beginning....

In this chapter we shall look at the absolute origination of anything and everything, first, from the point of view of physics, and then, from that of philosophy and theology. Two serious difficulties will be highlighted, in the light of which it may seem impossible to speak in any real way about beginnings. Suggestions will be made to overcome this impasse.

Some *warnings*: whenever we ponder our beginnings, we must be alert to our own narcissism. We rightly demand an ordered, reasonable, rational account of our early world; but we tend - even unconsciously - to expect it to be special, chosen for us, unique, even the only possible, and thus necessary world. That may be more than we can claim. 'Cosmogony' is the name given to the study of beginnings (and endings) of the cosmos. Cosmogonies abound, and they come from time almost immemorial, and are shrouded in myth. We must be alert to the depth in which we are conditioned by them, and still be prepared for truly critical thinking.

PHYSICS

In the past two decades, the *'Big Bang'* theory of the origin of the cosmos has moved to the centre of the thinking of most physicists.[1] It means that the cosmos began with an explosion, in a micro primaeval 'atom' that 'blew up', at immense density and temperature, and that it has been expanding, thinning out, and cooling ever since. I would like to summarise the scientific observational evidence for the Big Bang, and then to look at the theories behind the interpretation of the evidence, and in particular at the way in which they have been blended together to produce an imaginative 'story' of 'everything'. There are *four principal arguments* for the Big Bang: the expansion of the universe; the presence of radiation in it; the proportion of chemical elements in it; and the estimated age of the universe.

Despite Einstein's assumption that the universe was static, and homogeneous, astronomers since the 1920's have been able to observe a systematic redshifting of distant galaxies and quasars.   This indicates that the other galaxies and our own are moving away from one another, and that the farther away they are, the faster they are receding.   The speed at which this is happening is constant.   It is possible to speak of the 'flight' of the galaxies, as they speed away from one another.   The *expansion* appears uniform, at and from all points.   The natural assumption is that as you go back in time, all the galaxies were closer together.   If you go back as far as you can go, you get to a 'universe' of incredibly tiny proportions and see it as the origin of a dynamic 'explosion' outward - the Big Bang. However, even the word 'explosion' has to be used carefully: it is not as though the world blew up, and we are now riding on a piece of shrapnel (earth) from the original explosion.   It is rather that the proportions of the original micro-universe have continued to expand, like ink blots on a continually stretching rubber band.   The Big Bang did not occur 'in' any previously given space, the Big Bang was everything.   The very phrase 'Big Bang' was not originally used by the advocates of the theory: it was used derisively of it, by its opponents - steady state theorists who maintained there was no change in the average temperature and density of the universe.[2]

In our present universe, *micro-wave radiation* has been detected, from outer space, which is best explained as a necessary remnant or 'afterglow' of a very young, very dense, and very hot universe, that is, of the 'Big Bang'.   This radiation comes uniformly from all directions, like a constant 'noise', and no discrete objects can be indicated as responsible for its origin.   It seems best explained as a relic of the moment, about 300,000 years after the Big Bang, when matter was first freed from radiation.   The first real awareness of this radiation dates from 1964 (Penzias and Wilson, at the Bell Laboratories in New Jersey, with the help of Dicke and Peebles at Princeton).   Mathematically there should be small variations in the temperature of this background radiation, indicating the presence of variations in it from the very beginning, the precursors of a lumpiness needed for the ultimate formation of galaxies.   In April, 1992, a group of researchers in Berkeley announced that exactly such fluctuations had been detected by instruments aboard the NASA satellite COBE.   We seem to have been in touch with actual fossils of the Big Bang.[3]

In the universe, there is a detected proportion, and relative abundance, of certain *chemical elements*, in particular, of helium, deuterium, and lithium. This is hard to explain unless there was an epoch in the history of the universe, when the universe was at a temperature of over a billion degrees, and had a density and proton-neutron ratio suitable for the formation of large amounts of these elements. Again, this points back to a 'Big Bang'.[4]

There is a fourth consideration: the calculation of the *age of the universe*, on the basis of a Big Bang based on the data above, agrees substantially with the calculation of the *age of Earth* based on the rate of radioactive disintegration of uranium ore.

The scientific observational evidence for (at least one) Big Bang is then strong.

Two great scientific *theories* lie behind the interpretation of such a Big Bang: General Relativity, and Quantum Theory.[5]

General Relativity offers some positives and some negatives to the work of interpretation. *Positively*, it offers a coherent statement of why and how the laws of physics apply universally to all times in the history of the universe, and equally to all spaces in it. It shows that matter is distributed in it like a perfect fluid, it shows how the universe can look the same in all directions, and how its spatial homogeneity can be retained as it expands and evolves, so that its earlier stages were denser and hotter.

But there are at least three aspects of General Relativity which, enticing as they may appear, do ultimately present *difficulties* in the interpretation of the Big Bang. They are: its prediction of 'black holes', its admission of 'singularities' and 'false infinities', and difficulty in solving the 'horizon' problems in the early universe.[6]

In Relativity theory, attempts are made, through the Schwarzschild solution of Einstein's field equations, to impose a spherical symmetry on the geometry, and to give a relativistic description of the spacetime around a mass-object. There are ultimately objects with a radius inside which all is trapped by a gravitational field: the effective escape-velocity from the object would equal the speed of light. The radius then becomes an 'event horizon': no light, or event in terms of light, can escape from it, and no communication with or observation of it is possible from the outside. This is a *'black hole'*. The question must be asked, if you track back the early universe, in such Relativity theory, to its very earliest micro dimensions, have you gone back to an original black hole?

Even more, in the Schwarzschild solution, at the centre of any black hole, the radius would ultimately equal zero. This must mean that at least one parameter is *infinite*. At this point, the language and the mathematics of Relativity break down, and at root the theory is not applicable. This means that at the point of origination of the cosmos we are not in possession of an applicable physical theory.

That limit may well be reached earlier. Relativity is aware of the multitude of *horizons*, each incommunicable to each other, that must have been present in the early stages of the universe. They would all have the same density and temperature, but no causal contact or influence. This is a real anomaly given our knowledge of the further development of our universe. Relativity has recourse here to a theory of *inflation*, in which there would be an exponential expansion of the micro-universe for a definable but very short period. The energy for this inflation would have to come from an anti-gravitational force. It is not clear that Relativity theory can establish it.[7]

Quantum Theory has as its proper domain precisely those infinitesimal dimensions at which Relativity confesses its impotence. It is becoming clear, that, to interpret the Big Bang, we need to envisage a very early universe of dimensions of that kind. Early cosmological astronomy and theoretical Quantum Theory would seem to coincide here. Quantum may be able to help us see how we can get an originating universe at all. Relativity is in reality not helpful beyond dimensions of 10^{-8} m: after that, quantum 'takes over'. Quantum numbers themselves smear into unrealness at the Planck wall: at 10^{-43} s, 10^{-33} cm, 10^{94} gm cm^{-3}, etc. In between, what can quantum tell us?[8]

Basically, quantum is not interested in particular things or particular cases of its principles. It focuses on a *bundle* of latent potential properties that are only brought into being by the act of measurement. Quantum gives *predictions* for the results of possible measurements. The quantum state of a system is an attempt to say our complete knowledge about a dynamic system, by a *probability amplitude*, which is itself a *complex number*. The 'laws of quantum physics' would indicate all the *possible* states of the system; but the real contribution of quantum is to come up with a formula for all the *probable* states of that system.   To do this, it must go further than state the 'laws', it must also formulate the *'initial conditions'* or 'boundary conditions' of the system in which the laws operate and through whose sensitivity the laws express themselves in sometimes extraordinary ways.   In doing so, Quantum Theory expresses the *'space'* of states of the system: if it wants to know the particular state of the system, it has to invoke the act of *observation/ measurement*, which reduces the probability amplitude to a singular situation.

There are *two problems* in the application of quantum to primordial cosmology. *First*, there is only one case (our own) of the origination of a cosmos that is subject to our scrutiny: it is difficult to come up with probability amplitudes for a series of one! *Secondly*, even granting the possibility of formulating such an amplitude, it is difficult to imagine how there can be an act of measurement/observation which could reduce the probabilities into a singular situation. Most of the speculative work being done by quantum theoreticians about early cosmology attempts to resolve these two difficulties.

One approach is to suggest that 'prior' to any cosmos of our four-dimensional spacetime character, there must, by force of the mathematics, be a background of three dimensional space, called 'Superspace'. It would be the mathematical space of all curved three-dimensional spaces, and the domain space for the quantum probabilities of a 'quantum gravity'. It has to be considered logically, or mathematically, prior to our cosmos, since it does not include the parameter of time as we understand it.   It therefore has boundary conditions (at the logical boundaries of the system) rather than initial conditions which could imply temporality.   At the boundaries, the flux associated with quantum probabilities always points outwards, and this 'pointing' describes an orientation to the origination of a cosmos such as ours. *Others* would prefer to modify this insight, and to speak of an 'imaginary' time within or rather than 'Superspace', and to suggest a plausible description of the 'emergence' of 'real' time, in a classical universe, from this 'imaginary' time, in a non-classical background, while of course understanding 'emergence' symbolically, not temporally. *Others* again would prefer to speak of a special logic of this background, different from ours, which is reduced to our kind of logic by its encounter with an observing/measuring logic of human consciousness and introspection.   *Others* still would want to speak of the background as a 'quantum vacuum' which can exist in different energy states, as an 'excited' and 'fluctuating' 'false' vacuum - false, because in reality it has energy that sends the imagination reeling.   From such a substructure all present reality would emerge.[9]

The common factor in all these approaches seems to be the invocation of a kind of *mythic primordial pleromatic space* or region, somewhat like a 'womb' from which the cosmos would be born.   One must wonder, philosophically, whether this is rather an archetypal recurrence of *Platonic, Jungian, even Wagnerian* forms, than the result of strict mathematical reasoning.   In any event, the recourse to this style of imaginativity is significant, and I shall return to it as my argument develops.[10]

A *second* type of response to the two difficulties in applying Quantum Theory to early cosmology would envisage a quantum 'equation' for the cosmos, which had no special initial or boundary conditions at all.   There would really be no first moment, or initial event - the apparent 'phenomenon' of firstness would be the invention of the mind of any observer standing at any point of vantage.   The quantum equations describing the cosmos would include all probable states of the cosmos, and include also all probable transitions from one of those states to another.   So there is no real initiality, and no need to invoke any source 'outside' the cosmos 'intervening' to give an impetus to the cosmos to 'begin'.   In ordinary language, there would be no need for a Creator, and the cosmos could, to use inappropriate metaphors from machines, kick-start itself from and towards whatever starting points an observer discerns/ determines.   One consequence of this, is that the cosmos begins (from our viewpoint) *without any external physical impulse*;   and another is that there is *no womblike anterior state* 'prior' to the cosmos.   Again, this is a recourse to a different style of imaginativity from the one previously presented, and we shall return to it.   It might be noted, as a corollary, that this approach is congruent with the thought of those who speculate about 'many actual universes', indeed, as many as the mathematical probabilities of the cosmic equations.[11]

A *third approach* to the constant difficulties in the application of quantum to cosmogenesis, would suggest that at the point of meeting of the quantum domain with the domain in which General Relativity begins to be applicable and valid, there is as it were an objective reduction of the quantum probabilities.   The result would be the emergence of gravitational field-forces as we know them.   In effect, the point of meeting of the two domains would be equivalent to the presence of a measuring observer. There is a cleanliness of vision here that must hold its own appeal, but the grounds on which such a coupling of mathematical 'universes' occurs, is not as clear.[12]

This can lead us to the *nub of the problem*.   It relates to the simultaneous use of the two systems of thinking, General Relativity and Quantum.   It would appear that a number of theorists who work with one of these systems and get to an impasse which that system cannot solve, suddenly, and without manifested justification, switch systems, and invoke the other system to help them out.   *Three examples* can be mentioned.

First, when General Relativity suggests an anti-gravitational force to fuel inflation, but cannot come up with an energy source for such a force, Quantum theorists can suggest quantum sources for it, once the applicability of quantum to the assumed parameters of the case is admitted.

Secondly, when Quantum thinkers propose a natural transition from state to state, without initiality or boundary conditions in the equations, they do not explain how the transition can occur if it is to be actual and not merely mathematical.   Quantum cannot explain it.   General Relativity might explain similar situations, but there is a need to validate the analogous use of its principles in a confessedly Quantum domain.

Thirdly, to suggest that the domain of Relativity meets that of Quantum as a state-reducing measurement of Quantum, is to assume the emergence of Relativity from Quantum without possessing the explanation in Quantum terms.

In general, then, there does appear to be an *ambiguous*, if not *equivocal*, and *idiosyncratic* use of language in the switching of theoretical systems to get out of impasses into which each of them independently seems to arrive. When that occurs, there does seem often to be a falling back on the

Platonic imaginary and language of myth.   How valid this is to describe
the real beginnings of the cosmos is a good question; and how philosophy
and theology should respond to it is an even better one.   May I say at this
point that there is much in the language of those disciplines which needs
to listen to the manner in which science has forged its articulations in the
field, and to purify itself of similarly untested forays into a language of its
own.

However, once we can admit that physics has created a language of its
own, partly from myth, partly from relativity, and partly from quantum,
with a good dose of original intuition in the way words and concepts are
used, then we begin to possess the *instruments* with which to build a *story
of cosmogenesis*.   The hard part is the very beginning of the narrative, and
this is where the ambiguities lie.   Once they are glossed over, then it is
relatively easy for the plot to unfold in its manifold chapters.   And the
language is exciting, and appealing, and insightful.   It is to that story that
we shall turn in chapter 4, but now we must turn to what philosophy and
theology can tell us about the beginnings.

PHILOSOPHY AND THEOLOGY

My aim here is *first*, to state the basic reasons why an understanding of
absolute origination demands more than the best explanations of physics;
secondly, to affirm that, historically at least, the idea of a Creator is a
faith-assertion; and, *thirdly and principally*, to outline the various stages of
Christian thinking about creation.   I say 'thinking' because it includes at
the same time elements of philosophy and elements of theology.   It is best
not to separate them.

When philosophy receives the world view of physics in its ponderings about
beginnings, it has a sense that everything has not been said.[13] Some stages
of origination may have been described, but not absolute origination.   The
characteristic explanatory modes and strategies do not seem to tell the
whole and complete story.   It is not a sufficient explanation to say that a
'model' of the cosmos can specify and prescribe its own real and actual
existence: its real being is much, much more than the modelling of its
features.   And philosophy must look, beyond physics, for an intelligent
and sufficient explanation for precisely that mystery of real being, whose

realness is at root more than mathematical. This is not an argument from some alleged 'gap' in the scientific presentation: philosophers in the past have at times looked for such gaps, and science has eventually closed them. It is rather an argument from the metaphysical principles of the situation. Philosophy cannot sit back and say, 'reality just is, that's all'. Philosophy looks for the reason for the realness and actualness of real and actual being-in-cosmos.

On the principles of philosophy itself, it can be asserted that there must be at least *one self-sufficient being*: otherwise no being, anywhere, is sufficient in itself to explain its own existence. It adds that any being self-sufficient for its own existence, must be infinite in perfection, and that there can only be one such being. Philosophy would then respond to descriptions of the physicists concerning a quantum self-origination of the cosmos, that the cosmos, without a Grounding Intelligence or Source of existence not itself limited and so not identified with the material cosmos, cannot present itself as a self-sufficient explanation of its real and actual being.[14] Philosophy is then drawn profoundly to the mystery of this Being who is the *Absolute Originator* of everything, cosmos included. The classic word for such a Being, is the Creator. Philosophy would want to respect, and integrate, at its own level, the legitimate contributions of science to our grasp of the physical processes at work in the coming to be of the cosmos, but it would see its own main contribution in speculation about the identity and agency and style of relationship of the Being-Originator of the very being of the cosmos itself.

The Creator, in this sense, is distinct from the creation, but distinction is not the same thing as separation. In fact, if the Creator were separated and in that sense 'removed' from influence and relationship in regard to the cosmos, the cosmos could not and would not exist. What is asserted is a mysterious *connectedness* of self-sufficient Being and non-self-sufficient being: they *do* go together, or non-self-sufficient being does not go at all![15]

It is only a small step to think of the creative act as gratuitous, spontaneous and gracious. These are the aspects which the Abrahamitic faith-traditions have picked up and emphasised, in the languages of popular religion and myth rather than in that of metaphysics. In doing so, they have intuited aspects of the Creator that extend, in principle, the limit at which metaphysics exercises its own daring.   In *Christian history*, philosophy in itself falls short of the full picture of the Creator, which theology presents from its own revealed sources of faith, but in the language and principles it has learned from philosophy.[16]   If we look at the history of Christian thought about creation, there are variables in it, that come from *varying uses of metaphor* as different faith traditions and different philosophies interact.   It is necessary to track that history, and to show its openness to some of the metaphors suggested by contemporary physics.

The *stages* we shall look at are: the Patristic period, the medieval period, and the modern period.

The *Fathers of the Church* produced a mystical vision of creation, as the result of the encounter of Greek philosophical theory and Hebrew faith. Greek philosophy presented to them a First Source-Principle, that was One, and Good, from which everything emerged by way of 'emanation'. It was 'self-diffusive', pouring out its own goodness into cosmic patterns. (Some philosophies contemplated this as happening through various mediations, others did not.) The natural bent of this philosophy was to think of the cosmos as eternal, since the eternal First Good was always, and by its own nature, as it were necessarily, diffusing itself in emanation. This is short, technically, of the true philosophical notion of creation, to which Greek philosophy, even in Aristotle, did not arrive.

As a result, there was a popular impression taken, to say the least, that the cosmos was a participant in the divinity of the Source, and was itself divine, so that various particular items in the cosmos could be revered with the reverence due to divinity itself.   Christian faith encountered this attitude like a Hebrew sword in a pantheon.   The entire faith tradition of creation insisted that the cosmos needed the Creator, but that the Creator in no way needed the cosmos.   God does not need to create in order to be God.   Creation is not necessary on God's part, it is a free, spontaneous, gratuitous and gracious act to which the cosmos and the creation have no right.   Creation is thus contingent, and is reflected in the inadequacy of the creation to present itself as self-sufficient.   This is why in the popular forms for this faith-tradition, creation had always been presented not as eternal, but at a definite point in time.   God had always been, but the world had not.

The Patristic mind refused to look on the cosmos as a simple unexplained datum, and refused at the same time to look on it as a datum explained by its dependency on a Creative principle.   It would not look on the cosmos as a datum at all.   It was not a 'given', it was a *GIFT*.   And the mystery of a gift is that it comes from a *GIVER*, and effects in its own way the presence of that Giver to the Receiver of the Gift.   In this way, the Creator-Giver (free, spontaneous, gratuitous) became strangely present to the creation, which was the Creator's gift in one way, and yet in another way was the recipient of the Divine Creator both as *GIFT AND GIVER* at the same time.   This presence is not like other presences in the cosmos.   The Being of the Creator is not one more being, like other created beings.   It is a bit like saying that the presence of white light does not add any new colour to the spectrum.   The world is full of the glory.

Several things follow from this.   *First*, there is a demystification of nature, a defence of the reality of the world in its own right, a liberation of the creation to be itself.   God can be God, and the cosmos can be the cosmos.   This provides a foundation for the possibility of true science as a discipline distinct from theology, and autonomous in its own domain.   It also provides a basis for an emphasis in theology on natural things, like bodies, and conception, birth, death, burial, and resurrection, and for what we can truly call a sacramental vision of mystery.   Desacralisation, secularisation, and sacramentalisation belong together.

There is *also* a profoundly catholic optimism here.   The Patristic vision was developed as a reaction to gnostic pessimism.   The gnostics typically thought that there was an ultimate Depth that was incomprehensible (Bythos), from which emanated a Demi-Urge or Creator.   The Creator was not the ultimate mystery but an intermediate one.   From this creator came the cosmos, but as an accident, by way of unintended 'fall' from the divine sphere.   Into this cosmos that should not have been there also - by further accident - fell the human spirit, which was then trapped in the bad world, like a spark of divinity in the wrong place.   Its vocation then was to be released from all this and from the body, and to find its way back to a reunion with the divine.   This it could do through true knowledge of the situation (gnosis), given to a spiritual, esoteric elite.   This is a far cry from the position of the Fathers.

It is very important to realise the *profound personalism* of the Patristic vision.   It has synthesised the Hebrew and the Greek intuition.   A free Creator-Giver fruitfully gives, diffuses, dispenses itself as a flowing wellspring with no holding trough.   It gives itself as a self-pouring-forth in and to the creation.   The real words for this are *LOVE* and *SURREN-DER*.   An Original positive source of Being bestows its very Being, so that Being is revealed as *Bestowed-Being*: an Original font of Being declares itself not simply to be but to be-for the creation, so that Being is revealed as *Being-For*: the creation itself not simply comes into 'being' but comes into *'Bestowed-Being-For'*: and there is a binding together of givennesses, in which giving and receiving are in accord, and the overflow of this mystery of mutuality moves on in the universe.   When the Patristic tradition speaks of the Creator as almighty, it does not mean unlimited in the capacity to do anything, but unlimited in free power of self-bestow-al-for another.   This, as I see it, is a notion of personal love that is the antithesis of self-sufficiency and defensive autonomy.   Really, when we insist in our metaphysics that there must ultimately be one 'self-sufficient' Being as the source of all else, I wonder how we should understand 'self-sufficient' if we have heard the Church Fathers?

In a Johannine-style spiritual reading of the story of Jesus, the Fathers see *Jesus* as the living exegesis of the love mystery we have outlined.   The consent of the Son, in coming into this world, is required, in obedience; for this kind of 'obedience' is the essential creaturely form of the divine creative mutuality-outgoingness.   That is why and how the Son consents obediently to a 'being sent' from conception to death on the cross, so that his human life, in the context of cosmic history, is the sacramental revelation of the peculiar quality of divine love itself.   The word "Spirit" is rightly used as a key to the whole mystery.   The Spirit 'creates' the *openness* and the *unboundariedness* and the *givenness* of Jesus in life, and in death itself, as the Spirit raises the bodily Jesus into a transfigured form, in which he is no longer limited by the laws of time and space, or at the mercy of material semblance, but in which he is free to express in ways unknown to us now the *unlimitedness* of the kind of love that he has always sacramentalised from the Father in the Spirit.   It is the same Spirit that 'creates' in the Risen Christ that communion of the holy called church, which is catholic in the sense that it is communicative in and to and with all creation and all God.   The eucharist is its proper act, until through death and resurrection it enters into an eternally living involvement with the outpouring of Love that penetrates all communioned freedoms.[17]

If this Patristic mysticism was a synthesis of Hebrew faith and Greek emanationism, it was handed on to the *medieval doctors* as one member of a new encounter.   The other member was a new philosophy that went under the name of Aristotle, but that really was Arab, in their commentaries on Aristotle, and that was itself transformed by Aquinas into a metaphysics of being that was neither Aristotelian nor Patristic.   How did Aquinas look for a metaphysical realism in the mystical vision of the fathers?[18]

He did so by envisaging the creative act, in God, as an *act of vision in the practical intellect*.   This scholastic term means the actually practised knowing of a creative performative artist, but it needs introduction and explanation.   There is much daring in Aquinas here.

There are two kinds of knowing, speculative and practical.   *Speculative* knowing means thinking about things that might be, in relation to some prior reference field, in which they are possible in themselves.   It is like thinking about exemplars, or models, or archetypes that could give features to things.   Speculative knowing is a kind of musing: then the will would come in, and 'decide' arbitrarily on the possibles that have been mused about.   It would be something like selecting the winner of an architectural contest.   Actuality would be a subset of previously dreamed up possibilities.   I am sure that many thinkers, even in theology, implicitly assume that this is the way God operates in creation, without realising that it is not Aquinas, and that they are invoking a strong voluntarism.   One wonders about the state reduction of quantum probabilities by an observer!

Practical knowing is a different thinking, at least as Aquinas understands it in God.   Our difficulty is largely rooted in our anthropomorphism: we often do not see such a large difference between speculative and practical knowing in ourselves.   In God, practical knowing is the actual practice of thinking that thereby constitutes the things that are thought about and brings them into real being.   They are not even possible before God so thinks them into being: they come to be in the originating power of this thinking.   We are almost out of analogies for this: we can talk, but in a very limited fashion, of performative rather than assertive utterance, or of the en-acting vision of an artist (not an artisan) in the creative artistry of a moment - the wherewithal for the making of it was not even there beforehand!

The reason why we cannot imagine this kind of knowing in God is that it is not an act of production, but one of the emergence of being itself. Being is not produced, nor is a creature, formally as such, a 'product'. There is no 'change' in anything.   Rather, God by thinking like this, invites, allows, and enables a being that was not, to be, that is, to participate and to commune in God's own Being.   God's practical thinking is really the creative extension of relationship-in-being to what hitherto was not.[19]

It would be easy to highlight the freedom of God's act here, but I am not sure it is faithful to Aquinas to do so.   Bonaventure had felt that there was some kind of necessity in God to diffuse the mystery in this way. Aquinas seems to have moved to a position close to him in this.   Rather, he seems to have located the distinction between necessary and free at the level of the creature, and to have been reluctant to apply it to God. Norris Clarke speaks of the inevitability of a special *logic of love* in God, by which it would be out of character for God not to create, and this seems to capture the meaning of Aquinas.   Perhaps Eckhart was not so wrong in imaging it as a kind of 'boiling over' from within God (ebullitio)...[20]

Aquinas calls this creative knowing in God a *'scientia visionis'*. This is so different from what he calls a 'scientia simplicis intelligentiae' in God. In this latter knowing, God knows the 'rationes' of things that might happen, penumbrally and generally.   In the 'scientia visionis' God knows actively and creative-communicatively all that is actually happening and only that, i.e. all that God is actively bringing into being.   The language problem here comes from the fact that we have to use present tense verbs to speak about what God *is* thinking-doing.   Our present tense verbs have to be expanded to include 'all phases of time', and some of the phases of our time are past and some are future.   So 'when' does God exercise the creative act, of 'scientia visionis'?   The word 'when' has become ambiguous.   It is a 'moment' for and in God: but you can't date it.   The eternal present is not the same as the temporal now.   The 'nunc stans' of God is not the same as standing still.   We linguistically have to extend the idea of the present back and forward, in a time-line, and produce 'duration', but God's eternalness is not that.   It is a facet of the difference between being and Being.   It is philosophically correct to say that God knows actualities in their actuality: whatever else, God knows only penumbrally.   So in a technical sense, God does not know (in 'scientia visionis') contingent events 'before' they happen, and God does not similarly 'know' what has yet to happen and 'will' happen.   At the same time, God does not have to 'wait' to find out: God does not 'wait and see', God just 'sees'.   God's comprehensive vision in God's own present, does not mean that God peers wonderingly into the future (ours, not God's).   Nor is God 'surprised' when the future occurs![21]

By these mental and linguistic manoeuvres, Aquinas has attempted to safeguard the distinctiveness and the transcendence of God.   In a sense he has given a remarkable metaphysical sharpness to the Hebrew sword that originally cut through the Platonic forms of emanationist thought. He is saying, more than anything else, that the *relationship* between Creator and creature is not a relationship of the kind we think we know. But I wonder if he has equally explored and worded an accessibly languaged understanding of the new and different kind of relationship that does constitute creation?   Could he have put that in the more open-personalistic terms of the Patristic tradition?   Perhaps had he done so, the *further history* of the philosophical theology of creation might have been different.   In fact, it has gone in two unrelated directions.

The classic, standard, *'orthodox' direction* is the insistence that creation is a mystery and that there are no possible adequate analogies for it.   It is required to avoid metaphysical absurdity.   But in effect we cannot find our worded way into it.   We have abandoned both Plato and metaphor.   The *shadow side* of this position is the emergence, slowly, and especially in modern times, of attempts to language the unlanguageableness of creation, through metaphor and other devices.   The thinking efforts of scientists have often moved in this direction, and have made use of the work of philosophers who refuse to give up this attempt.   The chief 'school' of thought here is *Process Philosophy*, in the wake of Alfred North Whitehead.[22]   It has dominated the *modern period* of creation thinking.

Whitehead's intuition is that reality is a manifold waiting for synthesis. Every act of our knowing is a creative synthesis, a new unification of the manifold, an active making-one from what is there, turning it into a meaningful environment for us.   It is an act of 'concrescence'.   Reality comes to be then, and then perishes.   It is an ongoing 'Process'.

On all levels of reality, then, nothing is static: it is all a process of events, happenings, interactions and creative responses, between a synthesising subject and an 'actual occasion'.   The process is not always conscious.

Every actual occasion is intrinsically connected to the entire system of the universe: 'actuality is through and through togetherness' and every 'actual occasion' is a synthesis of the whole universe.   Reality is really nothing but these droplets of 'experience'.   There is no underlying 'thing' - only the networks of relationships, and 'societies' of these networks.   In our macro world, these societies are what we customarily call 'things', because they successively instantiate the same intelligible structure.   This structure is called an 'eternal object', and it alone perdures.

Eternal objects are equivalent to Platonic forms in the mind of God, who presents them as 'lures' to the ongoing occasions.   Each actual occasion, with its innate spontaneity, chooses its own form and contributes to making it real in a new way.   (The eternal objects as such are not 'real'.)

God is then a reservoir of eternal objects and a presenter of them as lures to each actual occasion.   God then respects the self-creativity of the cosmos in continuing to 'create' itself.   God has a primordial nature (described) and then a consequent nature (prehending what is actually going on in the cosmos).   In effect, God is not immutable but actually changes with the changes in the cosmos, that are not due to God as the originator.

There are *two problems* here, and with the tradition of 'Process' thought that stems from Whitehead.   *First*, there is a claim that new occasions create themselves by their own agency, in which the agency of God has no part.   This may appear to be descriptively true, but presents deep metaphysical difficulties.   *Secondly*, there is a claim that God at root is not the active creator of everything, and indeed that God is patient to change by influences that are not due to God.   This presents difficulties not only to metaphysics but also to theology.   However, there is a positive contribution as well in the process world view: God is thought of more on the analogy of internal and personal relations than as an omnipotent external cause.

We may pause here, and *review this history* of philosophical and theological thinking about creation.   When we move beyond the existence and necessity of creation to ponder its nature, I believe we can discover a constant if not thoroughly continuous stream of images to convey its meaning, and the gist of these images is deeply *personal*.   The Patristic vision is a mysticism of personal gift and giving; the Medieval vision is a transposition of personal creativity in an artist to the realm of the divine; and the Modern vision is through Whitehead one of a Creator who creates like a person among other persons.   Possibly because of the insistence of theology on the metaphysical niceties of the creative act, and on the transcendence of the mystery of creation, this tradition of a personalist interpretation of creation has at times been less than clearly presented. This may well square with the tendency to speak of 'being' in less than personalist ways.   It is time to retrieve the direction of the tradition and to allow it to speak to the scientific vision of our own times.

RECOVERING A LANGUAGE

I would like to suggest a personalist interpretation of Creation in *four steps*: first, the 'personalist' interpretation of causality, of John Polking-horne; secondly, the 'personalist' interpretation of the scriptural revelation about creation, of Marie Balmary; thirdly, the 'personalist' interpretation of the theology of God as Creator, of David Schindler and Norris Clarke; and fourthly, a critical pointing towards Aquinas' real contribution to the understanding of creation.

John Polkinghorne has attempted to put words on the difference between physical and *intentional* causality.[23]   Physical causality is the manner in which an efficient cause brings an effect into being, by way of the 'energetic exchange' of a physical motion or impulse.   Intentional causality is the manner in which an efficient cause brings an effect into being by way of *'active information'*.   The forms inherent in all material realities are really patterns of information.   If an efficient agent can truly impart a complex information bearing pattern to something, it is exercising a true causality and bringing it into being.   This does not necessarily imply the imparting of a physical impulse. Polkinghorne goes on to suggest that the physical model can be correlated with exchanges among the constituent parts of a system, whereas the intentional model relates to the *holistic patterns* of the system. The former could loosely be called 'bottom up' and the latter *'top down'* causality.

Polkinghorne applies this distinction to creation. He writes: "...it is entirely conceivable that God also interacts with flexible physical process through top-down holistic causality in a universe open to the future. Theology's language of the Spirit 'guiding' creation is beginning to find an hospitable lodging in the world that science describes."[24] He goes on to give a beautiful application of this thinking, in relation to *death and resurrection*.

"Both science and scripture encourage us to take a psychosomatic view of human kind, to see ourselves as animated bodies. The soul is then to be understood as the almost infinitely complex information-bearing pattern carried by the ever-changing array of atoms making up our bodies. Such an idea, of the soul as the form of the body, would scarcely have come as a surprise to St. Thomas Aquinas. That pattern which is me is dissolved at my death, but I believe that it is an entirely coherent hope that it will be remembered by God and recreated by him in a final act of resurrection."[25]

This concept of Polkinghorne invites me to make *two connections*. *First*, it offers a language in which to speak of the mystery of God's creative act as the 'scientia visionis' in the divinely artistic practical intellect, a language that is a little more accessible to us today than the language of mediaeval scholasticism. *Secondly*, it opens a way to understand something about creation that flows from the heart of the metaphysics of being, and which David Burrell has put in the strongest terms. Once the transcategorical nature of being is grasped, and the character of creation as a relation of dependence of the creature upon the Creator precisely in being, and the further task of describing the features of the created being is undertaken, then the Creator-Source not only can be but is necessarily 'factored out' of the discussion.[26] Precisely because we are - in dealing with creation - not dealing with ordinary predicates. I propose that this opens the way towards a partially sympathetic reading of the suggestion of quantum physicists like Hawking and Hartle, that the cosmos can adequately deal with its own origination without outside help.   If they mean that the outside help is by way of the ordinary predicate-categories of physical exchange as among constituent parts of a system, it could be conceded that there is no such thing in creation.   Aquinas would have put it that creation is not production, and that the creative act does not consist in imparting motion to the creature.   We would put it simply today that creation is not a physical impulse from God.   It is rather an intentional thing, in the divine Artist, excitedly imparting patterns of holistic meaning where none were.   This not only allows us to come to some understanding of a real meaning in the phrases of the physicists, but to purify the concept of creation and make it thereby all the more personal.

Marie Balmary has attempted to read the entire canon of scripture synchronically and holistically, and to hear, at a depth far below the surface, the *'real' message* of 'it all'.[27]   The message, she says, is about the *origination of men and women as subjects, or persons*, that is, as Je and Tu, speaking to and addressing each other.   Persons in this sense, she says in her scriptural study, are *not created by God*, but owe their origination to their mutually interactive address.   The bible is the story of that origination.   'Creation' (of the cosmos as environment for humans, and of 'humankind' - much less than distinct human persons -) is a setting up of the preliminaries for the different process of personal and interpersonal emergence.   But since that process is the ultimate intent of it all, and the model in mind in it all, *the dynamics of interpersonal exchange* ought to be found *mirrored* in the fashioning of creation.   Balmary's chief interest is in human interpersonhood, and that is why she sees scripture as an 'anthropogen' and so does not develop in any detail the mirroring of anthropogenesis in cosmogenesis, or 'creation'.   She takes the issue of creation at a descriptive, biblical, and psychological level, and not at a metaphysical one, but she is pointing us, in a different and challenging view of scripture, to be more careful, and more personalist, in our use of the very word 'creation'.

Norris Clarke, in his book, *Person and Being*, has opted for a radically personalist understanding of being, and has described, in its communional character in relationship, a *'receptiveness'* in the very mystery of being, which he insists is not an imperfection.[28]   His insight has been taken up by David Schindler, who phenomenologically relates this receptivity to a *'giftedness'*, and theologically connects it with the second person of the trinity as subsistent Receptivity or Gratitude, or Being-From the Father/Source.[29]   Both thinkers are pondering the Patristic tradition we have presented here, in the wake of Hans von Balthasar. Schindler goes on to suggest, and Clarke concurs, that through the mystery of creation, creatures image God *precisely as Son/Logos*, that is, precisely in the quality of receptivity/gratitude/being-from.   This belongs to the very being of the creature, indeed it is of the nature of being itself.   In their subsequent activity, creatures who 'are' the 'patience' of the Son, go on to image the 'agency' or 'pouring-out-ness' of the Father/Source.   In this proposal of a 'withinness' of receptivity and spontaneity universally in all being, what we have is a *metaphysics of love*, interpersonal love, trinitarian love. Metaphysics is not metaphysics without it. All being is primordially and trinitarianly relational, and personal, and creation is the primordial, trinitarian, relational outpouring that alone can make it possible as such. We are obviously dealing here with an intuition into *relationship* that is not familiar to many thinkers, but that is germane with the mysticism of the fathers of the church. It may well also be a highly creative, and faithful, retrieval of the metaphysics of Aquinas.   But it is reaching into the wellsprings of a kind of Platonism that is not usually presented as congruent with Aquinas.   We need to probe further into this relational-personalism of the creative act.   In their different ways, Polkinghorne, Balmary, Clarke and Schindler are demanding it.

Before attempting a positive suggestion in this direction, it would be useful to *review* our analysis of the language of physics, and of the language of philosophy/theology in the matter of absolute origination. The *language of physics* is an amalgam: it consists of an adroit but idiosyncratic blending of the language of quantum with that of General Relativity, plus that of 'Platonic' imagery. It is thereby doubly ambiguous, and tends to convey a sense of reality within those doubly ambiguous terms. The *language of metaphysics/theology* is also an amalgam: it consists of a balance between the language of mystical intuition and that of two contributing analogies, each of which is invoked to give critical enhancement to the sense of reality in the mystical intuition. The two analogies are: the analogy of practical knowing by creative vision, and the analogy of processes that take place in interpersonal relations. Immediately, each of the analogies has to be purified: the former, by insisting that its point is really true only if we are talking directly about God alone; and the latter, by insisting that the mutuality implied in the processes of relationship can be found only with difficulty in God.   When the two purified analogies are combined, they almost cancel each other out, and we are left with a fairly limp analogous instrument to put in the service of the mystical insight.   If the language of physics is doubly ambiguous, it could be suggested that that of metaphysics/theology is at least quadruply so.   Any attempt to combine the languages of the two disciplines would seem to lead to an exponential multiplication of ambiguities that is unhelpful.   It is in a linguistic situation of this kind that mysticism and imagination tend to win out, because of the uncritical and confusing use of any other language.

It is exactly here that we need to take up, critically, the *relational personalism* suggested by the authors and traditions we have reviewed, especially that of Aquinas.   It will be necessary, in the vein of Norris Clarke, to try a creative retrieval of the direction of Aquinas' thinking, rather than a repetition of his words.

First of all, Aquinas, I think, is clear that the kind of relationship involved between Creator and creature as such, is not the kind of relationship known by Aristotle.   It is not the *'to pros ti'* of Aristotle.   That very conception implies that there is - 'already' - a 'to' and a 'ti' and that the relationship is the 'added' 'pros' between the two.   The relationship of creation cannot be like that, because by definition before creation and its relationship there cannot 'already' be two terms.   What then is this relationship, and how does it differ from the Aristotelian one?   I would suggest that the implication is that the relationship is a *'pros'* that is there prior to any 'to' or 'ti'.   It is a connectedness that is there, before there are things to connect.   The terms of the relation appear if you like after, rather than before the relationship: they emerge, like clarifications of the webbedness, like nodal centres 'illustrating' the mystery of the 'field'.[30]

I would insist here that this is not to deny the reality of substances.   But it is to go a step further than to say that reality is substance-in-relation. That is true, but I think it might be more true to speak of relationships that demonstrate a substantiality and virtually demand that we conceive their reality in mutually terminal ways.   Our language systems are not geared to handling the almost ineluctible interweaving of the two dimensions, substance and relation, especially when it is not a question of 'to pros ti', and there will always be a leaning in one direction rather than the other.   I am simply leaning in the relational direction a little more strongly.

Secondly, when Aquinas insists in the name of Being itself that the creative act does not produce anything in the creature, or move anything, or change anything, what he is implying is that there is no 'to pros ti' relationship implied in or resulting from the creative act.   All instances of production, motion and change occur in 'to pros ti' situations.

Thirdly, what really happens in the creative act?   By an act of Being, being 'is'.   But how does big "IS" so act that small "is" is?   If we knew that we would understand creation, and I think we would need to be Being to do that.   It remains mystery.   But precisely at this point we do tend, by a natural congruence of language, to speak in terms of *'participation'*. Philosophers often do this without critical awareness of the linguistic manoeuvre they are making.   It is a case of a critically realist philosophy invoking the schema that is prototypical of Platonic and *emanationist* and Patristic thought.   But as David Burrell puts it, it is not invoked as an analogy, but as a *metaphor*.

> "That is, the outflowing is no longer patterned on formal inference, so that formal resemblances might be so explained; the participation is rather, existential: 'this is how things receiving esse from God resemble him: ..precisely as things possessing esse they resemble the primary and universal source of all esse (ST l.4.3.)"[31]

This is true, but exactly here there is a hint of a further ambiguity.   Is the metaphor of participation explained fully in the above way, or is there even *more in it*?   If the above explanation is adequate, then the metaphor is not saying much about the manner of the coming to be of the creature.   I suspect that the metaphysical manoeuvre implied in the appeal to participation is trying to say something about the manner of the coming to be of the creature.   How does finite, boundaried being 'come from' infinite, unboundaried Being?   Does 'participation' give a positive metaphorical hint about that *'how'* of the *'coming from'*?

Perhaps - perhaps - we could reverse the direction of our thought.   If we are dealing with a *'pros' relationship* (and not a simple 'to pros ti') and if precisely that kind of relationship instantiates its own realness by making the substantiality of its mutual terminalness emerge, could we perhaps invoke this very pattern as a metaphor of the emergence of being from Being? I suggest that this kind of emergence of substantial 'mutual-terms' is in a deep sense a 'participation' of these terms in the total realness of the relatedness in question. There are then *two paradigms of participation*: one, which is the participation of thing in thing; the other, which is the participation of emergent term in relatedness (which is prior to it). The *former* seems to me to imply change, and its application to Being and creation has to be made with much denial and purification of its content. The *latter* seems to me to imply no change or variation of realness in the 'pros'-relatedness 'from' which the emergence comes. Its application as a metaphor to the instance of Creation would seem to imply much less denial of content. It could be really contributing to the understanding of the manner of the coming to be of being from Being.

But there may well be *a price* in this. Can we then conceive the Creator, less immediately as a 'substantial entity' than as a 'pros-field' which is the active source of the emergence of all beings? Obviously, we can, and the implicit invitation to translate it into the theological language of the Creative *Spirit* is seductive. But it does seem to me that the opposition between this seductive option and the more naturally assumed one does not impose itself rigorously. How?

Before giving a direct answer, it is useful at this point to introduce the word *'person'*. The quality and character and inherent dynamicity of the 'pros-field', in its mutuality, and immediacy, and openness, is precisely and pre-eminently that of interpersonal relations. If we use the word adjectivally, the pros-field is profoundly 'personal'. But let us be careful about the very word 'personal'. There are *two ways* of understanding it.

First, and usually, I believe we imagine a person substantially as there and given, and another one as equally substantial and given. We then imagine them as relating 'interpersonally', and the conception is that of a 'to pros ti'. But there is a *second* possibility. We could imagine a pros-relatedness that had all the qualities we call 'personal', which expressed itself in substantive and mutual terms within the relatedness, which we would then call 'persons'. They would then imbibe into their substantiality all the relationality of the pros-field itself. It all depends whether we regard the noun-person as primary, with an addition of relationship, or whether we regard the noun person as emergent from the relationship-field, and integrative of the relational qualities of the field into its substantiveness. I believe that the direction of much contemporary phenomenology of person goes in this 'less obvious' way.

If so, I think we may have a metaphor here for a divine transcendent Being that *includes* into its Being, and into the very meaning of Being, all the 'adjectival' features of personalness and all the 'substantive' ones as well. It is in this sense that I would want to speak, with Norris Clarke, of *Person and Being.*

Now, to return to a *direct answer* to the question left unanswered, I think that Being itself is *both field and substance* at the same time. And I think it is so *as* Person. It is in this sense that a personalised metaphysics of Person-Being comes up with a better notion of Person than is customary and a better notion of Being than is customary. Thereby it is in a position to *justify* its use of participation as metaphor of creation, while remaining strictly a critical realism, and not falling back into the mystical and the imaginary. It forges a language which is not an amalgam of ambiguities, but a synthesis of truly complementary meanings.

This is why I would see the *emergence of persons together from and in interpersonhood*, as the best paradigm of creation. From the development of this chapter, I hope it is legitimate now to suggest that the principal metaphor of physics concerning creation, namely, the *'Big Bang'* and all that goes with it, and the principal metaphor of metaphysical theology concerning creation, namely, the *'practical knowing in vision of a creative artist'*, are legitimated by, and provide supplementary dimensions to, the personal paradigm. The 'Big Bang' asks us to see interpersonal emergence, or love, not as a quiet development or 'emanation' but as an *explosive excess* of outpouring discovery. The 'Creative Artist' asks us to see the same mystery as a *meaningful advent* of and to a *Seen-Truth* not seen before, so that mere energy becomes meaningfulness and desire knows it has always been directed. If we incorporate these supplementary dimensions into the personal paradigm, we could have an instrument with which we can - through a symphony of several disciplines - probe the mystery of Absolute Origination.

In doing so, we may also be developing a language with its own many-layered meaning, through which the tale of cosmic history can be told as the story of the divine persons.   But before we try to do that, we need to look at the 'end' of the story.

§ § §

NOTES

1.   B.Parker, *Creating: the story of the origin and evolution of the universe*. Plenum Press, London, 1988.

D.Overbye, *Lonely Hearts of the Cosmos: the scientific quest for the secret of the universe*, Harper Collins, 1991.

2.   S.Weinberg, *The First Three Minutes: a modern view of the origin of the universe*, Basic Books 1977.

3.   G.Smoot, *Wrinkles in Time*, Doubleday, 1993.   C.Powell, The Golden Age of Cosmology, *Scientific American*, July, 1992, 17-22.

4.   D.Darling, *Deep Time; the journey of a single subatomic particle from the moment of creation to the death of the universe and beyond*, Doubleday, 1989.

5.   P.Davies, *The Mind of God, science and the search for ultimate meaning*, Simon and Schuster, New York, 1992.   P.Davies, *The Cosmic Blueprint: new discoveries in nature's ability to order the universe*, Simon and Schuster; New York, 1988.   P.Davies and J.Gribbin, *The Matter Myth: towards 21st century science*, Viking, New York 1991.

6.   G.Ellis and W.Stoeger, Introduction to General Relativity and Cosmology, in *Quantum Cosmology and the Laws of Nature*, ed. R.Russell, N.Murphy, C.Isham, Vatican Observatory, 1993, pp.33-48.   One value of this study is that it deals exclusively with the contribution of General Relativity to cosmic origins, without introducing Quantum considerations.

7. W.Drees, *Beyond the Big Bang: Quantum Cosmologies and God*, La Salle: Open Court, 1990.

8. C.Isham, *Quantum Theories of the Creation of the Universe*, in Russell, Murphy, Isham, eds, *op.cit.*   n.6.   pp.49-90.

9. J.Wheeler, *Time Today*, Princeton University Press, 1993. A.Vilenkin, Quantum Cosmology and the Initial State of the Universe, *Physical Review*, 1988, 888 f. S.Saunders and H.Brown, eds., *The Philosophy of Vacuum*, Clarendon Press, Oxford, 1991.

10. W.Drees, A case against temporal critical realism? Consequences of Quantum Cosmology for Theology, in Russell, Murphy, Isham, eds., *op.cit.* n.6, pp.331-366.

11. S.Hawking, *A Brief History of Time, from the Big Bang to Black Holes*, New York, Bantam, 1988.

12. R.Penrose, *The Emperor's New Mind*, 1991.

13. D.Burrell, *Freedom and Creation in Three Traditions*, University of Notre Dame Press, 1993, p.14.

14. W.Norris Clarke, Towards a natural theology, in *physics, philosophy and theology, a common quest for understanding*, University of Notre Dame Press, 1988.

15. In this sense, God as Creator never 'intervenes' in creation: God's is a permanent presence.

16. D.Burrell, *op.cit.*   n.13, pp.12 ff.

17. H.von Balthasar, passim, as followed by Siewerth, Ulrich, Wojtyla, and now Clarke.   The insight, and its influence on the speculative discussion, can be pursued in the dialogue between Clarke and David Schindler, in *Communio*, Fall, 1993, 580-598, and *Communio*, Spring, 1994, 151-190.

18. D.Burrell and B.McGinn, *God and Creation*, University of Notre Dame Press, 1990.

19. D.Burrell, *Freedom*, cp. 2.

20. St.Thomas Aquinas, in *I Peihermeneias*, c.9, lect.14, n.22., a reference I owe to a personal communication from Norris Clarke.

21. D.Burrell, *Freedom*, pp.101-110.

22. A.N.Whitehead, *Adventures in Ideas, Science and the Modern World, Modes of Thought*, and especially, *Process and Reality*. This style of thinking is so widespread among the philosophising scientific community that quite frequently we see a 'modern Newtonian worldview' opposed in binary opposition to a 'postmodern Whiteheadian worldview', as for example by C.Birch.

23. J.Polkinghorne, Not just any old world, in *The Tablet*, 23 January, 1993, 102-103. Refer to the major writings of this author cited in chapter one, n.2.

24. Polkinghorne, *Tablet*, cit.n.23.

25. Polkinghorne, *Tablet*, cit.n.23.

26. I owe this expression to Burrell, *Freedom, p.39: "...once* we have the universe before us, the source-of-all seems able to be factored out, like a universal constant..."

27. M.Balmary, *La Divine Origine: Dieu n'a pas créé l'homme*. B.Grasset, Paris, 1993.

28. W.Norris Clarke, *Person and Being*, Milwaukee, Marquette University Press, 1993.

29. See n.17.

30. I am here consciously breaking from Cajetan, who posits the priority of an absolute ontological fundamentum to any relation. The consequences, for example, in a theology of hypostatic union would be significant.

31. Burrell, *Freedom*, p.36.

CHAPTER 3

GUESSING THE END

Beyond mythologies...
to a sense of
Ultimate Grace

We know little, and fear much, when we ponder the possible absolute ending of the entire cosmos. Our language about it has even more ambiguity in it than our language about our beginnings. Our individual emotive responses range from agnosticism to anxiety; our historically and culturally conditioned imagination turns agnosticism into desire and anxiety into fear. The whole speculation is haunted by the impression that 'the end' will be a return to 'the beginning', and parallels suggest themselves everywhere.

I shall outline the contribution of contemporary physics to the discussion. Then I shall look, philosophically, at the eschatological and apocalyptic imagination. It will then be appropriate to examine the character of our own dying. Finally, theology can teach us the mystery it knows and the humility we must all have in the presence of what we cannot know.

PHYSICS

When physics today makes *predictions* about cosmic futures, it relies principally on the laws of General Relativity and Thermodynamics. It assumes that cosmic background radiation is the same in all directions; that the average density, and rate of expansion of the cosmos are the same in all directions; and that the motion of the moving cosmos is simple and nonchaotic. On this basis, science is prepared to make predictions with reservations. It will make long, but not short term predictions about the cosmos as a whole; and it will make short, but not long term predictions about particular dimensions of it. It will be easier to look at some short term predictions first, and then engage the long term predictions that raise questions for philosophy and theology.[1]

The sun, in our solar system, is estimated to be about four and a half billion years old, and it is predicted that it will 'die' about 5 billion years from now.   Around that time, that is, around ten billion years from its origins, all the hydrogen fuel in its core will burn out and fuse into helium. The helium core is distended at first by the intense heat, and then begins to contract, under the influence of its own gravity.   Internal pressures and temperatures then rise, remaining unfused hydrogen gas around the core ignites, and the interior is hotter than at any time in solar history.   Over a few million years, the heat drives the surface layers out, and they cool to about two thirds of the current surface temperature.   The 'sun' then reddens into a 'Red Giant'.   It engulfs Mercury, kills all life, boils the oceans, and swallows Earth.   Cycles of expansion and contraction follow, until the outer layers boil off into space, and a naked core is left, a lump about as big as the Earth is now, glowing blue hot at about 120,000 degrees Celsius.   The fires never turn on again, and the Blue Giant becomes a White Dwarf, and then a Cold Black Dwarf, and eventually an Ice-Cold Cinder.[2]

Predictions can be made that *other small stars* in the cosmos will similarly become neutron stars.   Predictions can further be made that *larger stars* will eventually become Black Holes, millions of miles across, going 'around' once in a million years.   The *galaxies* themselves will in turn break down and disintegrate: in 10^{25} years for stellar masses, and 10^{100} years for galactic masses.   In due time (say 'long term') matter itself would self-destruct.   It is well to add that we do not presently know how rapidly the galaxies are slowing: the rate is not in proportion to the apparent changes in brightness.

Fascinating as these descriptions are, they are relatively unimportant in a scientific discussion of the *possible absolute ending* of the *cosmos*. Speculations about it in theoretical physics begin with the observed fact of the gravitational attraction of those galaxies now close enough to feel the effect of *gravity*.   Physics makes cosmic predictions on the basis of its understanding of gravity.   The cosmos is presently an expanding one. Gravity functions in it as a brake.   There are *two possibilities*.   *First*, gravity is strong enough to brake the expansion down and stop it completely and then turn its momentum into a contraction process.   In this scenario, contraction would keep on increasing, until ultimately there would be a 'Big Crunch' parallel to the original Big Bang.

Secondly, gravity may not be strong enough to brake the expansion of the cosmos.   Then the expansion would be perpetual.   It would never cease expanding.   The 'result' would be an ultimate state of the cosmos that is totally flat and bland.   There would appear to be no other possibilities. In General Relativity terms, the first scenario corresponds to a positively curved and so closed universe;   the second corresponds to a negatively curved and so open universe.   The first brings the universe to a point at which its density is virtually infinite;   the second brings it to a point at which its density is virtually infinitesimal.   One might be forgiven for thinking that neither possibility is tremendously attractive![3]

The interest of physics in all of this is to determine *which* of the two scenarios actually obtains.   To know that, we would need to know exactly the *gravitational force* in the cosmos.   To establish that, we would need to know the *relative density* of the universe.   And to know that, we would need to know how much *matter* there is in the universe.   It is very hard to know that.[4]

We can begin looking at this question by starting with the *observed and observable matter* in the universe.   That is, the stars, gaseous clouds, etc., that observably 'make up' the universe.   On present calculations, the amount of matter thus present in the universe would add up to about 2 per cent of what would be needed to 'brake' the expansion and bring about a Big Crunch.   But there appears to be other matter not so observed and observable.   Some galactic clusters seem to revolve around a gravitational force coming from a source that is not detectable but which must be highly dense and so contain a large amount of matter.   *Calculations* based on known situations of this kind would lead us to accept a further 10 per cent of the amount of matter needed to brake the expansion and induce the Crunch.   But there are still further considerations.   We do know from observation that there are galactic structures and even great cosmic 'walls' in cosmic space at present.   It is natural to go back to small fluctuations in the cosmic background radiation as their source and explanation.   Since 1992, and the COBE satellite data, it appears that they are insufficient to account for the clumping we know.   This leads physicists to develop a renewed interest in the hypothesis that there is *'other'* matter in the universe than the kind we 'know' from observation and 'Big Bang' calculations.   It is usually called *'cold dark matter'*.   Some suggest that it could comprise up to 90 per cent of the matter in the universe, and that, therefore, the density and gravitational force in the cosmos are much higher than we would otherwise estimate, indeed so high, that the likelihood is that expansion will be braked down and the Big Crunch induced. It is usually added that cold dark matter is not stellar or galactic matter: guesses are made that it could be made up of heavy neutrinos, Higgsinos, gravitinos, axions, photinos, wimps, etc.   (Note that this speculation implicitly opens the possibility of an origin of this cold dark matter that is different from the Big Bang we have come to know: could there have been more than one Big Bang?)   Perhaps cold dark matter and black holes have something in common.

There is a further consideration. It concerns the *initial conditions* of the cosmos. They have been *'fine tuned'* to an incredible degree of accuracy, seemingly with a view to giving the cosmos a future. If the amount of matter in the very primitive cosmos had been greater than it actually was by a ratio of 1:1000 billion, the cosmos would have experienced a Big Crunch collapse after ten years of its existence. If the amount of matter then had been less than it actually was by a ratio of 1:1000 billion, the cosmos would have spread out into an ultimate flatness and blandness by the time it was ten years old. You get an idea of the overall 'chances' of survival of the cosmos into a history such as we know it by multiplying the two ratios! The implied 'message' of such 'just right' proportions seems to be that we were always meant to be here: if the conditions had been even marginally different we would not be here to calculate them. This perception of some kind of *'Anthropic Principle'* in the mathematics of the cosmos itself from the beginning, leads some physicists to think that the amount of matter, the relative density, and the gravitational force in the cosmos have always been such that it would last this long and in process form stars, planets, ecologies favourable to life and human life, intelligent and loving beings, etc. Why should we not dare to think that the balances are right to continue to give us the existence they have always given us?[5]

Let me pause and *sum up* where we have come. Physics has - in working from General Relativity and Thermodynamics - been convinced that the cosmos will end and has wondered about the manner of its demise. It has experienced the limits of its present discipline in admitting it cannot answer the question of how the end will come. But in doing so it has been forced to raise other considerations, some physical, some philosophical, some human, that question even the assumption that the end is certain.   This last point has been reinforced by the introduction of *quantum* and *complexity* physics into the discussion.[6]   In all the variants of the view that the cosmos is moving to an absolute ending, a point is reached, at least in the time trajectory, where *Planck dimensions* are involved.   In other words, when we project to the 'final' moment of the cosmos, we are projecting beyond the 10^{-43} second Planck limit.   At this 'wall', the laws of classic deterministic physics, including those of General Relativity, break down, and the structures implied by them, including those of gravity, do not retain their meaning.   If the cosmos is to end in an ultimate singularity with dimensions that are infinite (or infinitesimal), can a science based on these principles make statements that purport to be real?   Is it better to say that it does not know?

There would appear to be problems *before the Planck Wall* is actually reached.   There is a minute arena in which Relativity has ceased to apply and the Wall has not yet been reached.   This is the *proper domain of quantum*.   The quantum dynamics operative here allow for massive fluctuations and oscillations in the forces at work.   They are very similar to those which a quantum theory sees in the origins of the cosmos.   Precisely here, then, 'before' an 'end' is reached, are we faced with the possibility of a new quantum origination of a new 'universe'?   Does the cosmos never absolutely wind down or disintegrate, but rather approach certain points where it would appear to be about to do so, and then revitalise itself?   This is one kind of thinking that has given rise to *'multicyclic scenarios'* in the total history of the cosmos.   It would be something like a Mother Universe which having engendered one 'generation' of cosmos, and seeing it 'dying', allows it in the act of its demise to present the next stage in cosmic process and allows it to begin the next epoch of cosmic history.   A still further possibility is that there have always been many universes, in their present dimensions incommunicable, and that in the 'ending' phase of one of them (ours) communication is established with another one, and entry into its dimensions.   We would be talking about a 'wormhole' from one to the other.   To put the matter in an image, is it possible to enter into a Black Hole, only to come out from a White Hole? that is, some'where' else, and some'time' else?[7]

For many, this sounds like science fiction rather than science.   There is of course no hard evidence for quantum fluctuations of the originating kind in the 'twilight' zone after Relativity and before Planck.   There is no known mathematics of access to other universes. But the speculation is intriguing. Some have even spoken of the need for a 'chronology protection agency' in such 'time travel': which is an imaginative way of saying that 'back' and 'forward' would not mean anything outside our world and our time. Does four dimensional spacetime still apply?[8]

Recent *chaos and complexity* theory, which we shall address in chapter five, would tend in its own way to confirm these optimistic wonderings. It deals with open, self-organising systems, in which the second law of thermodynamics does not apply, and in which entropy is converted and metabolised into a new creative expression of energy. In its terms, the cosmos could be such a system, and creatively recreate its own ongoing series of futures.

When all of these theories of physics are made to converge on the question of 'endings', there is a definite impression of *a single intuition*. It is one of a space dimension that is not our spacetime or unfolded space and time; it is one of 'imaginary' rather than 'real' time; it is one in which the logic that underlies the dynamics is different from the forms of logic known to us. This whole *arena* (if it may so be called) seems to have been always there, and our cosmos emerged from it and in a way returns to it. Indeed, just as in one theory the cosmos had no special or indeed any initial conditions at all, and in its own way accounted for its own 'origination', so it has no special or indeed any ultimate conditions at all, and in its own way accounts for its own 'non-annihilation'. It is a scenario that has a seductive human appeal coming from its optimism! (Of course, the optimism is balanced: there may be a future, but it is not as we know things now or can imagine them in the limits of an imagination conditioned by what is now.)

My interest in this study is particularly in the *analysis of language*. As a transition to the philosophical account of endings, I believe it is pertinent to comment on the kind of language used in the scientific account of endings today. It clearly has its own specialness!

I commented in chapter two on some *inherent ambiguities* in the physicists' language about beginnings. I believe they are to be found repeated here, with a new flavour. My comments in chapter two, were in reference to two things: the peculiar transposition of a realism that is proper to the world of Relativity and Classical determinism, into the proper domain of Quantum and even beyond the Planck Wall; and the regressive recourse to an imaginary and Platonic language to boost the inadequacy of the previous amalgam.   I think they are *here again*.

It is fairly easy, I think, to grasp the realism of the descriptions of solar collapse, and even galactic collapse.   It is less easy, but still reasonable, to go along with the well-argued scenarios of theoretical demise of the entire material cosmos.   It is precisely when quantum is invoked as a 'way out' of annihilation, that specific difficulties in the appreciation of the realness of what is proposed, seem to occur.   There seems to be a transposition of the realistic dynamics of the prequantum world into the quantum world, that is hard to understand on the principles of the prequantum world, and that is not offered a sufficient explanation on quantum principles.   It appears to be almost like having it both ways. The quantum language of revitalisation takes on the realistic contours of real relativity.   An *amalgam* is formed, and an *idiosyncratic* language.   Its inherent non-self-evident claim to assent is supported by the use of imagery that is *archetypal* and *Platonic*.

The new flavour in the use of this language, in the account of (non) endings, is *optimism*.   This makes one wonder if the optimism is arising from the scientific account, or rather coming from other sources (which philosophy and theology deal with) and then demanding a scientific story consonant with its mood.

Before looking directly at the philosophy, I believe we can grasp at this point how the emergent scientific languaging of cosmic futures is creating in the lay mind a new *'myth'* of how things are and will be.   The scientific contribution is much more than this, but it is really there at the same time.

PHILOSOPHY

A *cultural language* of cosmic ending has existed for a much longer period of history than that of the scientific community.   It has dimensions of speculation, and dimensions of religious conviction.   We shall look at it here from the point of view of *philosophy*, and reserve a discussion of it *theologically* until later.   It is called *'eschatology'*: the understanding of the 'last' or ultimate things and values.   It needs a critical analysis as a language.[9]

This quite distinct and indeed idiosyncratic eschatological language belongs to the world of *'myth'*.   This for me means three things: it does not intend to convey an accurate, empiric description of what it suggests; it is the instrument of a popular 'folk conviction' about things; and it touches the profound roots of reality that can hardly be expressed in any other way.   The word myth comes from the Greek muein, which means 'to be silent', as before a mystery that eludes ordinary language and articulation. Myth touches what is going on underneath, not what is happening on the surface of things.   That is why myth makes its own use of symbols, rituals, dreams, archetypes.   It is an oneiric 'sensing' of the depths, not a clear communication of what they are *'really'* like in the usual acceptance of the word 'real'.   The understanding of all eschatology as myth, and the development of a mythic sensitivity to what eschatology suggests, is essential to all eschatological study.[10]

I would accept the hypothesis that basically all such eschatological myth arises as an *unconscious projection* from the *collective unconscious* of peoples and cultures, and perhaps from that of humanity itself.   That does not mean that it is more 'true' than 'ordinary' myth: it means that all of us, collectively, can handle our ultimacies only mythically.

What is interesting about the language of such myth, is not how it came about, but what people have done with it once they had it in their possession.   Their *use* of it in their own communications to one another tells us much about its real value.   This use is a form of *'rhetoric'*: it is a vein of communication through speech that is meant to be persuasive. Not persuasive of empiric conclusions of verified research, but persuasive of certain desired behaviour in the social and political and cultural life of a people.[11]

Rhetorically-used eschatological-myth is of two kinds: commination, and enticement.   A *'comminatory prophecy'* is threat, in the form of a conditional prophecy, in which the condition is not expected to be fulfilled, nor meant to be.   A university administration can threaten a graduate group with expulsion/extinction unless more real cooperation comes from it here and now in the day by day running of the university.   When church orators preach that we will all go to hell unless we substantially improve our spiritual and moral performance (for example, in matters of fraternal charity and social justice), they do not actually predict that we will really go 'there': they are rather using the words to insist that we 'might', if we didn't, believing, hoping, and expecting, and almost knowing that we will. The rhetorical use of the myth is a mechanism for social control and behaviour change now.   Of course, such rhetoric would lose most of its impact if its internal linguistic and rhetorical character were explained to its audience at the moment of its use.   It is rather used *'unexplained'*, and the rhetor trades on the ambiguity created by such lack of explanation. There results an *'as if'* impression in the audience: it is impacted, and moved to change its ways, as it would be if what is preached to it were literally and empirically true.   There is then a sense, internal to the language exchange, in which an undiscussed realness of the mythic affirmations is presented as axiomatic.   Once the language data and its rhetorical use are critically examined, it appears that the alleged empiric or ontological reality of the material is neither affirmed nor denied: it is simply not the issue, the issue being the value of such myth for human improvement in a cultural community.[12]

An *'enticement prophecy'* is the contrary opposite of this.   It is a promise, in the form of a conditional prophecy, in which the condition is expected and meant to be fulfilled.   'Unbelievably' beautiful things are promised to those who act in certain ways now.   Because of the confidence in the community to respond to the enticement, the 'unbelievably' beautiful future is described with an unusual amplitude.   This does not come from privileged information about that future.   It comes from the enthusiasm and the excitement of the rhetorical plane of communication.[13]

This background makes it easy to understand why the most prevalent form of eschatological myth is *apocalyptic*.   The derivation of the word (apocalypse) suggests a revelation of something hidden.   What is to be so revealed is a way out of an impasse.   The impasse is that our entire present human (social, political, cultural, religious) situation is so irremediably bad in the eyes of God, that re-adjustment no longer has any point, and all we can now expect is a definitive intervention by God to destroy it all as it has been, and replace it with a new 'deal', a new 'heaven' and a new 'earth'.   Only those who are spiritually ready will survive the ordeal and enter into the wonders of the future.   Apocalyptic thrives on binary oppositions (two ages, two kingdoms, two spheres) and definitive interventions. It combines much of the two forms of rhetoric we have looked at. It is easy to grasp that eschatology lives happily as apocalyptic.[14]

Apocalyptic can become the *ideology* of a civilisation. It does so especially for early *literate civilisations*, when they are in transition from oral culture to *writing*. In such a 'phase transition', they need and create for themselves a disciplinary *world order* (that is, in their lifeworld or social world), and their apocalyptic myths help them rhetorically to do so. Because of the association of the inherent element of fear in all apocalyptic, with the burgeoning definitiveness of the written word, the emergent world order appears *moralistic*, and *penal*. This is promoted especially by a process of *externalisation*. The penal-apocalyptic horizon is imaginatively concretised into the image of a *'court'* of 'judgment'. Usually what is being judged, is the cultural patterns of a previous 'cyclical' myth, in the light and under the criteria of an incipient *'linear history'* myth (which writing fosters and expresses). In fact, in many such myths, the old cycles are thus thought to be *'redeemed'*.[15]

One salient characteristic of such a language system is the claim that it has *ultimate meaning*, but that the access of all of us to this ultimate meaning is *'deferred'*: we cannot quite have it now. This deference creates the basic difference between now, and some *'end-time'* in the future, after a duration of unknown length. The inbuilt *tension* between the already and the not yet then becomes a strong characteristic of eschatological thinking. It is at this point that we seem to have come to the kind of populist folk-religious understanding of the 'ending' of the universe that is widespread among many people today. The step from this into a *literal fundamentalism* in the reading and hearing of apocalyptic texts is a small one.[16]

It is interesting to compare and contrast this cultural language with the language of today's scientific community about cosmic endings. In effect, they agree on one thing: they *don't know* - in real and empiric terms - anything about the 'real' 'end' of the cosmos. They both speculate about it. The language of the *speculation* is for both disciplines, *mythic*. We are living with the encounter of a cultural myth and a new scientific myth. Both are redolent of *apocalytic*. Each has its *rhetorical* use, being put to work to persuade people to see the world in a different way and to live

differently as a result.   The old cultural myths are *anxiety* provoking (for
a purpose).   The new scientific ones are intended to convey a different
optimism.

For a long time in the cultural history of the west, especially the Christian
and European west, the eschatological myth has been radically *individualised*.   That is, the focus of attention has become the demise of the
individual rather than the disintegration of the cosmos.   In fact, the
symbols and metaphors used in the apocalyptic sources originally about the
end of the world have been transposed to relate to the death of the
individual.   In this sense, eschatology itself has been transmuted into a
'thanatology'.[17]

I believe consideration of the death of the individual is becoming the place
where the older cultural myths and the new scientific myths are meeting.
There is a new understanding of death.   A consideration of it will take us
to the limit of both systems of language, and will also show us the implicit
anthropological orientation of all our thinking.

DEATH AND DYING

It is recognised today that 'death' and 'dying' are culturally, and historically, *conditioned* experiences.   No one dies an absolutely, clinically 'clean'
death: cultural factors enter into the constitution of the manner of
people's dying, and dying occurs differently in different cultures in different
periods of history.   We have lived in the Christian European West for
many centuries now in a cultural model of death that could be described
as the *'terror of transcendence'*:   its recent denial and the advocacy of
agnosticism in the matter could be interpreted as its continuing shadow
side.   There is evidence that in the present generation of humanity we are
beginning a cultural mutation in the manner of our dying.   It could be
hesitantly suggested that a persuasion of the *'benignity of the beyond'* is
replacing the 'terror of the transcendent'.   It is in this transition that the
scientific vision of cosmic endings is exercising an influence on the older
cultural apocalyptic.

Before outlining elements of this process, let me say that the *existence of
life beyond*, for human beings, is not a matter of rationally proven

certainty: philosophically, it can at best be suggested, and theologically, it can be supported by reflection on the faith traditions of believing communities. What I want to probe here is a critical analysis of a cultural persuasion about death that includes philosophical and theological components.[18]

My belief is that it is useful to distinguish carefully between biological or clinical death (henceforth called *'death'*) and personal or existential dying (henceforth called *'dying'*). Death is a contingent, historical accident. Dying is an act, a personal act, perhaps the ultimate act of personal self-expression. It is easier to begin with a look at dying.

The simplest approach to dying, in this sense, is to see it as 'letting go'. There are in our psyches two conflicting instincts, one to *'cling to'*, the other to *'let go'*. In the former we tend to 'hold on' to resentments, to unshared pain, to our narcissistic and defensive attempts to contain what we do not want to share, and to the reinforcement of our isolation. In other words, we tend to 'hold on' and 'cling to' positions we take against the possibility of larger relationship, mutuality, and communion with others. In the second instinct in us, we also tend to 'let go' precisely of these things, and to open out, reach out, and relate communionally with the others we encounter. Our lifestory is a balance of the two, with, ideally, the second ultimately winning out. Our *'vocation'* in life, is to be ready, by the time the accident of death occurs to us, to make our final personal act of ultimate 'letting go' into a 'holy communion' with and in all reality. (Some traditions, for example, that of the Catholic Church, would add, in its theologising, the possibility that some are forever closed to this option, and so place themselves in an eternal and self-contradictory unfulfillment - 'hell'; and they would add the further possibility that someone might be not in principle forever closed to the letting go, but not quite ready at the unforeseen moment of physical death, and to meet such a contingency they develop the notion of a 'purgatory', with a catholic genius for middle terms in binary discussions.)

The *psychology* of such personal dying and letting go is developed today as an expansion of consciousness towards all the events that have ever been, are, and will be. It is an experience of synchronicity, and an extrasensory perception of a healing and reconciling protopathy with it all, in a new harmony. In that different sense, it is a kind of re-call of the whole life.

The experience is considered to be salvific as well as therapeutic, and it contains the seeds of universal salvation for all who go through the mysterious process of personal dying.   There is a sense of unboundaried-ness in it that removes all oppositions.[19]

Some thinkers in the scientific community extend their pondering of this moment of personal dying from subjective phenomenology to a more objective theoretical physics.   While they would agree that the salvific healing of all events in four dimensional spacetime (and in the three dimensional space and the time frame to which we are accustomed) does take place, they look for *something more*, perhaps as the very foundation of this experience.   They wonder if there is not a domain of reality, that has always been there as a kind of subset of the domains to which we have had access, to which we make connection through the personal act of dying and letting go.   It does not disappear when we die: rather it 'appears' to us through our act of dying.   It is perhaps a universe that is not 'three and one' or 'four' dimensional as we consider ours to be.   But it is still a 'material' universe of light, and energy, and information.   At death, perhaps our consciousness becomes a contemplation of such a differently dimensioned real-universe, in which there will be a differently-organised 'memory' of events that have been in the previous history of the person in a previous domain.   In this way, nothing is annihilated, everything that ever was, even in the material life of the person, is retained-reorganised. It is probably better to say that they are not in time, at least if 'time' is taken to refer to what we now mean by it.[20]

Are we back at what *physics* was suggesting at the beginning, and at the ending, so called, of the cosmos itself?

One of the difficulties in understanding what this language is suggesting, comes from its manner of conceiving the transition that death implies. The *popular myth* of death usually sees the transition as a 'temporary' dying to present world-conditions, to enter into a purely spiritual condition without material dimensions, and ultimately - if it believes in resurrection - to return to vastly improved world-conditions, which are essentially of the dimensions of the present universe.   The *new 'myth'* of death sees the transition as a permanent dying to regions of reality that are of the dimensions of our present universe, to enter 'immediately' (the temporality of our language is always deceptive) into a region of reality not of the dimensions of our universe.   An extremely interesting imaginative change is occurring here.

Another difficulty in understanding the new language, is that it often picks up an 'apocalyptic' style.   The classic repertoire of apocalyptic envisages an *annihilation* of all present reality, and its replacement by a different one.   The new language about death does see a passing over from one realm to another, but *without any annihilation* at all.   Indeed everything is retained in a different manner.

A third difficulty comes from the fact that the new vision would include the transition-in-difference of *all matter*, including the *bodily matter* of our body-persons.   This would implicitly mean that what older traditions have called resurrection, does not occur by an intervention of divine power at random, but in the inherent dynamics of the death process.   It would also mean that the transformation of the 'body' is so radical, since it becomes a component of a differently-dimensioned universe, that it would literally be 'unrecognisable' in our universe.   This causes problems with religious traditions which believe in appearances of dead persons in the very bodies they had in our world;   and it also creates difficulties, and ambiguities, in the way our imagination works to express our hunches about our own future.

Once this new vision is set up for the death of individuals, we can return to the question of the ultimate 'death' of the cosmos.   Is there a transition process, analogous to what we have outlined for individual death, in the final(?) transition of the cosmos as we know it?

If we reflect on a critical analysis of both cosmic and individual eschatology, one thing is clear: governing both dimensions of the understanding of ultimacy, is a certain perception of *Personhood*.   But for a sense of the ultimate dignity and indestructible being of the Person as such, the inner logic of neither individual nor cosmic eschatology would hold.   Perhaps we are talking less about the world or the body, than about the person, and the a priori conditions of possibility for personhood itself.   This is not to say that the claims are not real about cosmos and body: they are, but they are because of an even more central and even more real conviction of an even deeper realness of personhood.

At the same time, I would suggest that the model of person implied at the beginning of the above analyses is *modified* in the process of these analyses. At their conclusion, it is much more that of a *person-embodied-in-cosmos*, as an integral whole. And if the insight has developed like this, so has the language peculiar to the philosophical (and scientific) discussion. It is indeed a *special language*, tolerating its own special ambiguities for the sake of the special probings into reality that it wishes to undertake. The wellsprings of that language lie in a meeting of two mythic traditions: an old, popular one that becomes progressively individualised and personalised; and a new, scientific one that gets personalised and then returned to the cosmic dimensions which are the trigger of its first reflection. The use of that language is also peculiar: it is less trying to say something as if the saying were the point of it all, than trying to suggest a way of being *(person in cosmos)* that eventually transcends all accurate saying. Such is the limit, and the grandeur, of human speech about being fully human.

THEOLOGY

There has necessarily been some introduction of theological data into the preceding discussion of eschatology. Here I would like to hear the theological voice by itself. I shall ask, *first*, what theology is really trying to say when it treats eschatology; *secondly*, how Christian theology has historically treated eschatology; *thirdly*, why the question of the meaning of the resurrection of Jesus has affected the theology of the eschata; *fourthly*, how the question of cosmic history is theologically the question of the missions of the persons of the Trinity; and *finally*, what is the peculiar quality of the language of theology in these matters. What is theology trying to say? Let us look at its *data*, its *aim*, its *instruments*, and its special *style* in making its contribution.

Theology, as I understand and practise it, is a servant discipline. It serves the *myths* and popular expressions which articulate the faith of believing communities. The faith of those communities does not ultimately depend on theology: it is much deeper than any theology. Pastoral teaching authorities in those communities are there to protect, and render as functional as possible in a practical sense, the body of symbols and myths which the believing community uses in its faith life. They are the stuff of folk life: encrusted with cultural accretions, roughhewn, unpolished - but diamonds. Theology is there to serve the people who use them, the authorities who protect them, and especially the inner meaning they enshrine and sometimes conceal.

The aim of theology is to conduct an integral hermeneusis of this tradition, and to use it as a launching pad, to probe into the realities it points to, rather than captures, and to elaborate their full meaning. It thus in a way helps the tradition to do what the tradition cannot do without it. For this purpose it needs instrumentalities that do not come from the tradition.

The chief *instruments* which theology uses are human sciences (natural and social), and philosophy. The more they themselves are integrated, the more they can offer theology the rudiments of a language that can probe the reality beyond them all. When theology uses them, it is not simply 'repeating' them. It is not claiming that they express fully and better what the myth tradition was trying to say. Nor is it saying that they are mere academic footnotes to a text that can never be more than mythic. Rather, when theology engages the meeting point of the tradition and the combined instrumentality of human thinking, it *'realises'* something of its own. The verb is a happy one, because what emerges is a sense of *'the'* real, an intellectual experience of a realness not touched in the same way either by the tradition or by human thought, and often not focussed or located in the same way. When theology does this, it does something peculiarly its own.

In the theology that serves the Christian tradition, this properly theological sense of a realness not otherwise touched is focussed on the *life, death, and resurrection of Jesus Christ.* There is a unique realness about the way it speaks of Jesus, that transgresses the limits of all human disciplines and dares to have a knowledge of reality, in quality and mystery, not otherwise accessible. It claims in effect that at root, all reality is, to coin a word, *"Jesus-ised".* Historical sciences have said historically real things about him, and the tradition of faith has said mythically real things about the way he lived. Theology picks these up, and in using the word *"Person"* about him, uses it in a way all its own, a way that gives utterly new depth to the sense of the word, and that insinuates that in and through Jesus all reality is at root a self-communicating overture of reciprocal communion. The claim that this is so is based not on any philosophical argument, (which at some historical periods of theology has actually been lacking), but on the properly theological form of conviction I am suggesting here.   In reverse, once this happens, the philosophical instrumentality (theory of person) that theology has used, returns to its own metier, and in full confidence identifies the supreme reality of being as personhood itself, and henceforth cannot speak of the real, or of being, without introducing the nuance of 'personal'.   The tradition always had a faith in such a mystery, but in its own opaque forms.   Theology has made them translucent.

It is in this sense that for theology proper, the lifestory of Jesus is *a parable and a paradigm of the person*.   Real faith in Jesus is not the collection of symbols and rituals about him, but the living in personal communion and self-giving which all those symbols and rituals really suggest.   That is what theology is 'really' 'all about'.

When it comes to *eschatology*, Christian theology sees its language as one way of asserting the irremovable beauty of the person, even in the face of death and possible cosmic destruction.   That is what it really wants to say, theologically, in the matter.   Theology then works on coherent ways of penetrating the meaning of the eternal life of person-embodied-in-cosmos, using available tools of myth and science and philosophy, but always probing into its own 'more'.

At present, theological eschatology seems to be at a critical stage of its own development.   It is only recently that it has achieved a more explicit sense of its specific style and message.   (This has become even more delineated as science and philosophy have been more assured in their own domains.) It is also only recently that it has possessed a more accurate, and a more critical history of its own use of its mythic data.   *For example*, it has tended in the past to rely quite heavily on apocalyptic, and to elevate apocalyptic into a governing matrix of large segments of its endeavour. It has now come to realise that historically, much of this theological reliance on *apocalyptic* has been uncritical.   It is therefore moving in a direction that criticises naive apocalyptic, and inquires into the real referent of the symbols contained in it.   In doing so, it runs counter, in the short term, to the 'sense of the faithful', in the folk-religious use of apocalyptic.   At the same time, it is thereby learning a new openness to dialogue with the sciences and with philosophies of language.[21]

Another example of the present theological situation here is the rediscovery of the *historical Jesus*.   It had been assumed for a long time that the message of the historical Jesus was apocalyptic.   The recent work on Jesus suggests this may not be so, unless one vastly redefines one's idea of apocalyptic.   Jesus seems to have conceived, in his own historical ministry, a sapiential and peasant openness to the present, and not to have been so directly and primarily concerned about the eschatological future. Theology is having a difficult time in assimilating and assessing this change of appreciation of Jesus.   It may mean that it will shift its own primary emphasis to a kind of unlimited openness in relationship after the model of the historical Jesus.   This may mean that theology will tend to claim less knowledge of the eschata, and propose any understanding of them in terms of interpersonal communion now.[22]

A *third example* of the current situation comes from the understanding of the *passion and resurrection* of Jesus, which Paul has left us.   It is being appreciated anew, that, for Paul, when Jesus in dying entered into a state of permanent crucifiedness, he became an utterly unboundaried person, since not even the boundary of real death could limit him.   This condition of crucifiedness as *unboundariedness* was eternally sealed into his very being in resurrection, so that the risen Christ is forever the *Xristos estauromenos*, the Christ in a permanent state of unboundaried openness. It is this kind of Christ that Paul wants to live in him, and thus he will carry in his body the death-state of Jesus, so that the life of Jesus can be found unlimitedly in him.   This is why for Paul, for those who are in the unboundariedness of the Crucified, there can be no divisions of gender, or race, or status: we are all where there are no boundaries.   The paschal mystery is a passing into such a condition.   It is not clear whether Paul's thought remains a phenomenology of a subjective experience of this kind, or whether he also envisages an entry for the Christ and for us into a real space-time world where such unboundariedness is possible.   But there are at least indications that the latter is germane to his central vision.   Once theology assimilates this, it will discover a key focus of its eschatological reflection, that is different from much of Christian history's explicit thinking.   After the time of Paul, sources other than Jesus and Paul appear to have become dominant in theological eschatology.[23]

In this period of theological transition, interpretations of the real bodily *resurrection* of Jesus by those who deeply are committed to faith in it, have begun to differ significantly.   Theology had until recently been ready to accept a resuscitation of the cadaver of Jesus in the tomb, within a larger process of the transfigurative glorification of his body-person.   Almost all popular religious mythic understanding of the mystery is in the same vein. Indeed, although *exegesis* is not unanimous in the matter, there are fine exegetes who would sustain that at least some of the texts say exactly that. They do not raise the issue about the function of the texts: do they simply reflect the primary naivete of folk thinking, or are they making a theological statement in a critical sense?   In other words, are they referring really to what limited and simple language of the time would superficially indicate?   However, *recent theology* would seem to show some sort of preparedness to discuss an interpretation of resurrection that did not assume resuscitation or 'use' of the materials previously composing the body of Jesus, and that saw the mystery as an entry of the body-person into different dimensions of existence from ours, with a corporeity (still truly that of the one body-person Jesus) appropriate and commensurate to the new cosmic situation.   The *theological* jury is of course still out on this question, and the *pastoral* implications must surely be handled with extreme sensitivity.   None the less the possibility of a real dialogue with contemporary science and philosophy is obvious.

There are actually some *hints* in the theological tradition itself in this direction.   *Aquinas* has two principles which are in point.   *First*, his understanding of the human composite would demand that there can be only one true body for each human person; but it would not demand that one true body be always made up, as of 'raw' materials, of the same 'stuff'. If then there were another world (of different cosmic dimensions from our own) in which a human person existed, having passed through death, and therein had its own bodyliness, that bodyliness would both be the one true body of the person, and would look, dimension wise, utterly different from the way it looked in our cosmic (present) situation.   In fact, we would have no way of knowing or imagining how it would 'look'.   *Secondly*, Aquinas has understood the process of animation of the human composite as open to two quite different interpretations.   In the original creation of the human, he sees matter moving to such a qualitative degree of sophisticated sensitivity that it almost 'begs' the infusion of an informing soul to constitute it as a human composite.   In the resurrection, he sees the direction of the process reversed: the Holy Spirit grasps the soul that has passed through death and transforms it in glory, and the inSpirited soul then reconstitutes for itself its own appropriate bodyliness.   In such a dynamic there seems no reason to impose on the Spirit the demand that the same raw materials be made use of.[24]

In fact, if there is any credence to be placed in the suggestions of contemporary *physicists* about a cosmic situation of different dimensions from our own, these new interpretations may have a larger plausibility. On those scientific assumptions, the retention of the materials of the former body would seem impossible. Indeed, if the recent interpretations are followed through in their own logic, it would seem that any appearance of a risen body-person to people in our world would have to be symbolic. Should the presenting image be 'real' in the sense of the real dimensions in which the person really is, then there would seem to be no possibility of cognitive perception on our part.   On the other hand, on these assumptions, should a risen person appear in a real body of our kind, and be recognised as such, it would be evident on the logic of the situation that such a person had not truly passed into a different world, and in that sense was not 'risen'!

A. Grib has suggested that this other world operates according to a logic that is not isomorphic with ours.   When we project our kind of logic on it, it is something like the quantum collapse of a wavepacket: we share in the construction of what we see and where we live.   This is still a realist interpretation but not a naive one.

Theology, at its best, prefers to look to a *larger horizon* than these particular issues.   In the centuries when *Platonism* was its workmate, it reached back to a consideration of the divine persons of the trinity and their involvement in creation.   The interest was actually in a framework even larger than creation itself.   The second and third persons were seen as being sent out from the first, into creation, accompanying the emer-gence of the creature from the Creator.   Their role was not simply to be Gift-with-the-gift, but to become dynamic principles directing and empowering the return of the creature to its Source, namely the first person of the trinity.   In this way the ancient myth of emanation and return was taken up and transposed into the very life of the trinity, in the doctrine of the *divine missions*.   Theology was not so much about creatures in their relation to God: it was about God as God is in Godself, not statically, but dynamically - the dynamism of the entire creation's movement to its fulfilment in the presence of God is only a glimmer and a result of the much more profound dynamism of the return of the sent divine persons to the source and sender of all personhood.   If the ancient theology was anything at all, it was a mystical contemplation of the divine outgoing and returning life of the divine persons.   Perhaps today in retrieving it we should say that it was a profound insight into the trajectory of *all personhood*, divine and human-in-the-cosmos.

Aquinas inherited this, and willingly accepted it as the basic framework of the Summa.   But with a significant modification at that!   A careful reading of his texts shows that he did not envisage the 'return' of the persons of the trinity: he saw them as forever moving outward.   And in a sense, that means that he did not see them as 'sent' in quite the same way as the tradition behind him.   They are not sent to be Gift exactly, nor precisely to make possible the return of the creation: rather, as action is the self-manifestation of being, so an energetic ecstasis is the self-manifestation of divine personhood.   The going forth of the persons (rather than their going 'out') is the condition of the possibility of the persons' being known.   Neither they nor the creation ever goes 'back'! They are always going onward, always self-manifesting, always unfolding. What Aquinas has really done here, in his reslanting of the Platonic tradition, is a further insight into the trajectory of *personhood*: it is forever active, self-revealing, and seeking to be known in the reciprocal love of interpersonhood.   Aquinas' vision does sit better than the Platonic one with the best intuitions of modern science and philosophy.[25]

Hegel should not be lost sight of here.   Though coming from a tradition that is philosophically contrary to Aquinas, his framing imagery can be seen as somehow complementary to that of Aquinas.   He saw all process as one *Aufhebung*, or sublation: thesis, antithesis, synthesis.   The permanent outreach of personal action includes into its dynamism the tendency to seek rest and 'go back', and modified by it, moves on and forward.   Again, the varieties of a phenomenology of *personhood* are slowly appearing and becoming integrated.

It is easy, in conclusion, to state that the language of authentic theology is all its own.   It is not simply a series of abstruse philosophical footnotes to accurate exegesis of folk-religious myths.   Its endeavour is to communicate a peculiar sense of the real that comes from a humbly successful exploration into the divine life that is in our midst.   It is ultimately not eschatological, and a fortiori not apocalyptic.   It is not interested in visions of the end, because in its sense of the real, there can be no end of the action of the divine persons.   It is *never 'over'*.   But the actual words in which theology tries to convey that, are taken from human languages and betray the limits of their origin.   Theology's best attempts degenerate into formulas, and the formulas become myths of their own, within perhaps distinct theological communities.   The mystery is never captured, and so never ends.

ULTIMATE GRACE

In this chapter, I have outlined the contribution of Physics, Philosophy, and Theology to our understanding of the ending of the cosmos.   I have tried, in each section, to lead the discussion to an analysis of the special language employed by each discipline.   They all have their ambiguities, they are all amalgams of many things, they are all idiosyncratic, they all fall back, for want of anything better, into an archetypal imagery of a Platonic mould. Each has its own distinctive mood, style, and 'flavour'.   In the sense we have developed, each discipline creates its own myths and unfolds its own mythic language, useful for the purposes humans have in mind when they make human use of myths.   The myth to which all disciplines seem to come is that of 'region' or 'universe' of different dimensions than our own customary one, towards which we seem to be 'going' (if not 'returning'). The best theology would seem to see this as a suggestive (non-descriptive) parable of the ever-outgoing action of the divine persons, and perhaps of personhood itself.

Some conclusions deserve their drawing here.

First, no one knows anything really about the 'ending' of the universe. When it comes to clear knowledge, there is none.   We don't know.   Not even the faith-traditions of folk-religion - assertive as they are in form - really 'know' anything.

Secondly, in all disciplines there is an increasing sense of positivity and optimism in regard to 'endings' or 'ongoings'.   Not only is there no need to be afraid, there is a positive invitation to be hopefully excited.

Thirdly, from *all disciplines*, there is an increasing invitation to a mystical contemplation of the 'more' involved in it all, a 'more' that theology would like to name as God.

Fourthly, the dynamics discerned in the acting God, and in the acting cosmos, are parallel, and the actions are linked in a profound communion.

Fifthly, these dynamics have as their best model and paradigm, what we are increasingly coming to know as the mystery of the person. I say, 'the' person, to cover both divine and human persons. But 'the' person is a defective term: what is really meant is the communication of person to person, the reciprocity of action-reception of one and the other that constitutes mutuality and is named communion.

Sixthly, this personal mystery is what is going on in the real life of God, and in the real life of humans, and all this is going on in the cosmos.

Seventhly, the cosmos is more than a home for this activity: in real ways, the dynamics at work in the physical cosmos mirror the interpersonal dynamics of human and divine life.

Eighthly it may well be more possible, and more valuable to us, to track the parallels in these dynamics, than to try to tell an adequate story of the cosmos and predict its 'ends'.

But over and above all this, there is something - something that is almost impossible to name, but something that is ineluctibly there. It is beyond all the myth systems. It is not the result of 'guessing the end'. It is the sense of ultimacy that does not end, the feeling of benignity of person to person, of divine to human, of divine and human to cosmic, that never ceases to impart and convey and unfold an inexhaustible beauty. It is perhaps not wrong to call it *ULTIMATE GRACE*. For there is an ultimacy that is more than eschatology, and there is a grace that is more, much more, than a random gift to enable us to do something we could not do without it. Grace is Loveliness, and it is the Ultimacy of Loveliness that is in point here. The learning for us from all our inquiry about ends, is that the real issue is LOVE. A Karis and an Agape that are the same thing. A Hesed and an Emeth.

We have looked at the incomparable beginning of the cosmos in creation, and we have looked at the unknowable 'non-ending' of it all in the ultimate grace of Love. Is it still a matter of telling the story in between beginning and ending, or is it now a matter of unfolding the dynamics and the aesthetics of love, as we see them in a personalised cosmos in which we now live ?

§ § §

NOTES

1.   E.R.Harrison, *Cosmology, the Science of the Universe*, Cambridge University Press, 1981.   W.Kaufmann, *Universe*, Freeman, 1991 (3rd.ed.) T.Snow, *The Dynamic Universe*, West Publishing Co, 1991 (4th.ed.).

2.   See reports of the collision of a comet with the planet Jupiter on July 16, 1994.   *U.S.News and World Report*, August 1, 1994, pp.54-61.

3.   G.Smoot, *Wrinkles in Time*, Doubleday, 1993.   D.Reanney, *The Death of Forever*, a new future for human consciousness, Longman Cheshire, 1991.

4.   M.Reordan, D.Schramm, *The Shadows of Creation*, dark matter and the structure of the universe, W.H.Freeman and Co., New York, 1991.

5.   N.Murphy, Evidence of Design in the Fine-Tuning of the Universe, in *Quantum Cosmology and the Laws of Nature* ed.   R.Russell, N.Murphy, C.Isham, Vatican Observatory Publications, 1993, pp.407-436.

6.   C.Powell, The Golden Age of Cosmology, *Scientific American*, July, 1992, 17-22, R.Russell, N.Murphy, A.Peacocke, eds., *Chaos and Complexity*, scientific perspectives on divine action, Vatican Observatory Publications, 1994.

7.   P.Davies, *The Cosmic Blueprint*, Simon and Schuster, New York, 1988.   S.Hawking, *A Brief History of Time*, 1989.

8.   J.Gribbin, M.Rees, *Cosmic Coincidences*, dark matter, mankind, and anthropic cosmology, Black Swan, 1991.

9.   Z.Weblowsky, Eschatology, an overview, *Encyclopedia of Religions*, ed. M.Eliade, et al., Macmillan, New York, 1987, vol.5, pp.148-151.

10.   K.Rahner, *Theological Investigations*, to this analysis.

11.   N.Perrin, in his commentaries on the apocalyptic sections of the New Testament, especially of Mark, and in particular, *The Language of the Kingdom*.

12.   J.P.Kenny, Hell - the meaning of its everlastingness, *Compass Theological Review*, 1978, 25-39.

13.   J.Delumeau, especially *Guilt and Fear*, and *A History of Paradise*.

14.   The Society of Biblical Literature Seminars on Parable, and on Apocalyptic, expressed in the journal *Semeia* and the writings of John and Adele Yarbro Collins.   Also see R.Funk, in the Jesus Seminar of the Westar Institute;   and recent commentaries on the book of Revelation.

15.   D.Cupitt, in the Cambridge University Press edition on predictions.

16.   The influence of French deconstructionist theory can be seen here, in Lacan, Derrida, Foucault,etc.

17.   Ph. Aries, *The Hour of our Death*, N.Y. 1981.   P.Delooz, Death and the Hereafter, *Pro Mundi Vita Dossiers*, Brussels, 4/1985.

18.   H.Kung, *Eternal Life?*, life after death as a medical, philosophical, and theological problem, Doubleday, N.Y.   1984.

19.   G.Blandino, Modern science and the immortality of the human person, two trends of thought in Christian anthropology, *Teresianum*, 38, 1987, 305-323.

20.   A.Grib, Quantum Cosmology, the Role of the Observer, Quantum Logic, in *Quantum Cosmology and the Laws of Nature* eds.   R.Russell, N.Murphy, C.Isham, Vatican Observatory Publications, 1993, pp.163-184.

21.   R.Funk, cited above, n.14.

22.   J.D.Crossan, *The Historical Jesus*, the life of a Galileean Jewish Peasant, 1993, and *Jesus: a revolutionary biography*, 1994.

23.   Commentaries on Paul, but especially the work of S.Lyonnet, B.Ahern, D.Stanley, and F.X.Durrwell.

24.   One of the more valuable discussions of Aquinas here is that of M.J.Nicolas, *Revue Thomiste*.

25.   T.O'Meara, Grace as a Theological Structure, in the Summa Theologica of Thomas Aquinas, *Recherches de Théologie Ancienne et Médievale*, 59(1988) 130-153.

CHAPTER 4

TELLING THE TALE

An appreciation of the
personal and historical
'now'.....

We have looked at beginnings and at endings. It is time to look at the middling of things. In between the absolute origination and the perhaps non-ending future, how does the Ultimate Grace manifest itself? Can we tell the story in such a way as to unfold what is really going on underneath the surface and obvious dimensions of the 'story'? This is perhaps a different style of doing 'history': less narrative than meditative of the meaning that seems to be striving for clarity in every 'now'; less evaluative of one period in relation to another, than appreciative of the striving within them all, once we get a glimmer of what they are striving for.

PHYSICS

I should like here to focus on four things. *First*, a clarification of the perspective I am taking; *secondly*, an insight into the basic dynamics of cosmic and personal history; *thirdly*, a discussion of the variables always present in the interpretation of this history, and the different emphases that always occur; and *finally*, a sketch of the way in which these issues are working out, in our present stage of history.

First, the *perspective*. In recent years there has been much discussion, stimulated by the work of Barrow and Tipler, of what is called the cosmological *Anthropic Principle*. It is an attempt to take full cognisance of the presence of life, human life, intelligent life, personal life, in the universe. In simple form, it states that we were meant to be there from the beginning: there is a finality, a purposiveness, a teleology in all creation from its first moments that intends the final presence of human and personal life. Without that the universe would not be meaningful. There are two forms of the Anthropic Principle: *strong and weak*. In its *weak* form, the Principle reflects on the fact that we can observe the universe only from places and times where intelligent and personal life can exist. For 'us' to be 'here', there must have been a specific determination of the laws of physics and the initial conditions of the universe from the beginning. In particular, the universe would have to have had, from the beginning, a rule of 'locality' (local systems are able to function independently of other local systems, within the whole); an 'arrow of time' (and hence the second law of thermodynamics, without which consciousness might not have developed); a 'quasi-equilibrium' state of physical conditions (without which the delicate balances that allow evolution would not have occurred); and the emergence of a 'classical era' from a previous 'quantum era' (needed for the appearance of forms of life anything like the ones we know). Only on such a basis could heavy elements have appeared, and had time to evolve into advanced forms of life, in regions neither too hot nor too cold, with the 'right' constants that control chemistry and local physics. In its *strong* form, the Anthropic Principle states that intelligent and personal life must exist in the universe: it is necessary, for the consistency of quantum mechanics and the possibility of a quantum era itself. This means that the values of all the fundamental constants governing the universe from its origin must have been such as to allow, and even indicate, the future emergence of human personal life.[1]

Scientists express *hesitations* within their own disciplines about the Anthropic Principle, especially in its strong form. I shall neither pursue it nor depend upon it here. I would like to move away from estimations of 'conditions' and 'finalities', and to ponder some *fundamental parallels* between the dynamics of the *cosmos* (at all times of its history) and the dynamics of *interpersonal life*. It seems to me that this extraordinary consonance of dynamics makes the cosmos home to the person, and creates the concept of 'person-in-cosmos'.

It would appear that in the cosmos, there are *two* basic 'forces' or directions of development: one, *'centrifugal'* and the other *'gravitational'*. From the Big Bang onward, there has been an *'explosive'* dimension and an *'attractive'* dimension. The former is essentially a *'diversification'* process, and the latter is essentially a *'containing'* process. The two are woven together to form the curve of cosmic development. Examples are everywhere. A very interesting one goes back to the very early 'moments' of the cosmos. After the initial quantum fluctuations in the original vacuum, shortlived or 'virtual' realities began to appear: like 'puffs' or 'whimpers' of an 'excited' vacuum.   There were lots of them, and most of them failed to develop into any 'permanent' reality.   In the inflation period, there was in effect a 'spacefoam' or 'sea' of such particles.   They were there in pairs: each one with its mirror image, and the normal rule was that when they encountered each other they self-destructed.   The normal rule: the exception to the rule occurred when one escaped destruction, and the chances of this were one in one billion.   It was this 'escapee' that was the first photon.   It then linked with other such photons (or quanta of light) and moved on the path to a universe of light.   It came from a centrifugal, explosive, diversification process, balanced by and intertwined with a centripetal, attractive, containing process.   This seems to be the basic dynamic pattern of the cosmos.[2]

The 'history' of the cosmos has been divided by Karl Schmitz Moorman into *three periods*: in the *first*, when particles become molecules, there is a unification of small entities into larger ones; in the *second*, when life emerges, there is a self-replication of the formed larger entities; and in the *third*, when human life occurs, there is a simultaneous claiming and sharing of intelligent information.   These phases can be seen as varieties of containment and diversification.[3]

What is really happening, then, in every phase of cosmic existence from its beginning, is a process of 'genesis within communion', or *'cosmogenesis'*. It is probably better to speak of this cosmogenesis than to speak of a 'cosmos' which suggested a static, finished product.   We could call the 'whole thing' a mystery of *'differentiation in and through communion'*.

I believe that this is exactly where there are intriguing *parallels* between cosmos and person.   Interpersonal relationship operates on exactly the same dynamics, namely, dynamics of 'differentiation in and through communion'.   They were mirrored in the cosmos from its very beginning, and from the micro to the macro, they always are.   The story of the cosmos is the story of the changes in these connections.

Particular scientific disciplines tell this story from their own point of view, and sometimes lose the overall picture by legitimately stressing the particularities.   There is emerging among scientists at present, a desire to *'write large'* again and to recover the big picture.   As they do so, there is an inevitable pendulum swing of *interpretation*, from an emphasis on differentiation, to an *emphasis on communion*. The former is less popular than the latter.

It is usual, at present, to find interpretations of cosmic history which strongly *favour the trend to communion*.   The history is divided into various periods: paleolithic, neolithic, classic-traditional, scientific-technological, and ecological.   The classic-traditional, and the scientific-technological, come through as differentiation processes that have been too severe.   They are presented as disturbing the communion intended by nature.   The coming *'ecological'* period is presented, with some advocacy, as the right one, restoring the processes of communion.   We are presented then with a choice: to become even more technozoic or to retrieve an *ecozoic* way of living.   We are encouraged to discover the new connectedness, or bondedness within the cosmos, between all the elements in it, the divine, the human and the material-cosmic, and to see that the deepest symbols of our languages, especially our deep dreams, unite all three as one.   There is here an eternal dimension in the temporal, and the need is for 'shamanic' visionaries who see this, and can lead us to 'redeem the times'.   This often includes a repentance from the autism of androcen tric and patriarchal thinking, and a return to a new respect for 'mother earth'.   There are inevitable influences in this, of a rhetoric that does not emerge exclusively from the considerations of science.[4]

It is always possible, though at present less popular, to read the history in a way that puts the positive emphasis on *differentiation*.   The goal would be to do so without losing the valid points made by 'communionists'.   At all events, I believe that all such canvasses of cosmic history bring out one thing: the history is a disclosure of the difference and the inter-connected-ness of these two great principles of being itself.   It is valuable to *illustrate* these underlying peronal principles of cosmic history, by focussing on *one period of history* in which we are still involved, namely the period that begins in the 14th century and concludes at the end of the 20th century. I shall offer a *schema* of how it has unfolded, with indebtedness to Jean Delumeau and Thomas Berry, and additions of my own.

SCHEMA

BLACK DEATH (of biological soma)
    Classic cultures
      'Protestant' cultures: philosophy of *awesomeness*
      Transitional subcultures:
        scientific secular community (civil religion)
        redemptive healing community (therapy)

    'Enlightenment/Modernity' cultures: philosophy of self
    Transitional subcultures:
      mission-commitment community (colonialisation)
      devotional-piety community (respectability)
        Failure of all above: critical nihilism
        Failure of the critique: beyond meaninglessness?

GREEN DEATH (of ecological soma)
    Neo-classic cultures
      'Global reorganisation' cultures: philosophy of *control*
      Transitional subcultures:
        transnational superpower community (IMF - world bank)
        living-in-deeper-debt community (third world)'

    Re-centration' cultures: philosophy of *centredness*
    Transitional subcultures:
      transcendent truth community (fundamentalism)
      alternative life-style community (neo-gnosticism)
        Failure of all above: critical pointlessness
        Failure of the critique: beyond criticism?

RAINBOW RESURRECTION (of personal-cosmic soma)
    Post-classical cultures
      'Communional' cultures: philosophy of *interconnectedness*
      Transitional subcultures:
        'new physics' ecological community
        'feminine bonding with poor' community

    'Differentiation' cultures: philosophy of *distinctiveness*
    Transitional subcultures:
      'person-discovery' community'
      'systemic-nodal' community

The *value* of looking at this period is that it shows how the interpretation of history, and even the unfolding of history, is governed by the search for synthesis of the two great cosmic and personal principles, differentiation and communion.   It would suggest that since the 14th century, there has been an excessive swing of the pendulum towards differentiation, and that recently the swing has been strongly in the opposite direction.[5]

The *Black Death* ravaged Europe, and left in its wake a collective obsessive-compulsive neurosis, in which the culture felt sure it was being punished, but not sure what it had done to deserve the punishment.   This resulted in a profound sense of duty (without a clear idea of what the duty actually was), and a punctiliousness about ceremony and detail (without a clear idea of why it had to be so exact).   This heightened the presence of 'classic' forms of culture.

A *classic culture* is taken here to be one flowing from a single central governing insight.   This is its 'hallucinatory fantasy', and the basis of its self-conception in energy terms.   Classic cultures generally consider themselves to be 'right' and 'chosen'.   They tend to separate themselves from others: they differentiate.

In Europe after the Black Death, *two* classic cultures emerge.   The first is *Protestant* culture.   It is a sense of awe in the presence of a demanding God of Duty.   This implies a profound interiorisation of the experience of the sacred, and a *differentiation* of it from the domain of the secular. In the consequent transitional subcultures, the scientific secular community then is freed to move into its own work unhindered by religion, and the religious community becomes one that increasingly seeks therapeutic healing from its inadequacy in the presence of the divine.   The *Enlightenment/Modernity* culture then discovers the transcendent self as subject, and is fascinated by its autonomy and independence.   The political projection of this idea gives birth to the European nation state of the period, a further index of extreme *differentiation*.   Consequent transitional subcultures are colonial imperialism, and bourgeois respectability.   It is clear that such extreme tendencies to *differentiation* have engendered their own criticisms.

The *Green Death* is the death of the ecological body, a death inflicted upon it especially by technology and warfare.   Technology became as it were an instrument that allowed the differentiating fantasy to act out its dreams on a global scale, to compete with nature, to dominate and master it, and to force it into slavery for the production of profit.   War, especially in Europe in the 20th century, ravaged the land, and led to nuclear pollution of the atmosphere.

The immediate historical response has been the re-emergence of classical forms of culture in a new form. *'Global reorganisation'* cultures are really Enlightenment cultures endowed with global capacity, through new technologies of information control. *Differentiation*, in the extreme sense we take it here, is the result of such control. The consequent transitional subcultures are the expression of power and powerlessness in the face of a new global economics. *'Re-centration'* cultures attempt to use the same dynamics, not in the field of economics, but in that of value systems and life styles. They want to create an old/new centre - in the recovery of certitudes, and in the legitimation of what were once called marginal alternatives. It is clear that as usual, extreme *differentiation* engenders its own extreme criticism, which enhances the *differentiation*.

Rainbow Resurrection is a vivid way of suggesting that something different from all the above is beginning to show itself. It is the emergence of a new aliveness in the whole soma, personal and cosmic.   *Post-classical* cultures are beginning to be envisaged in it, in which there will be no single central governing insight in the culture, but rather a mandala of multiplicity. There are two kinds: *'communional' cultures* - which are the contrary opposite to the extreme differentiation of the epoch - believe in the web of interconnectedness that constitutes reality. We can see them, transitionally I think, in the new sense of ecology that claims the new physics as its theoretical base, and its own congruence with the new feminine type of bonding in solidarity with the poor of the third world. The rhetoric is one of a *communion that overcomes all differentiation*.

This is hardly possible without a reaction, and the reaction is in the form of a *new sense of differentiation* itself. Perhaps the expression 'philosophy of *distinctiveness*' suggests it.   It claims that communion itself does not exist without presuming and promoting the distinctiveness of those in communion.   The past sense of extreme differentiation virtually equated differentiation with *separation*.   The new sense of it insists that distinction is not separation.   Separation is inimical to communion; distinction is essential to it.   There is then a new quest for true personhood, not in autonomy but in community, and a new grasp of the way the vision of physics (systemic thinking) gives rise to the 'nodes' of systemic webbing that are distinct, and different entities.   It is too soon to evaluate this position.

Thomas Berry proposes that the last 600 years, which we have taken as a focus for our reflection, can be understood truly only against the wider background of the *last 3000 years*.   He believes that 3000 years ago, there was formed in the human mind a *'story'*.   It was the story of an original harmony of all things, a cosmic communion.   Through a primordial human fault, it was lost.   The human community then embarked on a historical journey to repair the tragedy, a journey of *'redemption'*.   From the 14th century on, as we have seen, this redemptive journey took two complementary forms: that of personal 'redemption' from the tragedy of the primordial fault and its personal consequences;   and that of the cosmic or secular 'restoration' and remodelling of nature through technological mastery.   Berry would think that the story was unhelpful and brought more damage than good in its train.   It ought to be replaced by a *new story* of original cosmic communion that perdures.

Though I much appreciate this wisdom, I am not quite proposing the same position.   My suspicion is that the very concept of original perduring cosmic communion bears the traces of a onesidedness.   I believe it always needed to be complemented with the principle of differentiation, not as separation, but as distinctiveness within communion.   We are searching for the tools to do this.

At the conclusion of this review, there may well be an impression that we have not being doing 'physics' but rather 'history'.   In a way, we had to. When we approach history at this depth, we inevitably touch principles or dynamics of history that are valid in, and are often learned better from, other disciplines than history.   The two disciplines most in point are a phenomenology of personhood, and cosmic physics.   There is an extraordinary convergence of the principles and dynamics of all three - *history, personhood, cosmos*.   That is why my focus of interest here has been and remains not the details and the describable data, but the dynamic underflow.   It is close to the reality of 'it all'.

It is important to note that this dynamic is not made up of a single principle, such as the principle of communion alone, or the principle of differentiation alone.   It is really a fascinating dialectic of the two.   It could perhaps be suggested that history, personhood, and cosmos are three (complementary?) attempts to get them together, and that the telling of the tale of all three is the story of their seeming asymptotic convergence.

PHILOSOPHY

It is the task of philosophy to ask *'why'*.   Why is the deep story like that? In particular, *first*, why are those the dynamics, and which of the two is the more ultimate?   and *secondly*, why is it so hard to get the two of them 'together'?   Are they trying to come together, really, or is it just that we imagine it to be so?

Philosophy itself is caught up in the same tension of the same two principles (communion and differentiation) that it attempts to interpret. There has always been, in philosophy, a romantic or idealist tradition, and a critical or realist tradition: they represent our two principles.   The *Romantic tradition* goes back to Plato, and reaches its height in the idealism of the German Enlightenment.   It includes at its extreme fringe, the entire 'mindset' that goes under the coverall name of gnosticism. Much of current New Age writing comes under its umbrella.   The entire mood of the mind in this tradition is an enormous attempt at synthesis. It is a refusal to believe that all things cannot in the end become one, one in a Source of meaning and beauty, with which they are finally in communion.   There is a slippage from the rigidity of insistence on the limits of metaphor, to a sleight of hand in which metaphor slips into the full realism of proper statements.   Distinctions tend to disappear, since separations are anathema.   The human is ultimately swept up into the divine;   the material cosmos is said to be conscious and alive;   the boundaries are down, in the name of unity.   In the expression, 'being with', there is so much emphasis on the 'with' that the distinctiveness of 'beings' is virtually lost.   Identification takes the place of presence, with an accompanying loss of identity.   All is one.

There are traditions in *depth psychology* that mirror this romanticism in philosophy, and are psychologies of communion.   They place a high and perhaps ultimate value on fusion, into an oceanic totality. They are traced back to the ontological security of symbiosis with the original mother. An entire language vein comes from this - one that the French psychoanalysts love to call 'imaginaire'. It is best expressed in myth.

In contrast, the second major tradition in philosophy is that of *Critical Realism*. It is critical precisely of the tendencies to unification and the pretensions to synthesis in the idealist tradition. It is realist precisely because of its metaphysical convictions about the primacy of being. For this tradition, reality is being: it is not ideas, or visions, or possibilities that might be. Reality is the actual real-ing of real be-ing, and real being now is distinctive from all other being, and removed as act from potency from possible being. Real being and real differentiation go together. Of course, what is meant here is *existential differentiation*, not the particularisation of features that is the field of phenomenology. That is why the principle of differentiation, which goes with the conviction of the realness of actual being, is for this tradition a metaphysical principle, and applies to all real being.

A *psychological tradition* that is consonant with these metaphysical persuasions would stress distantiation rather than fusion as the precondition of relationship. It would insist that real speakers submit themselves to the real order of language, with its necessary differentiation of subject, copula and predicate, and not remain in the vagueness of the 'imaginaire'.

In the Christian tradition, this critical metaphysical realism is at the service of faith in *creation*, and takes new inspiration from its sense of creation. If creation is the absolute origination of being from Being, then creation is at the same time the absolute differentiation of being from Being. Without such differentiation, creation would not be real. True, there is a communion between created being and Creator-Being, without which their relationship cannot be conceived, but the communion is set up by the differentiation and not vice versa.

The manner in which being is 'from' and 'with' Being, in and through the creative act, is far less explicable, metaphysically, than the necessary differentiation of one from the other. It is this basic sense of ontological otherness that founds, in this philosophy, the sense of *analogy*: analogous beings are 'simpliciter' different, and 'secundum quid' the same.

I applaud the robustness of intellect in these perceptions, but I also give attention to the *language* that this tradition must inevitably use to convey its appreciation of creation and of the created reality.   After saying the fundamentals, there is literally not much more that can be said.   And yet, there is a human need to keep on saying, when the topic is almost unsayable.   That is why, willy nilly, the strongest realist tradition develops its own idiosyncratic language to keep on talking.   It gets it by having recourse, in its own way, to the language of the romantic or idealist tradition, and bending it to suit its own purposes.   It retrieves the language of the 'imaginaire' and of 'oneness' and puts this language at the service of the insights about differentiation.   I think it is precisely in this way that it makes use of the repertoire of participation and relationship.

The language of *relationship* which the realist tradition uses, is implicitly at least ambivalent.   A real relationship of dependency is sustained in the creature towards the Creator, but, in a technical sense, there is no such matching real relationship in the Creator towards the creature.   At the same time the Creator is said, with emphasis, to be really related to the creature.   This looks like having it both ways at the same time, and is true only within the technical language appropriate to the context.   But the purpose of using such niceties, is to suggest without outright affirmation, that there is an almost absolute ontological connection between Creator and creature that provides the fundamentum in the creature for the relation of dependency that is at the heart of creaturehood.   I cannot help suspecting that we have an adroit balance, or amalgam, of the precise language of metaphysics in the realist tradition, with the romantic language of the idealist tradition.   They have been wedded for a purpose, that of engendering some idea, beyond the niceties, of the mysterious 'how' of creative origination.

Similar comments could be made about the use of *'participation'*.   Once again, it is suggestive of what cannot be affirmed, and affirmative of what should not be suggested, in the refined principles and language of the realist tradition.   And again, the vagueness is tolerable, and positively put to work, to convey something of the unsayable 'more' of the mystery.

At all points in the *'story'* of creation, when we tell the *'tale'*, it is this differentiation that needs supplement from a sense of communion that is always happening.

The overall purpose of this book is to make some *suggestions* at the point at which the romantic and the realist traditions come to an impasse.   In Chapter 1, I indicated that I would try to do so in the wake of the recent work of Norris Clarke.   In Chapter 2, I offered some nuances towards an understanding of both relationship and participation on the one hand, and of person and interpersonhood on the other.   I would like now to use those points already made, and show they can help in developing a sense of *'communion that includes differentiation'* which is a different meeting of the romantic and realist traditions.

The three points on which I am relying, are: *first*, that relationality is a mystery prior to the terms that appear to be related;   *secondly*, that participation is to be understood as emergence from the matrix of this prior relationality;   and *thirdly*, that interpersonhood, or interpersonal mutuality, as a mystery of participative relationality, is prior to the persons - the distinct persons - involved in it.   In their light, I am sustaining the *priority of communion*:   a communion which is a pulsing oneness that self-engenders its own self-expressions.   It is thus a communion that demands, engenders, and creates *differentiation*, so that the 'what' that is 'differentiated' is a revelation of the quality and beauty of the prior communion. This position is not entirely within the romantic and idealist tradition: that tradition would tend to absolve communion from differentiation.   Nor is it entirely within the critical realist tradition: that tradition would sustain so strong a differentiation that it would limit, if not deny, communion.   It is a moderately critical position.   It is worked out on the principles of a personalist metaphysics, and when it looks for a language in which to amplify its essential points, it turns to the phenomenology of personal love, to the physics of the cosmos, and to the novel dynamics which both personal and cosmic history reveal to us.

Personalism is the guiding and underlying thread of this book.   Cosmic matrices have already been elaborated, and will be more so in the following chapters.   When we attend here to *history*, and to its two fundamental principles of differentiation and communion, we no longer need posit a dialectic between them, nor an analogy of one to the other. The differentiation is the unfolding of the communion, in history, and the novelties of history 'show' us 'how' the differentiation comes from the communion.   If we read history in this light, we would see it as pulsing with this double energy, almost in a quantum fluctuation.   It is that dynamic that we are narrating every time we truly tell the tale.

What then is *reality*?   What is being?   It is not, in isolation, the distinct and discrete 'things' we seem to perceive.   It is all of these, as emergents from and still within the matrix that has engendered them.   Solidarity is more than a secondary metaphor.

It is sometimes asked, is the bonding or relatedness of created beings primarily to the Creator, or primarily to one another?   Romantic traditions would lean one way, and realist ones the other.   I am suggesting a third or middle position.   It is *already*, *all*, a communion.

Is the Creator then as it were a secondary factor, if even the Creator is somehow 'emergent' from the matrix?   No.   It is precisely the mystery of the Creator that in the Creator and in the Creator alone, a substantive personhood does not emerge *'from'* the matrix, but *'includes'* it into the substantiveness.   And having done that, the Creator re-shares the matrix with the matrix itself, so to say.   This is exactly why the Creator is Being, and not being, that is, the Undifferentiated and Unemergent from the energy matrix, not the differentiated and emergent from it.   And this is *'what happens'* when Being acts, and there 'is' being: in something like a quantum fluctuation of the Creator-Being-Undifferentiated-Unemergent One, there differentiates and emerges a 'being' that does not, and cannot remain within the matrix, in the sense of being fully identified with it. The created 'being' is still within the matrix, but not in the sense of inclusive identification with it.   That is why it is inherently *dependent* upon not only the matrix, but upon the one Being that alone can and does remain so fully and inclusively identified.   I think this is germane to the thinking of Aquinas, that the Creator is one with its own Esse, while the creature cannot be so.   We have tried to put some words on the manner of the participation of the latter in the former.   The being of 'being' is a fragile arrangement, impossible literally and metaphysically without 'Being's' act in regard to it.   The price of its very being is its dependency.

I have chosen to develop these points here, in a chapter in which we are trying to appreciate the personal and historical *'now'*.   Whenever that 'now' is, the fullness of the creative mystery is occurring.   History, understood, is always an *interpretation of creation*.   Perhaps only history, cosmic and personal, can really interpret it.

THEOLOGY

Can theology add to this interpretation of the depth of present history? I believe it can, through its understanding of the act of seeing God (*beatific vision*), and the implications of this theory for the mystery of the *divine missions*.   It is through these insights that we can enter into the presence of Ultimate Grace in the historical now.

Aquinas believed that the ultimate 'end' or finality of the human, was to come to an immediate insight into God.   That is, to know God as God is in Godself, face to face.   In this final act, there is communion with the Infinite.   But the subject that enters into this communion remains differentiated from the Infinite, and is still a finite, created being.   The whole endeavour of Aquinas, in pondering this matter, is to keep the balance between *finite and infinite*.   It is not easy to do.

Aquinas is quite clear that the human soul or spirit, in its own essence, or from faculties that flow from that essence, does not possess the potency to see God face to face.   He is also aware that the act of knowing God in ultimate immediacy demands an intentional conjunction of the finite human mind with the Infinite that is known, without the mediation of any concept or 'species'.   For some of his partners in dialogue, especially among the Arabs, that was enough - I am thinking of Al Farabi.   But for Aquinas, marvellous as it was, it was only the beginning of a deeper question.   Intentional conjunction with Uncreated Act lies at the heart and at the term of the act of knowledge: but where comes to the human mind, the capacity to perform that act?   Aquinas is insistent, as usual, that it is the finite human mind that sees the infinite God.   Whence comes its potency?   He calls that potency a gift, a grace, a 'light' - the *'lumen gloriae'*.   He says it is something added to the human spirit, coming to it by 'adjunction'.   That is about as far as his technical language can take him, but he then develops three metaphors to unfold what he really means.

The first is the metaphor of *'call'*, or *'creative voice'*.   From the depth of God, there comes into the human spirit and mind a 'call' - an invitation, a request, an empowerment, not simply to 'perform an act otherwise beyond capacity', but to come towards God.   For every call is a call to a person.   God, as it were, yearns and desires to be seen face to face, and empowers the person to come to God by calling the person to God.   It is an *invocation*, an address to the personhood of the person, that is also and thereby an *evocation* of capacities that the person as such did not have, but that the person now does have precisely as a divinely invoked person.   Could we say that the *call* echoes through the fibres of the personality and brings out from them something that was never there, but is there only as the echo of the voice?   Such is the source of the power to see God.

The second metaphor is that of *'drawing'* or *'attraction'*.   One is tempted to fall back here on the idea of a gravitational field.   There is a kind of gravity exercised by Infinity upon the finite mind.   There is a 'drawing', an 'attraction'.   And that 'drawing' includes and begins with a *'touching'* of the depths, that is a sort of 'awakening'.   Nemo tractus nisi tactus, as Augustine wrote in the commentary on Jn 6.   It is a drawing away from all limitations and boundaries of self-focussed, so that there is an awakened openness to something beyond all possible limit and boundary, the Infinite itself.   The *boundaryless*.   One draws the boundaried beyond its boundaries into the *boundaryless-ness* that It alone knows by nature. We are only a short step away from 'seeing' God.

The third metaphor, in the notion of 'lumen gloriae' is the idea of *light as glorification*.   The person is called and drawn into a Beyond that is not dark.   The person sees in a way never done before.   The seeing to which the person has been accustomed has been a seeing of distinct and discrete 'objects' in 'concepts' and 'ideas'.   This new seeing is not any 'object' and the person has no concept or idea of it.   The Infinite is too close for that.   What we have is the mystery of closeness as illumination.   If an Infinity were to be so close to a finite entity, that as it were its very infinity filled the finitude of the finite thing, the finite thing would 'see' into the infinity.   But the closeness cannot be illuminative without being in a true sense a *'glorification'* or transfiguration or transformation of the finite.   We might even risk the formula 'transformative identity' of finite with infinite, as long as infinite differentiation remains as the support of the realism of the infinite communion.   We shall be truly like God, because we shall really see God as God IS.

What does it mean to be called, drawn, changed so that we *see the Seer*? It means that we really know even in the manner in which we are known. We see the unboundariedness-entered-into-us even as the Unboundaried-One sees himself as entering into us. *Intimacy is the capacity to see the reciprocity of intimacy.* We are at the threshold of a kind of metaphysics, or metaphysical theology of intimacy as *mutually illuminative.* The 'scientia visionis' of God creatively and actively sees us as entering into the unboundariedness that God creatively and actively draws us toward. This is how we know God in the very act of God's creativeness, in us! And God knows us, not as distant any more, but as close as God has always been to Godself.

It is this double movement, this *mutuality of active engagement,* of ourselves in God and God in ourselves, that is really going on when the 'lumen gloriae' is conferred and we are able to 'perform' the act of beatific vision. Aquinas calls it our beatitude, but I believe he really prefers the word *'felicitas'* - there is more aliveness, and 'happiness' suggested there, that really echoes what is going on, for both human and divine seers.

It is virtually impossible to grasp this, without realising that we are at a point where the difference between knowledge and love has disappeared. This mutual seeing-intimacy is *love.* Perhaps it is only in God and in us, endowed with the lumen gloriae, that this is so.

When we get to the point of seeing it as love, we are already at the point of seeing it as *personal.* But I think in doing so, we are changing our previous notion of 'person' a good deal. We could almost think that we become persons, in this full sense, only through the gift of the 'lumen gloriae'. It is only then that we and God become intrinsic factors together of a mutual unboundariedness that is reciprocally illuminating. I am not sure that mutuality in the full sense occurs elsewhere.

This is where my thinking is drawn to the idea of the *missions* of the persons of the Trinity. I have said before that the persons, as sent, are not in Aquinas' mind guiding principles of a return to the Father, but rather themselves sources in our midst, put there by the Father, to *go forth without ever going back.* I would now suggest that in the forever going forth, there is an *oscillation,* a *pulsation,* a *'fluctuation'* if you wish, a 'quiver' within the onrush ad 'extra'. What I think it is, is the visual reciprocity in the mutual unboundariedness.   It is something like the *excitement* (Spirit?) of the sent Son in our midst, as the Son goes on further (in 'mission').   To capture the excitement we have to have recourse to the word *'joy'*.   The energy of creation and Creator is the vibrant joy of both together, visually.

The point of all reality, then, when it comes to its own ultimacy, is the breakdown of all boundaries so that there can come a breakthrough of light, and a resultant radiance of joy in that light.   The first of these processes is precisely *communion*;   the second is the *differentiation of communion*, or within communion, not of distinct elements, but of a distinctive joy.   The first is *'epiphany'*, the second is *'jouissance'*.   The two - intimately - go together.

When I speak of the breakdown of boundaries, I am thinking in anthropological terms, of the progressive removal of the tendency to possess, and even of the capacity to possess, that is to adhere to a 'thing' as if it were not in a network or a node of a relational matrix.   This shows us the difference between a false 'pleasure' in the use of a 'thing' and the true 'happiness' in the co-being-with of relationality.   The latter goes with the joy.

The breakdown principle, which is the initiation of the total process, could be called by the theological term *'kenosis'*, or emptying.   In classic Greek theology there is a kenosis of everything that would aspire to or claim autonomous subsistence, that is, a kenosis of every would-be *'hypostasis'* or 'person' in the Enlightenment sense of the word.   Only at the price of such a radical kenosis can there be the *perichoresis*, or circumincession, or dancing-around-together of all reality, without boundary limitation. Nature, in the Greek theological thinking, is always moving towards this situation of togetheredness, always aiming at this *anakephalaiosis* or heading-up-ness away from limitation.   It is there that the *synergy* of all-natures-together is meant to take place.   Greek theology would see a paradigm of this is what it is pleased to call the 'miracle' of *Chalcedon*: that wondrous openness of Person (Jesus) which allows the divine and the human in him to concur without inhibition and without distortion.   It is a paradigm of all reality, human and cosmic: and the ideal, or eschatological, fullness is a *koinonia* of holy people in holy things that are not separate.   When this occurs, there can indeed be sung a cosmic *Exultet*.

When this occurs... I hope I can be forgiven for this long theological seeming digression from the principal point of this chapter, the *telling of the tale of history*, cosmic and personal.   My thought was, that once we can see where the whole of history was going, and see the dynamics that were leading it there, we would be in a better position to appreciate the *'now'* of every moment of that history.   Every such 'now' is much more than a step towards such a result.   The 'now' of every point in time *already contains all the principles* (communion and communional differentiation) and *much of the end-result*, anticipated (the unboundariedness and the joy).   This is not an interpretation or vision of what the individual moments might be, in some mystical perspective, it is a statement of the reality as it is.   When we discuss any 'now' of any point of history, we are talking about the real actuality and real being of it all, and that means, in effect, that we are talking about the mysterious coming together of the processes of communion and differentiation at that time.   In theological terms, it is the dawning of the lumen gloriae that is happening as history unfolds now.   It is the pulsing of the persons in missions, as they go on to the fullness of it all.

David Braine and David Burrell have spoken of a *'dramatic'* now of God, in relation to all history.   Might not we extend this phrase to every 'now' of history itself: is it not dramatic in the sense that it *encapsulates and reveals* the drama of the convergence of cosmic principles, the drama of the calling-drawing-enlightening-pulsing-in-love of it all, the drama of the release of the joy as the divine mission of the divine persons unfolds?

It is the contention of this book as a whole that an attentive reading of the evidence of *contemporary physics* can lead - through philosophical reflection - to an appreciation of *how*, in detail and in particular, each 'now' of creation actually does encapsulate and reveal the mystery.   To introduce that insight will be the task of the subsequent chapters of the book.

NOTES

1.   J.Barrow, F.Tipler, *The Anthropic Cosmological Principle*, Oxford University Press, 1986.

2.   K.Schmitz Moorman, in *Evolution and Creation, a European perspective*, eds. S.Andersen, A.Peacocke, Aarhus University Press, 1987.

3.   Schmitz Moorman, n.2.

4.   T.Berry, *The Dream of the Earth*, Sierra Book Club, San Francisco, 1990.   Also T.Berry, T.Clarke, *Befriending the Earth*, a theology of reconciliation between humans and the earth, Mystic publications, Conn., 1991.

5.   J.Delumeau, *Le péché et la peur, la culpabilisation en Occident, xiiie-xviiie siecles*, Paris, 1983 (ET: Guilt and Fear).   J.Delumeau, *Histoire de la consolation*, Paris, 1989.   J.Delumeau, *Histoire du paradis*, Paris, 1993.

I have attempted to integrate the thought of Delumeau with that of Berry.

CHAPTER 5

IS NATURE ALIVE?

An aesthetics
of
the beauty of everything

It is time to look deeper than at beginnings, endings and middlings. Beyond the story and the unfolding, what is it that unfolds, and what makes it unfold? What is the nature of nature? What is it made up of? How does it 'work'? The research is full of surprises, and science itself is coining new metaphors to voice its growing convictions. The cosmos is not a machine, and we are groping for an aesthetics of its mystery.

PHYSICS

What is nature made up of? What are its 'building blocks'? They are much smaller than atoms, or even atomic nuclei and electrons. The word *'quark'* has been adopted in physics (from the writings of Joyce) to describe what purports to be the most fundamental (sub)-particle that makes up 'everything'. It is believed that there are six families of these quarks, all of which can be identified except one, known as the 'top quark'.

There are now claims that it has been found (April, 1994). This has led to questions: are there smaller items even than quarks? Attempts are made to recreate the conditions of the primordial cosmic soup in the first micro seconds of the universe's history: massive underground supercolliders could do so, and perhaps would give experimental evidence of infinitesimally small 'particles' not yet known. If this were successful, it might contribute to an unsolved question: why does matter have mass? what does it mean to make that statement? Some have had recourse to a "Higgs" particle, a theoretical device, not necessarily appearing as an actual particle, which would allow other particles to acquire mass. Some now believe the "Higgs" is an actual particle, of a very large mass, and that is why it functions as the source of mass for other particles. Whatever the varieties of interpretation, there seems to be a consensus that nature is basically some kind of *particles*.   Perhaps we are not far from the thought of the ancient Greeks![1]

How does nature 'work'?   What are the fundamental forces within it, that direct it?   The consensus speaks of four: the electromagnetic force, the weak nuclear force (that causes radioactive decay), the strong nuclear force (that binds together the components within a nucleus), and gravity.   There is a consensus that at the earliest moments of the universe, these forces were all one force, and that it broke up into different forces at various early stages of cosmic development.   Physicists are working at a mathematical statement of the unification of these forces at earlier strata of history than our own.   There is agreement that the electromagnetic force and the weak nuclear force can be so unified (Weinberg, Salam and Glashow).   There is some agreement that the strong nuclear force can also be integrated.   If it were, we would have a *'Grand Unifying Theory'* of forces.   Gravity is proving the most difficult to bring in, and if the attempt to synthesise it were to succeed, we would have a *'Theory of Everything'*.   Other thinkers are beginning to speak of a possible 'fifth' force.   Whatever the varieties of interpretation and stages of unfinished research, there seems to be agreement that the impetus in nature is a matter of integrated and separating forces.[2]

Particles and forces: is that the nature of nature?   While the endeavour to find them still goes on, some things have been happening in the field of theoretical physics that vastly change the centrality of its questions.   It seems to have come in four steps: *first*, a perplexity; *secondly*, a discovery; *thirdly*, a hypothesis; and *fourthly*, a daring guess.

First, perplexity.   It has come from attention to what are called *'diverse unpredictables'*.   The movement of flame in fire, in a fireplace; the falling of snowflakes; the drift of mist in a waterfall; a vortex of white water; a gulf stream; cloud formations; weather patterns; population variations in fish, flies, ants; the 'redspot' on Jupiter; fluctuations in the stock market; darts, roulette balls, loose steering wheels, dripping taps... all of these are so inherently unpredictable that reduction to particles and integrated forces will not explain their inherent diversity.   Laplace once said: give me your position and velocity, and I will tell you your past and future.   Such predestination thinking, and fatalism (your number is on it) comes from a determinism that does not apply to 'diverse unpredictables'.

In a clockwork universe, there is really no novelty: nothing genuinely 'new' ever happens.   But the new is happening all around us, unpredictably...[3]

When physics discovers a phenomenon, it usually tries to find a *'model'* for it, and to express it in an *'equation'*.   The diverse unpredictables defied physics, because they refused to be modelled, and could not be captured in an equation.   At least, in the kind of models and equations that applied to other areas of the cosmos.

With diverse unpredictables, physicists attempt to draw a *'phase portrait'*. Imagine a multi-dimensional space (for example a cubic graph) whose coordinates are the variables of a system.   Each point in the space would then represent a whole set of coordinates.   Each possible state of the system would equiparate with a point in this 'phase space'.   When 'phase' occurs, it can be indicated, and as various phases occur, they can be indicated, and a 'portrait' can be drawn of the ongoing phases.   You can get a global picture of all possible phases.   In the case of diverse unpredictables, the phase portrait is unusual.

The unusualness consists in the mystery of *'symmetry' 'breaking'*.   A symmetry of a physical theory arises, if, when some of the parameters are replaced, or if there is some different combination of them, then the theory remains unchanged.   It just 'looks the same' if it is turned around in some way and looked at from another angle.   Symmetry is usually taken to be exact.   In cases of unpredictables, it is not: there occurs, under certain conditions, and in certain cases, a *'spontaneous'* 'breaking' of symmetry.   This is close to what could be called pure chance, randomness, novelty.

One way of expressing this strange energy of the system is to consider it in terms of the system's *hypersensitivity to* extremely refined *initial conditions*.   As the system evolves in its own time frames, the effect of that sensitivity appears to be so massive that the symmetry of the system has been broken.   It would be like a delayed response to instructions, by the system, which forgets the fact that its response is a delayed one, and that there has been a time lapse between receiving the instructions and acting on them.   If the situation were expressed mathematically, it would imply complex, irregular numbers, but still within the linear equations of a deterministic system.

It would appear that there are points in the evolution of the system when in effect it could go 'either way'. They are *'bifurcation'* points. At these points something seems to attract the system, something which is not predictable, but which does provide a meaningful point of attraction. This *'strange attractor'* itself moves asymptotically in relation to the coordinates of the system. The result in the phase portrait is that the hypersensitive system, when the symmetry breaks, expresses itself at the bifurcation points in randomly beautiful patterns - a *chaotic* movement of *fractals* and Mandelbrot sets. It is as if the information in the system, left unimpeded, has a natural beauty not contained in predictable equations. In fact, it is necessary to change language in speaking of it, from a language of energy, to a language of *information*. It is also interesting to note, that in the fractal patterns, there are no points and no loops - no particles and no waves! It is strangely perplexing for a science engaged in detecting ultimate particles and unifying fundamental forces... the issue may not be particles at all, and the mystery may not be a 'force' but an information flow.[4]

Secondly, discovery. In the complexity of this mind-boggling expression of the system into chaotic fractals, like foliage on a tree that keeps on having more and more leaves, in an unceasing 'printout', the information in the system allows it to become 'self-organising'. These systems are actually referred to as *'self-organising systems'*. This concept seems to challenge certain fundamental laws of thermodynamics, especially the second law. The new discovery was of the existence of systems which did not obey the second law.

Thermodynamics sustains that all matter and energy is constant, and that one is transformed into the other. A good example is the transformation of work into heat. There is a change then from usable energy into unusable energy, from available energy into unavailable energy, from energy ordered to use to energy that is disordered and useless. The second law demands this process of depletion of 'good' energy, and describes the accumulation of 'unavailable' energy in a condition of *'entropy'*. You can see it in a machine: friction will make it run down. It is an irreversible process, towards a 'stability' and an 'equilibrium' of the kind in which nothing further can happen, because there is no available energy to make it happen.   In simple terms, there is a tendency in every system to wind down, to lose energy, to lose adaptive organisation, to lose whatever level of complexity it has, and so ultimately to become simply bland and at rest, in an equilibrium, where it rests in peace.

Ilya Prigogine discovered the existence of systems in the cosmos which did not obey this law.   He distinguished these systems from 'equilibrium' systems which do obey the law, and called them *'far-from-equilibrium'* systems.   In them there are sudden, unpredictable, inhomogeneous, giant fluctuations and oscillations of energy.   When they reach a critical size, they perturb the whole system, and at that bifurcation point the system makes new interconnections and bondings, and 'escapes' into a 'higher' wholeness.   The whole system is like a fluid web that overarches into novelty of this kind.   In metaphorical terms, it is *'alive'*, like a living organism.[5]

Prigogine calls such a system an *'open'* system.   He is creating a new sense for the adjective 'open' as applied to systems.   In the first half of this century, von Bertalanffy had given us a language of closed and open systems: closed systems did not interact with their environment, open ones did and were known as 'interactive' systems.   Prigogine would specify that a closed system may indeed interact with its environment, and in the process pick up chaotic information that leads it to a state of entropy: in other words, it is an equilibrium system.   An open system in the new sense is one that does all that, but which then makes use of the received information that would lead to entropy in a different way.   Instead of allowing itself to be led to a final stability and equilibrium, it *metabolises* the whole syndrome, and *transforms* the energy implied in it into a capacity for the *creative expression* of a *new complexity*.   In this sense it is a *'dissipative system'*.   It does not escape contact with the entropy-inducing syndrome: it just does something creatively different with it.

Eric Jaentsch thought through the whole process of evolution in this light. Is it a matter of survival, adaptation, and natural selection?   Or could it be more a matter of interaction with others, that leads to a different and more interconnected existence?   Do systems not 'survive' but rather 'self-organise'?   He developed a language for 'self-organising structures' that were more frequent in the cosmos than previously suspected.   David

Bohm spoke of a *'holomovement'* and Rupert Sheldrake called it 'morphogenesis': Hubert Maturana names it *'autopoiesis'*.   It is as though some things can catalyse themselves, so to speak, into novelty.[6,7]

Could we suppose that at a deep level all nature is like this?   That is was not running down, but running up, in the joy of a self-expressive creative dance?   Can the heart-beat of the cosmos beat faster than we have measured yet?   Are we close to a glimpse of the cosmos as such as such a system, a *'Gaia'* system perhaps, as James Lovelock and Lynn Margulis would call it.   Does its biosphere actively create the environment it needs?

Is the *whole cosmos* active, altruistic, holistic, ongoing?   One is tempted to wonder what difference such thinking might make in fields like psychology, which tries to apply some systems theory to its own work: is the family, and perhaps the psyche itself, a dissipative self-organising structure in this sense?   We are getting further away from particles and forces.[8]

Thirdly, a *hypothesis*.   The hypothesis is that 'self-organising' might apply to the *quantum* domain as well as to the arena of diverse unpredictables in the fringes of the classic domain.   It would appear that it is not possible for pin-point units, or particles, to behave in the manner of self-organising systems: there would, as it were, be too much containment there, for adequate interactive metabolic transformation to occur.   Now Quantum Theory cannot deal with points: at the singularities implied in General Relativity, false infinities occur.   Quantum deals with precise discrete values that are not so pin-pointed.   Perhaps the notion of ultimate minute particles is too small and too foreign for quantum thinking.

Now, if by hypothesis, we were to draw these two lines of analysis together, we would have both a self-organising theory and a Quantum Theory that demanded that reality was ultimately of *larger dimensions than points*.   The imagination starts to wonder if 'points' may also mean *'particles'*.   The hypothesis we are really introducing here is known as *'string theory'*.   Could the cosmos be ultimately made up of entities that are precisely between the Planck length (10^{-33} cm) and nuclear length (10^{-13} cm)?   (Note that the Planck scale as to an atom is as an atom to the solar system).

Could these extremely small but definably 'long' entities be not particles but 'strings'?   It is assumed that there would be various lengths among these strings: they would not all be the of the same length: rather, some would approximate the Planck length, and others would approximate the nuclear length.   When the word 'string' is used, the image conveyed is not that of inert rope but that of a violin or guitar string - *a vibrating string*. It is always in a dynamic state, a state of fluctuation.   This is why, if we could change the metaphor from the auditory to the visual sensorium, we can never get a clear 'picture' of what nature is exactly like, or where exactly it is at a given moment.   It dissolves into a *binocularity*, a bit like an Aboriginal drawing or a Van Gogh starry night.   It is as it were in a permanent state of dynamic *phosphorescence* and is meta-metric: it cannot ultimately be measured accurately.   But let us return to the auditory sensorium.   If the 'violin' strings are vibrating, we are not far from *a metaphor of music*.   It is worth pursuing.[9]

Could it be that what we perceive to be a micro-particle, say, *a quark*, is the lowest mode of vibration of one string?   Could it be that *a quantum*, say, a photon, is another mode of vibration of another string?   Could it be that a wave is a higher mode of vibration of either, or of both together?   Could it be that *nature* is basically made up of musical notes, that each atom is in reality a symphony orchestra?

Is *'matter'* a matter of harmonics, and each *element* a musical score?

Is this a way of comprehending, in metaphor, why the Heisenberg Uncertainty principle, and the Pauli exclusion principle, are necessary for the harmony of nature?.

Could we even hypothesise that the vibratory character of the strings is the reason they exert what we call *gravitational attraction*?   Is a quantum of gravity (a 'graviton') a certain mode of vibration of the strings?

Is this metaphor of music a way of integrating the reality conveyed in the theme of *energy* and the reality conveyed in the theme of *information*?

Are we really saying that the self-organisation of *chaotic* and *complex* systems, which remains within the limits of determinism and linear equations, and the self-organisation of *quantum* systems, which does not, can be seen as coming from the same root?

Is our previous discussion of the *origination* and of the possible *ending* of the cosmos too dependent on the validity of the second law of thermodynamics?   Does the music of a self-organising orchestra ever end?

Fourthly, a daring guess.   PERHAPS it is not illegitimate - after pursuing matters this far - to hazard what can only be stated as guesswork: there is no possibility of verification.   Some are 'guessing' in this way that the cosmos in its most primordial state was *a 'ball' of 'strings' of ten dimensions*.   In the Big Bang, six of them compacted, and four extended to create what we call four dimensional spacetime.   In other words, our orchestra plays one possible kind of music, not every kind of music, or the only kind of music.   The dimensions are like musical scales.

Could there be other scales in other universes?   And if there were, would we be able to 'hear' their different music?   More radically, is it possible that 'prior' to the Planck wall, was there *a basic two-dimensional universe* from which 'came' even the Planck limit and what is on our side of it? Is there a mysterious symmetry there, which is 'broken' at the Planck wall and beyond - a 'SuperSymmetry'?[10]

This kind of physics is highly speculative and does not command universal assent.   It is heavily dependent on metaphor.   Our interest in it is precisely there: what does it suggest, in its metaphors, to philosophy and to theology?

PHILOSOPHY

There are two issues here, *one* in the metaphysics of being, especially Being that is the source of all being; and the *other* in epistemology, the understanding of what understanding really means.

First, metaphysics.   At the beginning, we can say without demur that there is nothing in the concept of self-organisation that presents a problem to the basic principles of philosophy.   Sufficient reason and causality are intact, as explained in chapter one.   In fact, there is a remarkable consonance between - a relational understanding of being, such as we are developing, and the vitality of the self-organising systems.   The perspectives developed in physics seem to be a kind of physical resonance of the inner 'aliveness' and communicativity of being itself.   There is no problem, but there is much confirmation of insight, and a good deal of challenge to the language that has become customary.   Especially in regard to God-Being-Creator, it has been too static and insufficiently 'alive'.

Norris Clarke has penned his insight into a Creator who would fit well with such a universe as has been hinted at:

> "Let me conclude by suggesting as a fascinating task-challenge-opportunity for natural theology today to speculate creatively and imaginatively as to what the 'personality' or 'character' must be like of a Creator in whose image this astonishing universe of ours is made, with its prodigal abundance of energy, its mind-boggling complexity, yet simplicity, its fecundity of creative spontaneity, its ever-surprising fluid interweaving of order and chance, law and apparent chaos, and so forth.   Must not the 'personality' of such a Creator be charged not only with unfathomable wisdom, power and exuberant generosity, but also with dazzling 'imaginative' creativity - might we say a daring Cosmic Gambler, who delights in working out his providence by a creative synthesis of both law and order, on the one hand, and chance, risk, spontaneity on the other - a 'coincidence of opposites', as St. Bonaventure put it long ago ?"[11]

Gerard Manley Hopkins captured what is surely the same intuition in his poem, *God's Grandeur*.

> The world is charged with the grandeur of God,
> It will flame out, like shining from shook foil;
> It gathers to a greatness, like the ooze of oil
> Crushed.   Why do men then now not reck his rod ?
> Generations have trod, have trod, have trod;
> And all is seared with trade,
>   bleared, smeared with toil;

And wears man's smudge and shares man's smell;
  the soil
Is bare now, nor can foot feel, being shod.

And for all this, nature is never spent;
There lives the dearest freshness deep down things;
And though the last lights off the black West went
Oh, morning, and the brown brink eastward, springs -
Because the Holy Ghost over the bent
World broods with warm breast and with ah!
  bright wings.[12]

Secondly, epistemology. If the world is as described, what does understanding of the world really mean?   What does it mean to 'know' the music of the cosmos?

Much work is being done at present on the functions of the human *brain*, and to this I shall return in a later chapter.   But for now it is necessary, if we are to sense what grasping the music means, to look at some metaphors of how it operates.   The brain may look like a bowl of cold porridge sitting in the midst of cosmic spaghetti.   But - it thinks!   What does *'think'* really mean?

The principal characteristic of the human brain to which I shall draw attention is its plasticity.   Its neurons, dendrites and synapses are part of a mysterious growing and shrinking.   It images, almost too physically, the process of reaching out and bringing something in.   It touches, takes, condenses, crystallises, actively uses, re-expresses the world with which it makes contact.   *How?*

I suggest that there are *three complementary phases* of this process.   *First*, the brain reaches out and brings in, and in doing so functions like a *computer*.   *Secondly*, it rests tranquilly in and with what it has interiorised, and in this it functions like a *holograph*.   *Thirdly*, it actively articulates its own informed sense of what it has received, and in this it functions in a *quantum* manner.[13]

In the *first stage*, the brain is drawn towards the real world, touches it, and brings it home.   The condensing or crystallising implied in bringing it home suggest some kind of translation such as the translation involved in a computer program. The dynamics-aesthetics of a musical creation are transposed into messages within the brain that the brain can sustain. It is, as it were, the computational character of the brain that is able to effect this.

In the *second stage*, the brain rests tranquilly in what is known as a Beta state, which is pre-oneiric and pre-thematic and pre-conceptual. It is not a computational process, it is a non-algorhythmic. It is like a *'ground-state'* of consciousness, without being conscious of any discrete things in particular. It is like musing with the music perceived. You are the mus-ing while the mus-ic lasts like this. The whole of the music is there, holistically, much in the manner of a hologram. In holography, every object scatters a wave field of light as an original pattern. The pattern is recorded on a plate by laser, like a kind of photographic record of the original pattern. In a coherent light beam, it is regenerated and appears as three dimensional: any piece of it will reconstruct the whole: it is a holo-gram. The brain seems to be like this in this stage of its functioning: it takes in the musical reality holistically, it as it were brings together in harmony all the varied instruments that make up the orchestra, and sits with the entire symphony, able to reconstruct the whole from any 'piece' of the orchestra.

In the *third stage*, the brain actively articulates all this experience by creatively unfolding what it has held within it. It is like an active making of its own music, which is the music of reality made its own, and joined in by the music-making ability of the brain. The full music of reality isn't really there until we make the music with the music that has been made independently of us. Reality is a kind of overture, and we play its variations.

In this last, third, stage, the brain would seem to operate as a quantum state, in that the 'music' it articulates in its knowing comes in micro, discrete 'packets', and the conjunctions from one to another mirrors the 'quantum leap' of quantum systems.

To *sum up* the metaphor: the brain is a respondent to the music of the universe. It picks up the 'score', it orchestrates all the possibilities of instrumental symphony, and it 'makes music' with the original music. In this latter mode, it is something like a quantum observer in the active sense, perhaps bringing, as Grib would have it, its own Boolean and Aristotelian logic (or music?) to the non-Boolean, non-Aristotelian logic (or music?) of nature, and causing a collapse of the wave function into a 'real' and 'really perceived' state.

The underlying suggestion here is that our intellectual life is meant to be *contemplative and mystical* in an active sense.   One can only regret the excessive technologising of our minds through education!

Three concluding remarks.   *First*, the manner in which the cosmic music amplifies and extends itself into and through the music of the mind, must remind us of the way the relationality-matrix of the universe self-expresses itself into the realities that we discretely know.   *Secondly*, we might well ask if the only kind of 'knowing' that really matches this deeper understanding of 'knowing', is interpersonal knowing.   Do we need to include the thematics of this music into our notion of interpersonhood?   *Thirdly*, is the universe 'alive'?   Yes, at least in a metaphorical sense: at least, because we need to look again at the notion of 'aliveness' and perhaps loosen it from the analogate of life that we call primary, namely, carbon-based life.   These questions can remain.   Meanwhile, we need to pursue the theological implications of the musical metaphor.

THEOLOGY

Theology is challenged by these new insights of physics and philosophy into the make-up and the manner of functioning of nature.   The challenge can be located at two levels, one, spiritual, and the other, sacramental.

At the *spiritual* level, there must be questions about the imaginative understanding of providence, and consequences about the conception of prayer, especially the prayer of petition, and of freedom.

Providence has usually been presented in theology after the manner of God's continuing care for creation, often through 'direct' intervention. The new insights in no way question the reality of God's continuing and active care.   But they do ask about the manner in which it occurs.   They would not want to conceive it by way of intervention, but by way of a permanent and all-pervasive active presence, indeed very close to the presence of Being to being.   Such a presence is one that allows and catalyses the intrinsic and in-built energies of nature to express themselves in their own way, with all the self-organisation and surprise they own. What we have so often called 'providence' and linked to God, may perhaps better be looked at as the *self-expressiveness of the largeness of nature.*

I can readily imagine nature as a vast symphony orchestra, without any conductor, which, in response to the presence of audience participation, spontaneously breaks into free variations of the theme it is playing. Providence is a word that expresses two things, almost contradictory, at the same time: first, the fact that we deeply want to look forward into the future of systems and see, from the distance of our present, what is going to take place; and secondly, the fact that we can never quite predict or foresee what is going to happen next.   We are always in a stance of fascination and frustration!   It comes from *the nature of nature*!

This openness to the real, on the basis that it is not all clear yet, and not fully predetermined, is what *prayer* has always been 'all about'.   I mean of course an actively participant openness.   The traditional language of prayer puts this as openness and opening up to God.   It could be suggested today that one way of opening up to God is exactly to open up to the energies of the universe, and to its unpredictable self-organising patterns.

Can we open up to the novelty of the vision, of the music, of the patterns, and listen - with respectful and hopefilled attention in a new way? Words are secondary, but if there were need to express them, a 'prayer' might go something like this: "Here I am, God, in your cosmos. I'm trying to open up to it all and to you in it all.   I'm trying to remove all the blockages to life and beauty that are still there, in me-in-it-all.   You know, God, how at the beginning of creation you smiled the loveliness into it, and whistled the music into it.   Could you show me now, through the energies you gave it then, how it still lives with the free life you gave it?"

Critics of the teaching about prayer, in the past, have made us humbly alert to the possibilities of narcissism in it.   The new 'cosmic' type of prayer is much less open to that criticism.   Prayer is much less an 'asking' for individual needs, as if creation could stop so we could be attended to, than a kind of *spiritual networking*, involving solidarity with all other persons, all other natures, all other events of cosmic history. It is entering into the 'divine milieu' of the cosmos, to use Teilhard's phrase.

One of the paradoxical features of this understanding of prayer, is that it emphasises the prayer of *petition* as central.   Such an attitude of prayer is like the permanent presence of an 'observer' in the cosmos, whose very 'prayer' always collapses the wave function in favour of the cosmic and human solidarity...

In this sense, asking is a form of music.   Could we change the image of the symphony orchestra, and place a conductor in it?   The conductor is totally alert, listens to everything, evokes music, but is separately and individually the source of no sound?   Is the conductor the person who prays?   It is perhaps a pity that many people, especially those with a sensitivity to the new science, who almost live in this attitude, have been so conditioned by a limited use of the word 'prayer' in certain religious traditions, that they do not recognise and name the experiences they already have.

A word about *freedom* here.   Freedom has been taken to be identical with autonomy, independence, unencumbered and unrestrained personal action. That is a very partial access to the real mystery of freedom.   Freedom is rather the full access to the intra-systematic aliveness of it all, freedom to be co-responsive with and to the communion of persons in the communion of the cosmos.   It is a function of that mutuality and reciprocity.   It is not freedom from being musical, but a freedom to be part of the music!   This is true, not simply for us, but for God as well.

At the *sacramental* level, there are questions in theology about the amplitude of the paschal mystery, and about the iconicity of all creation.

It could be said that the paschal mystery is the most significant theological (re-) discovery of this century.   It is an insight into the ultimate mysteries of Jesus, namely his dying and his rising, an insight which integrates them into a unity.   The model for this synthesis is exodus, that is the passover of the Jewish people from Egypt to the Land.   In the intuition of this century's theologians, it was understood as a *'passing through'* the red sea of death and an entry into the new life of resurrection.   (I am not sure if this is entirely faithful to the original meaning of the Hebrew word pesah or to the original biblical sense of the phrase in the Hebrew scriptures, but it was certainly the meaning grasped and spread in this century's theology.)

This idea of 'passing through' changed the perception of death as an endpoint, and integrated, upwards so to speak, the human life we have now with the human life we shall have in resurrection. The 'passing through' mystery applied primarily to Jesus, but extensively and eschatologically to us as well. The inherent dynamics of the mystery were positive: the breakdown of death is the shadow side of the breakthrough to resurrection.

This *dynamic* was then amplified to every subjective and spiritual experience, in this life, of equivalent breakdown and breakthrough, and a 'spirituality of the paschal mystery' was developed. The implications for a reconstruction of the liturgy of Easter are obvious. The Spirit of God was then conceived as the mysterious power which made the breakdown and breakthrough occur as one.

In many ways, the taking of centre stage by this paschal theology was one step in the longer history of the breakdown of a certain kind of *'redemption'* theology based on guilt and fear.   A more recent step in this breakdown, has been the advent of a *'creation'* theology, a positive move, but one which needs much more integration into the thinking of the paschal mystery and indeed into the more sophisticated dynamics of the new cosmic physics.

What does the vision that comes from the physics and philosophy I have sketched in this book mean to paschal mystery theology? I suggest that it means that the dynamics we have discovered in the dying and rising of Jesus, and by extension in our own participation in his life, are actually in all nature, from the micro to the macro. The *cosmos itself is a paschal mystery*. Whatever appears in the cosmos as substantive and perduring, in its own time breaks down, and the ongoing matrix makes it reappear in new forms and patterns. It is a - metaphorical at least - dying and rising. Theology must attend to this: not perhaps by amplifying the referent of its language about the 'body' of Christ to make it a 'cosmic' body, but rather by questioning the exclusivity of the application of the dynamics of the paschal mystery to Jesus alone, or to Jesus and us, alone. Do we have to recognise a *hidden anthropomorphism* in our enthusiasms about the paschal mystery?   Have we allowed this sense of 'resurrection' to isolate us from the cosmos itself?

Theology has tended, in its concentration on the paschal mystery, to speak as if the miracle of resurrection had virtually no analogies.   It has tended to present resurrection as blocking out whatever death did to Jesus.   It has seen the power of resurrection as coming from 'outside', from 'God', and not to have parallels in any human or cosmic system.   There is at least some modification needed in those statements, when we ponder the reality of self-organising systems, of morphogenesis and autopoiesis in the cosmos.   Is the dynamic in Jesus that makes him pass through death into life, *extrinsic or intrinsic* to Jesus?   Is the life that is in him capable of a 'quantum' leap from death into resurrection?   Is all life as such capable of doing that?   What is life?   Is it inherently overcome by death, or does it in some marvellous way not realised by us have an intrinsic capacity to enter into death and still find a form of life beyond the death-state?   These questions have not been taken seriously by our theology; indeed the answers to them would usually be assumed in the standard direction.   But they must be asked, and given a more serious response, if we are in the end to appreciate the wonder of nature, and the distinctiveness of Christ.

In the ancient theological texts, 'paschal mystery' is rendered 'paschale *sacramentum*'.   If we extend the idea of the paschal mystery to the cosmos, are we actually developing a 'sacramental' vision of the cosmos, and at the same time, a 'cosmic' vision of the primordial sacrament, the rising Christ?   Indeed, while it is tempting to think of the cosmos, in its own energy, as a sacrament of the paschal mystery in Christ, would it not be true, at least in this historical moment of our theology, that the paschal Christ is a kind of sacrament revealing to us the mysteries of the cosmos?   Which is the sacrament of which?

If the Latins speak of sacrament, the Greeks speak of icons. If an idol is a vision at which we become fixated, an icon is a vision of a transparency through which we see the unseen.   Is the whole cosmos iconic of the rising Christ?

At the heart of much Jewish theology is the axiom of the *aniconicity* of God: God cannot be imaged.   I wonder if the real function of that beautiful principle is to remind us that we should not look for, or attempt to create, isolate and particular would-be images of God, when in fact we have them cosmically all around us? Perhaps we have been too protective of a certain exclusivity of God, and of ourselves really, and too little ready to open our eyes to the icon of nature. How do all three, God-in-Christ, we, and nature, sing in harmony?

It would not be inappropriate here, to turn to *St.Paul*. There are seven texts in which he leaves us seed-thoughts that are meant to germinate in our minds, now more amply tilled by recent gains in science. They are: 1 Cor 8,6; Phil 2,6-11; 2 Cor 5,17-19; Gal 6,14-15; Rm 8,18-22; Col 1,15-19; Eph 1,10.[14]

In *1 Cor 8,6*, Paul makes his own and adapts an ancient credal formula, which itself reflects Jewish wisdom spirituality's understanding of the Shema. Christ and God (the Father) are seen side by side in creation. In the following translation I have rendered ta panta as the 'everything':

> Yet for us there is one God, the Father (ho pater)
> from whom (ek hou) is the everything,
> and towards whom (eis auton) we exist,
> and one Lord (Kyrios) Jesus-Messiah,
> through whom (di hou) is the everything,
> and through whom (di hou) we exist.

In almost hymnic rhythm, Paul is suggesting that we-in-the-cosmos are from and towards God, 'through' Jesus.

In *Phil 2,6-11*, we have the Christological hymn (carmen Christi) that Paul is using as his own characteristic confession of faith. It is interesting that the exegetical tradition has always called it a 'song':

> at the name of Jesus every knee should bow,
> in heaven and on earth and under the earth,
> and every tongue confess that Jesus-Messiah
> is Lord (Kyrios) to the glory of God the Father.

Paul is envisaging all created nature, the cosmos itself, as entering into the explicit acknowledgment of the glory of Jesus which believers make in faith.   This post-resurrectional recognition of Jesus is the glory of the Father.

In *2 Cor 5,17-19*, Paul is arguing against the backdrop of Stoic thinking, which saw every cycle of time ending in a conflagration (purosis), after which the seed-word (spermatikos logos) returned to the divine Fire-Word (Logos).   There would then be a new cycle (apokatastasis), in which a new seed-word would leave the divine fire for a new age.   Paul does not agree with this.   For him, since the resurrection of Jesus, the one cosmos is not in a process of dying, but of *'coming together'*. The Greek root katallassein is usually translated 'reconcile', but I prefer 'come together' to capture Paul's sense.

> If anyone is in Christ, that one is a new and different sort
> of creation.
> All this is from God, who through Christ has made us 'come
> together' to himself,
> and has given us the ministry of the 'coming together', that is,
> God was in Christ making 'come together' the cosmos to himself.

There is then, for Paul, really only one process going on, that of the *'coming together'*, and it goes on in us-in-the-cosmos.   It is interesting that Paul uses an imperfect inchoative participle, to suggest an act that is beginning to unfold, and continuing.   It is we who 'do' it...!

In *Gal 6,14-15*, Paul's thought needs to be understood in the light of his interpretation of the meaning of 'being crucified'.   He sensed that crucifixion brought Jesus into a permanent condition of *'unboundariedness'* and 'openness' which resurrection sealed into him.   Here he uses the word 'crucified' in that sense.   I paraphrase the text in that vein.

> But far be from me to glory except in the cross of Our
> Lord Jesus Christ, through whom the cosmos is unbound-
> aried towards me and I am unboundaried towards the
> cosmos, for neither circumcision counts for anything nor
> uncircumcision, but there is a new kind of creation
> (Kaine Ktisis).

Even the most significant differentiation hitherto known to Paul, that between Jew and gentile, is of no relevance, in a 'new' world that is constituted by the principle of unboundaried and open communion.

In *Rm 8,18-22,* in the midst of Paul's great hymn to agape, he sees the fullness of all things to be a disclosure of divine filiation, in humans, but also in a certain real sense, in the cosmos itself. For the cosmos is - with and through the human - brought to this apocalypse. The personal and the cosmic together are at present in a state that is described as 'waiting' and 'eager longing'... as if they were together peering into the future to see if it is coming.

> I consider that the sufferings of the present time
> are not worth comparing with the glory that is to be apocalypsed into us;
> for the cosmos itself is waiting with eager longing for the apocalypsing of divine filiation.
> For the cosmos was subjected to futility
> not by its own will
> but by the will
> of him who integrated it into the trajectory of hope:
> we know that the whole of creation has been groaning in travail until now..

For Paul, there is no inherent evil in the material cosmos: if there is futility, or vanity, there, it is of human making, and has been definitively transformed by the dying and rising of Jesus. He indulges in an extreme metaphor when he compares the drive in creation to that of a woman in pain of giving birth.

Col 1,15-19 is a hymn in honour of the cosmic Christ. It is not an 'answer' to questions about the origins of the cosmos. It is a statement about the ultimate finality and meaning of the cosmos, which is to be found in Christ. This is a Christological mysticism of the cosmos.

> He is the image of the invisible God,
> firstborn (prototokos) of all creation.(v.15)
> He is the beginning (arche),
> the firstborn even of the dead, so that in everything

> he might be the pre-eminent one(v.18b)
> For in him the everything was created,
> in heaven and on earth,
> visible and invisible,
> whether thrones or dominations or principalities or authorities,
> the everything was created
> through him and for him(v.16)
> For in him all the fullness of God was pleased to dwell,
> and through him it was pleased to make *'come together'*
> the everything.(v.19)
> He is before the everything,
> and in him the everything 'holds together'(v.17)
> He is the head of the body, the church(v.18)

Paul is really seeing the risen Jesus as the prototype of all cosmic existence, and the absolute primacy of the meaning of cosmos is to be found in Jesus.   Jesus is thus *arche*, not protos - protos is the first of a series (1234567....) while arche is a qualitatively absolute origination that sums up all meaning in itself.   The one-and-only meaning point.   You could say that Jesus is the raison d'etre, and magnet that attracts all creation. Cosmos, in the sense of a creation with an integrated meaning, is impossible except 'in' Christ.

> In *Eph 1,10* there is mention of
> a plan for the fullness of time,
> to unite all things in him,

But the translation does not do justice to the sense of the original.   It is not a plan for the final stage of history, whenever that would come; it is rather the deep meaningfulness of all the stages of history whenever they occur, in so far as they form a total unit called 'cosmic history'.   And their meaning is that they be 'headed up' in Christ.   'Headed up' (*anakephalaiosis*) suggests that their own intrinsic value finds its natural centre and consummation in Christ, that is, in the dynamics of the paschal mystery.

In other words, it is impossible to speak of an integrated cosmos ('the everything') without including it in the Christ of the paschal mystery.

NOTES

1. W.Broad, *New York Times*, 4/26/94, Top Quark, last piece in puzzle of matter, appears to be in place. S.Weinberg, *Dreams of a Final Theory*, Pantheon, New York, 1993. Review of Weinberg by R.Penrose, Cosmic solution proves elusive, *The Australian*, 10/20/94.

2. References in n.(1), and (26), chapter 1.

3. M.Waldrop, *Complexity*, Doubleday, 1993.

4. J.Gleick, *Chaos*, Penguin, 1987.

5. I.Prigogine, *From Being to Becoming: Time and Complexity in Physical Sciences*, New York, W.H.Freeman and Co., 1980. I.Prigogine, I.Stengers, *Order out of Chaos, Man's New Dialogue with Nature*, Toronto, Bantam, 1988.

6. D.Bohm, *Wholeness and the Implicate Order*, London, Routledge, Kegan,Paul, 1980.

7. R.Sheldrake, *A new science of life*, the hypothesis of formative causation, Collins 1987. R.Sheldrake, *The rebirth of nature*, the greening of science and God, Century, 1990. Also D.Bohm, *Unfolding meaning*, Ark paperbacks, London, 1987.

8. E.Jaentsch, The *self-organising universe*, scientific and human implications of the emerging paradigms of evolution, Oxford University Press, 1980. M.Kafatos, R.Nadeau, *The conscious universe*, part and whole in modern physical theory, Springer Verlag, 1990.

9. P.Davies, J.Brown, *Superstrings*, a theory of everything, Cambridge University Press, 1988. P.Heelen, Nature and its transformations, *Theological Studies*, 33, 1972, 486-502. R.Penrose, *The Emperor's New Mind*, concerning computers, minds, and the laws of physics, Oxford University Press, 1989. D.Hofstadtter, *Metamagical themas*, questing for the essence of mind and pattern, Penguin, 1987.

10. S.Weinberg, *Dreams of a Final Theory*, Pantheon, 1993.

11.   W.N.Clarke, Is natural theology still viable today?, in *Prospects for a Natural Theology*, ed. E.Long, Catholic University of America Press, 1992, p.181.

12.   G.M.Hopkins, *The Poems of Gerard Manley Hopkins, Oxford University Press*, 1952,p.70.

13.   D.Zohar, *The Quantum Self*, 1990.   D.Toolan, *'Nature is a Heraclitean Fire'*, reflections on cosmology in an ecological age, *Studies in the Spirituality of the Jesuits*, St.Louis, 1991.   D.Zohar, I.Marshall, *The Quantum Society*, 1993.

14.   M.Neary, The cosmic emphasis of Paul, *Irish Theological Quarterly*, 48, 1981, 1-26.

CHAPTER 6

FLOWING WITH MYSTERY

Contextualisating the beauty
in time

We have come to know a cosmic mystery: a self-organising 'music', a communion that demands differentiation, a reflection of the undying holistic vision of the Creator. There is a real sense in which this mystery *'flows'* and the context of its beauty is the 'ongoingness' of *'time'*. But, does the cosmos and its mystery really 'flow'? does the beauty have a real temporal 'history'? Do we flow with it and in it? do we have a real part in real cosmic ongoingness? The spontaneous answer to these questions would seem to be 'yes'. But the questions touch issues that are very central to the speculations of physics today, and they relate to extremely sensitive themes of philosophy and theology. Let us look closely at the sense of *'time'* in the music of the universe.

PHYSICS

When we speak about the 'flow' of things, we are asking questions about events in space and time. The very word 'flow' immediately evokes a sense of the flow of *'time'*. At the *macro* level, there is clearly an irreversible arrow of time. At the *micro* level, it is disputed: some would contend that it does not exist there, while others would say that it does, and then subdivide into those who see the arrow as entropic and those who, like Prigogine, see it as negentropic. All this is an invitation to look more closely at what we mean by 'time'.

To do so, it is useful to remind ourselves of some of the *basic* systems of physics, e.g. Newtonian physics, Special and General Relativity, Quantum physics. In each of them, time means something different.

In *Newtonian* physics, both space and time are universal and clear concepts - infinitely extendable continua. In *Special Relativity*, it could be argued that there is no such thing as universal simultaneity of time, and time is beginning to become less clear.   In *General Relativity*, it appears that time cannot be conceived as infinitely extendable, without coming to singularities that are meaningless.   In Quantum physics, there are really no fundamental states of time: the theory is equally open to any of them. There seems to be no agreed notion of time in all the basic systems of physics.   Each of these systems is thought to be a valid interpretation of certain levels of reality: Newton at the more macro levels, Quantum at the more micro levels.   It would seem that the idea of time gets more vague as we get more micro, and that it changes in meaning as we cross the frontiers that divide the domains appropriate to each system of physics.[1]

In general, scientists seem to *coalesce* several of these different perceptions of time and come up with a composite attitude to time.   There are *two* such *attitudes*: narrativism, and atemporalism.   The *narrativists*[2] are basically critical realists: they believe that science gives us real knowledge of a real world beneath its phenomenal manifestations.   They also believe that that real world changes: there is a real succession of real events. Thus they believe that a 'story' can really be told, of the happening of things, one after another, in real time.   They would regard the change (or phase transition) of the cosmos from quantum to relativity to Newtonian dimensions as a prime example of this.   Their mindset is thus in a broad sense at least 'evolutionary'.   Process is real.   This is apparently a majority view today.   It is roughly the assumption in the pedagogy of this book.

The *atemporalists*[3] hesitate precisely at all the key points the narrativists maintain.   They are not as sure about the sense of the adjective 'real' when there is talk of a 'real' world and of 'real' change and of a 'real' succession of 'real' events.   They are often more strongly influenced by quantum thinking, and resist a coalescence of quantum and non-quantum understandings.   They would like to know more about the meaning of 'time' and where the idea of it comes from.   They seem attracted to a timeless, Platonic, perhaps gnostic perception of reality. They feel such a perception is more germane to the data of quantum physics, and that we need to check the unsuspected naivete of our world views that imply narrative.   In many ways they would like to 'deconstruct' the story!

It seems already clear that a real influence is coming into the thinking of scientists from both *philosophy and theology*,   and that the two persuasions about time are not entirely and exclusively the product of scientific investigation.   The kind of realist philosophy advocated in this book, would extend its investment in actual being, as the core of the real, to temporally factual being, in history.   Any challenge to it would be a challenge to its foundations.   On the other hand, the Platonic mindset often mentioned with reservation in this book, would seem to sit well with the persuasion of an atemporal universe.   Theology has an equal sensitivity to these questions: it needs to protect the eternity of its Creator God who acts in time, and the historical framework of salvation made possible by such acts of God.   In fact the very distinction between infinite and finite is so linked in the theological imagination with the distinction between eternity and time, that a question about the latter is a challenge to the former, and the unquestionable status of the former is an influence on the formation of opinion about the latter.

In any event, the *meaning of time*, and the *origin of our sense of time*, are central issues, for physics, philosophy, and theology.

It is best to present, *first*, something of a case for the non-narrativist, atemporal vision of the cosmos, and *then* to unfold some recent work that attempts to support the narrativist cause.   In the first part, I shall draw upon the work of John Wheeler, Christopher Isham, and Willem Drees.

Wheeler[4] begins his study of time in General Relativity.   He looks at the world of *four dimensional spacetime* that Einstein first discovered for us. It is not the familiar world of three dimensional space, plus a very different thing called time.   Rather, neither space as we are accustomed to it, nor time as we think we know it, are retained as such in Einsteinian 'spacetime'.   There is a four dimensional geometry there that sets up a different 'world'.

Wheeler contends that the dynamics Einstein worked out in General Relativity apply primarily and directly to *three dimensional geometry*, not four dimensional geometry.   A four dimensional geometric world (of 'spacetime') is simply one frozen step in the working out of the dynamics of three-dimensional geometry.   It is the three-dimensional world that is important in our inquiry.

The dynamics of three-dimensional geometry unfold in what Wheeler calls *'SuperSpace'*. It theoretically consists of an infinite number of points, each point representing one three-dimensional geometry or possible three-dimensional world. Each one of these is like a single bent leaf from SuperSpace.

In each such leaf, there are *two kinds* of three-dimensional geometry. One is called a "YES", the other a "NO". A "YES" means that it conforms to prescribed initial conditions, a "NO" means that it does not.

Only the "YES"es can be the possible building blocks of a four-dimensional geometry like spacetime.

Wheeler asks us to imagine SuperSpace as a landscape foliated by non-intersecting hypersurfaces. They could be imagined as fences. Each one of them is spacelike, and the intervals between them are also spacelike. Each one of them is a three-dimensional geometry. Wheeler then asks us to imagine a rogue three-dimensional geometry *intersecting* them all at an angle, and to imagine a second, and a third, such rogue intersecting at different angles. The result would be a definite *point* that would belong to *four* hypersurfaces. It would be a point in a four-dimensional geometry. This means that a point, or event, is a selection from pre assigned three-geometries in SuperSpace, a *selection* which itself sets up the four-dimensional geometry. *'Spacetime'*, as Einstein called it and we know it after him, is a collection of such point-like events.

Now if you pushed the first slicing hypersurface forward, it would intersect the sheet with a different numeration: you could then *arbitrarily assign* number coordinates to such experiments and speak of the succession of them as... *time*!

Wheeler then moves his frame of argument from General Relativity to Quantum Theory. Here, things are different again. In the three-dimensional geometries, there are no outright "YES"es and no outright "NO"s. Each one has a probability amplitude of Quantum fluctuations: in fact, each one has its own. This occurs at the Planck length.

If you remember this, there is *no objective* way of getting the building blocks of a four-dimensional geometry like spacetime. Only by overlooking it and choosing to act as if it is not so,   do you fit three-dimensional geometries into a frozen state called four-dimensional geometry or spacetime.   Spacetime, for all the reverence we owe it since Einstein, is then an *approximation*.   Really, there is *no such thing*!   This means of course that really there are *no events* and *no intervals* between them. There is *no time*.

Further, even when we look at what we call spacetime itself, (and not how we constructed it), Quantum gives us more reasons for hesitation. Because of the complementarity principle, we cannot give a geometric field-coordinate and a geometric field-momentum at the same time.   That is, we cannot give a dynamic variable and a rate of change, at the same time.   Therefore it is impossible to make a prediction concerning spacetime.   In effect, then, in Quantum thinking, four-dimensional geometric spacetime does not exist since it has *no predictable meaning*. At best, it becomes a (very useful) *approximation*.

Time, then, is not a primary concept in physics, and there is *really no before/after/next*.

Wheeler's thought can serve as introduction to the view which has developed among physicists under the name of the *'Block Universe'*.   It is well presented by Christopher Isham and John Polkinghorne, as a central matter of current debate.[5]

A *'Block Universe'* is a set of points, all of which are meaningful, and all of which have equal ontological status.   In it there is no fundamental meaning of 'past', 'present', 'future', or 'now'.   All these are illusory, as is the idea of an open future.

The Block Universe is connected with the idea of a Light Cone of events. Event E can be represented in a three-dimensional graph with a cone that represents its future, and a cone that represents its past.   'Around' it is its 'elsewhere'.

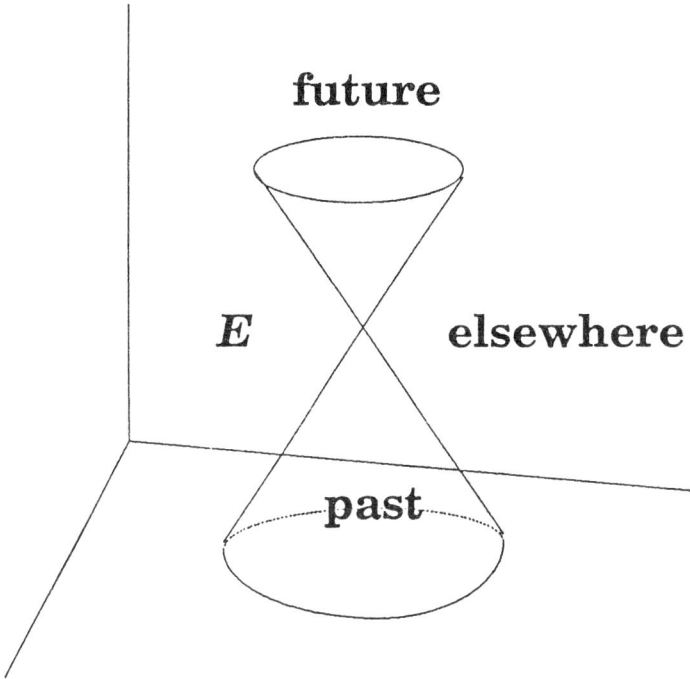

future

E   **elsewhere**

past

(From: C.J. Isham, J. C. Polkinghorne.   The debate over The Block
Universe, in R.J. Russell, N. Murphy, C.J. Isham, eds., *Quantum Cosmology and The Laws of Nature,* Und Poems, 1993, p. 136.)

You can only identify the future and the past of the event E in the light
cone of the event E, and not in the 'elsewhere' of that event.   If we were
to graph a distinct event E-1, we would have to give it a distinct light cone,
which did not overlap with the light cone of event E.   This means that
there cannot be an unequivocal meaning for *'simultaneity'* of events. And
no unequivocal meaning can be assigned to *'time'*, or *'future'* or *'past'*.
There can only be an infinite family of possible definitions of time, in
relation to determined initial reference frames.

In Special Relativity, the reference frame has to be selected from a
potentially infinite set.   In General Relativity, this selection takes place
through the particular and arbitrary 'slicing' or intersecting of spacetime,

as Wheeler has shown. There cannot be a scientific justification for the choice of these particular selections.   In effect, the role of what is called 'time' can be and is played by a chosen dimension of space.   The construction of planes of simultaneity is retrospective and artificial. Events in principle don't 'happen': they are 'there'.

Polkinghorne and Isham show us the range of the debate about this notion, but in doing so they bring out the mindset behind the atemporalist and non-narrative version of the universe that we are trying to explore.

Willem Drees[6] has raised explicit questions to the critical realistic narrativ ists along the same lines as Isham and Wheeler. He insists that the notion of time has been extracted from other (non-temporal) variables.   It is a derivative notion.   The derivation is from SuperSpace: a collection of all possible configurations of curvature (geometry) and matter (material) on a three-dimensional manifold.   Within this SuperSpace, there are subsets and *'paths'* which can trace various possible *'histories'*.   In some such regional subsets the notion of time is extracted coherently.   The regional subset of General Relativity does not clear ly allow this extraction.   But when we look at the *Quantum* region, the most we can get is a probability amplitude describing a number of paths and a whole set of possible (classical) histories: the probability amplitude peaks within them.   Here there appears to be *full parity* between space and time.   Drees notes that some in describing the Quantum domain prefer to retain the word 'time' and speak of *'imaginary'* time not 'real' time.   Vilenkin would seem to approach creation as the transition from one to the other.   Drees notes that it is really a matter of taste whether one speaks of *imaginary time* or drops the parameter of time as *meaningless*. This raises serious questions about where and what reality ultimately is: temporal or atemporal? He suggests that the tendency to atemporality is *more germane* than its opposite with much of present theoretical physics.   It is no wonder that there is an attraction for Plato in philosophy - or is it an influence from Plato upon it?

As the scientific debate continues, there seems to be increasing consensus that science alone, whether that of General Relativity or that of Quantum or of some combination of both, cannot resolve the issue.   Philosophy must enter the discussion, but it must first be able to hear the question as the scientists are putting it.

Before we turn to philosophy, we must introduce a vein of thinking in science which affects the argument.   It attempts to *'get underneath'* even *Quantum Theory.*

This thinking assumes the validity of Quantum Theory, and asks *'why' questions* about Quantum Theory.   Is reality at roots made up of small discrete units, or quanta, and if so,   why?   Why should the precise numbers that define the quanta be these numbers?   Why does 'phase transition' occur from a Quantum domain to a General Relativity domain and why at the precise mathematical moment indicated in Quantum and Relativity theory?   Why is there mass at all? why is the speed of light exactly what it is? what is light? why are there anomalies and paradoxes in all the theories?   These questions would clearly have further implications in other fields of science to which the basic mathematical theory has relevance - astronomy, biology, studies of the brain and consciousness, etc.

The general response of thinkers like Erwin Laszlo, Milos Lokajicek, and David Bohm and Basil Hiley is in the direction of *field theory.*   Some understanding of field has been about at least since Faraday and Maxwell and electromagnetic fields.   General Relativity is a field theory, demanding its own different geometry.   We talk commonly of matrices and systems.   Among them we have seen the interest taken in self-organising systems and morphogenetic fields.   String theory is a form of field theory. These thinkers are trying to discover a basic cosmic field that underlies even quanta and explains the emergence of quanta.

To create his kind of field, Laszlo makes use of *two theories* that need their own explanation.   They are solitons, and virtualities.[7]

A *soliton* is a solitary wave in turbulent media.   Scott Russell discovered one, in 1845, when riding beside a narrow channel of water.   It was a wave rolling with great speed, a large solidary elevation, a rounded, smooth, and well-defined heap of water.   It continued its course along the channel without change in form or speed.   Since then solitons have been discovered in tidal bores, in atmospheric pressure waves, in heat conduction in solids, in complex electrical circuits, in the human nervous system, in superfluids and superconductors, even in the Great Red Eye of Jupiter. They are considered to be solidary waves in a non-linear medium.

A *virtuality* is a real entity that is not detectable by a device that observes and measures gravity and electromagnetic phenomena. The expression 'virtuality' thus has its own meaning, which is different from the use of the same word in computer studies and in philosophy.

Laszlo begins by envisaging the basic cosmic field as made up of *quanta in a vacuum*. But he suggests that the quanta are really *solitons*, and the vacuum is a vacuum of *virtualities*. The advantage for him in considering quanta as solitons is that they are *not discrete and discontinuous*, but continuous with the medium in which they are solidary waves. In effect, they are not by definition 'quanta', and he is talking about a stage of reality prior to quantised appearances. The advantage for him in considering the vacuum as a vacuum of virtualities, is that it is not 'nothing', nor described as filled with marvellous energy, but precisely described with the technical properties of virtualities. Among these properties is the property of being *massless*. The quanta-solitons are *massed*, while the vacuum-virtualities are massless, and as such they can form an integrated field.

The original quantum-vacuum is a dense structure of energy, oscillating. At the Planck length, the oscillations break up the four-dimensional spacetime continuum, into 'spacetime segments', or 'quantum foam'. This is the equivalent of a pure massless charge-flux. But when the oscillations do not breach the level at which the creation of quantised particles and antiparticles occurs, the realities remain massless, or virtual energy charges, or *'virtualities'*. It is in this vacuum of virtualities that the solitons occur.

The solitons, and the virtualites, are really two different kinds of *'wave'*. One is a *vectorial* wave, the other is a *'scalar'* wave. The vectorial wave is the ordinary manner of propagation of charged, massed particles. The 'scalar' was discovered by Nikola Tesla at the turn of the century, and is something like a sound wave. A scalar is a quantity completely defined by magnitude alone, without reference to displacement. They have neither mass nor specific spin. They are not transverse waves, but 'shadow' vector waves, that is, in a virtual state.

Soliton-massed-vectorials are limited in their *velocity* by the speed of light. Vacuum-virtualities (massless) are not so limited, and in principle can aspire to infinity.

When the calculations are done mathematically for each of these two factors, it is seen that they can be integrated into *a single field*.   Laszlo calls it an *Interactive* or *Interinformational* field.

It is something analogous to a *holographic* field. Any pattern in spacetime is transformed into a series of waves.   Each wave has a characteristic frequency and amplitude. A photograph maps three-dimensional outlines of objects on a film or plate. A holograph maps the coefficients of the interference patterns created by the wave transforms at the intersection of the wave fronts.   The sites of the intersections are nodes of various amplitudes, and are recorded as a pattern on the hologram.   A three dimensional picture can be recreated from them.   An interactive field is not a holographic one, but there are similarities.

The similarity consists in the *transforms*.   A transform is a pattern in spacetime that gives rise to a set of regular periodic oscillations that differ in frequency, amplitude, and phase.   From the transforms, exact representations of three-dimensional objects can be obtained.

A good example of a field in which transforms are encoded is the path of a ship at sea.   It leaves a pattern of waves behind it.   Suppose another (smaller, almost weightless) craft crosses the path of the ship, with its own patterns behind it.   The two patterns intersect.   It is possible that they can also integrate.

The integration can be such that it (the field) is able to give rise to various patterns that are precisely encoded in the integration of the transforms of the two waves, vectorial and scalar.   Seen this way, the primordial cosmic field is some thing like an ether of virtualities with defined trajectories in it.   It is able to *give rise to the discernible patterns* we call real entities. As such it is a creative communion, able to give rise to 'downward causation' and *ontogenesis*.   There is a value in the field, mathematically, that could be called?   *Universal Integrated Differential*, and that expresses how exactly the field is constituted.

Laszlo would want to argue that the *values* of the quanta, of the photons, the value of the speed of light, the value of mass, the values of the transitions from pre-quantal to quantal to relativity to Newtonian domains, could all be illustrated from this basic cosmic field.   Because the field is not quantal, it is not subject to the reduction of a probability amplitude by an observer/measurement.   Rather the truth of that principle and its boundaries can be established by pre and non quantal principles in the cosmic field.

Implied in Laszlo's theory is the *reality of time*.   Perhaps not of time as we ordinarily conceive it, but of time none the less. His universe is not a block universe, but a *process* one.

Other thinkers are moving in the same direction.   *Stapp* has queried the Copenhagen interpretation of Quantum Theory, and sustained that the probability distribution is ontological.[8]   *Bohm and Hiley* speak of an ontological interpretation of Quantum Theory.   They would speak of an 'implicate order' enfolded as it were holographically, like information given for navigation to a ship by radar, in the woof and web of all reality.[9]

Milos Lokajicek would argue in a similar direction, from an analysis of the mathematics involved, that all reality of space is in fact a reality of double space, an integrated set of *two subspaces*, and that it is in the meeting point that light is transmitted.   He ponders the meaning of *light* itself.[10] Perhaps, in too simple a form, the insight behind this vein of thinking is that any integrated field manifests itself in discrete particles or units.   If then there are quanta of light, there must be such a photonic field that gives rise to the photons.

So, *where are we?*   It seems a long 'time' since we began our ponderings about time.   We have learned that there are two quite different approaches to time among the physicists.   One group sees it as a subjective perception and perhaps projection upon a physical reality in which at root there is no time.   The other sees it as real in the very make-up of the real itself.   And yet, even if the latter group is right, the notion of time that they advocate, and especially the sources from which it appears to them to come, are not nearly as obvious as most people imagine.   The scientific jury is still out on these matters, possibly permanently, since many think it is at root a matter of philosophy, and perhaps theology.   The result is that we really do not understand time, and we do not have clear positions to present to philosophical and theological analysis.   Perhaps that is the real message to these disciplines.

A question that is intimately linked to these issues about time, is the *nature of nature*, that is, of the nature of anything that lives and exists in space and time.   If we cannot define such natures without including the time dimension, and if we cannot get clarity about the time factor, can we legitimately speak of the nature of anything?   What does it mean to *'exist'* if not in time?   Does the tenacious advocacy of real being in our critical philosophy face an insurmountable problem when it cannot work with scientific assurance about time itself?   Does *being itself* recede into the mystical darkness of some atemporality?   These questions should remain with us, as we move to our study of philosophy.

There is some agreement all the same here.   An agreement about a kind of oneness from which we all come in our distinctiveness.   For some, the oneness is real, and the coming is more imaginary.   For others, the oneness is imaginary, and the coming more real.   It is impossible to deal with scientific objectivity in such preferences.   It is good to sense a natural preference for the reality of time, yet to temper it with a new hesitation about the exact boundaries between the real and the imaginary.

PHILOSOPHY

Philosophy might well focus on *five problems* here: *first*, the problem of a time-frame for reality; *secondly*, the problem of naming the real; *thirdly*, the problem of anchoring our knowledge of the real; *fourthly*, the problem of 'inclusive language'; and *finally*, the problem of styles of cognition of the real.   They are fundamental questions, and agreement among philosophers is never supposed.

First, *a time-frame for reality*.   When philosophers consider the mystery of creation, they know that the core of it is the relation between Being and being.   This relationship is capable of two different emphases: on the infinite difference between them, and on the incredible bondedness between them.   You have to keep both in focus!   It has often been true that a critically realist philosophy (and theology) has tended to put a greater emphasis on the former than on the latter.   There is a tendency among many thinkers today to recover the latter emphasis, and in doing so, they need to be careful to retain the former as well.

Being and being: transcendence and bondedness.   When these deep values are translated into a time frame, the older traditions in critical philosophy made them virtually equivalent to *Timelessness: time*.   I say, virtually, because that philosophy was always fully aware that created finite being was more fundamentally characterised by its finitude than by its temporality.   None the less, its temporality was as it were the natural property of its contingency, and translated it into more tangible terms. When God the Creator, Being itself, was referred to, the notion of eternity as timelessness was invoked, again as the natural property of Transcendence.   More recent thought attempts to speak of the bondedness of Being and being in these terms, and runs into difficulty: it is hard to establish a bondedness between timelessness and time.   There is a demand that God be more in touch with time than that, in order to be able to sustain a temporal being in being.

A classic philosophy can legitimately *reply* to this query by insisting on two things.   *First*, as we have outlined in chapter two, eternity is not timelessness at all.   It is the condition of Being proper to Being, and never to being, and as such is neither timefull nor timeless.   It is of another order. *Secondly*, there is no radical problem in establishing the connectedness of Being and being: being cannot even be existentially conceived without the actual, dynamic presence (and actuating contact) of Being to it.   It would appear that behind the more recent trend (of equating eternity with a form of time) there may be a sliding from the authentic conception of eternity as a property of Being to a conception of it as infinitely extendable *duration*, which would be a property not of Being but of being.

This being said, and these distinctions retained and insisted upon, there seems to be merit in *listening* to what the recent trends are trying to say. They may well be picking up, at the philosophical level, some of the intuitions of some currents in science.   Science envisaged the possibility of some arena of the real in which time could be called either imaginary or illusory, in other words, an arena where time was not the kind of time we ordinarily know.   Philosophically could there be such a thing?

Wolfhart Pannenberg considers the feasibility of a *'background time frame'* of the universe, which is not a subjective projection but an objective reality, which is not a finite time-span but a virtually infinite duration, a fundamental time-frame from which all other time-frames of a more limited nature are derived and to which they approximate. It is still a time-frame, as it were the accomplishment of all the unfinishedness and waiting for fulfilment in other modes of time. Any temporal 'now' must include this, for without it there is no such thing as temporal presence. He speaks of it as an image of the omni-actuality of God, and indeed has recourse to rarely used older theological sources to attempt to equate it with eternity (but of course not timelessness).[11]

Pannenberg goes on - almost following the trajectory of the scientists - to speak also of a *space-frame*, of the universe, which is non-subjective, nor of a geometry that we can express, which as it were enfolds all other space-frames of a more limited nature and extent. It is a fundamental space of a different kind from the space we are familiar with. It reflects, for him, the ubiquity of God, as incommensurable omni-presence.

Pannenberg then attempts to integrate these two insights, concerning time and space, and comes up with the idea of a 'field'. We have seen how central the notion is to contemporary physics. He tracks its philosophical roots to the pre-Socratics and Stoics and sees traces of it in Tillich and Teilhard. Tillich had grasped the ecstasis of the human spirit towards the Divine Spirit, as it were in one 'field' together. Teilhard had sensed or intuited a radial energy, 'inside' matter, through which all things material were self-transcending and converging towards Omega, as one Spirit. There are clear parallels in the psycho-dynamics dear to Jung. Pannenberg sees the cosmos as emergent from this fundamental force-field of space and time, and tends to *identify* the field with the Spirit of God.

The tradition in which I am writing cannot accept that identification. Infinite 'extent' is not infinite Being. But perhaps we should pause, and recognise the possibility of a (metaphysically finite) background force-field of space and time, from which all the dimensions of the known universe come, as not necessarily incoherent from a philosophical point of view. Such a notion would actually go far towards explaining why some trends in physics say that time is an illusion (because at the physical roots of the universe it is not the time that we speak of), and other trends speak of a 'deep' time, more real than the one we know.   As long as the Creator-Being is its Source, and is not identified with it, there seems no problem in principle about it.   It would represent the convergence of many disparate trajectories of thinking that cannot terminate in their own disciplines: such as those of physics, depth psychology, mythology, and Platonism.   It is of course a further question, to ask if it actually exists and how we could know if it did.

This brings us to our *second problem*, that of *naming the real*.   There is an insistence, in any realist philosophy, on naming the real as actual being. There is a natural slippage from the metaphysical notion of actual being, to a description of actual being as historically factual being, that is, actual being in time.   There is a refusal to extend the notion of actuality to any background region of Platonic ideas or shadows!   If any of the probings we have examined are valid, what do they suggest differently about naming the real?   Does the 'real' include the 'background' from which it comes, not as idea or shadow, but as integral to the whole actuality itself?   Can we describe actual being with the help of what we can know about the 'background'?   This raises the *problem of description* in the metaphysics of being.   Most realist metaphysicians would appear to refuse any attempt to perform a 'phenomenology' of being: being is not a feature, and a phenomenology is a delineation of features.   Norris Clarke has broken ground here, in his attempt to describe being as personal.   In effect he has accepted the metaphors that come from the realm of *interpersonhood* as valid in the interpretation of being itself.   This is true, as Gerald McCool puts it, of the 'higher instantiations' of being:

> "In Clarke's metaphysics, person is not considered a new perfection added to the perfection of existence.   Personal being is rather the form in which existence reaches the fullness of its own reality in its supreme spiritual instantiations: God's Infinite Esse, the esse of pure angelic spirits, and the esse of the lowest spiritual creature, the incarnate human spirit.   In those higher instantiations, wholly or partly freed from the restrictions imposed on it by limiting matter, the act of existence can unfold its own intrinsic plenitude in the knowledge and love of consciously self possessing and self-transcending

persons.   To be a conscious, self-possessing person, in
Clarke's metaphysics, means simply to be most fully."[12]

Clarke is then willing to metaphorise being from *interpersonhood*.   And
he limits the metaphorisation to the *higher instances* of being.   The
question must be asked: can you metaphorise being from other sources
than interpersonhood, and can you do so for even lower instances of being,
in the material cosmos?   In particular, I ask: can you speak of the
metaphysical being of the *material cosmos* in metaphors taken from *time
and space*?   Is physics usable as metaphor for metaphysics?   For some,
this is precisely, a contradiction in terms, but I would suggest that it is not
necessarily so.

If we are dealing with the parameters of space and time as we usually
know them, in positivistic terms, the objection to their use obviously
stands.   Because in that sense their sole function is the limitation of being,
not its expression.   But if we are dealing with space and time, in a
background cosmic field from which more particular parameters of space
and time then come, we may have room for hesitation.   I suggest that we
do not focus directly on the 'contents' or 'space and time' dimensions of
the 'background field', about which not much knowledge can be available
to us except projectively from our obvious world.   I suggest rather that we
focus on the *emergence* of our kind of time and space dimensions from
such a *background-field*.   I am trying to imagine that kind of emergence
as something like the emergence of interpersonal activity from being in its
higher forms.   If the latter is a metaphor for being (in its higher forms),
could the former be a metaphor of being in all its forms, even its lower
ones?   The former would not be a physical and material dimension as a
limitation of being, but a physical and material dimension as an expression
of being itself.   It does seem to me that what we are dealing with in both
cases of emergence (personal and cosmic) is the *unfolding of a primordial
oneness into differentiated terms*.   The realness of the differentiated terms
is a participation, or unfolding, or instantiation, of the prior realness of the
original oneness.   What being, or reality, really is, is that act of emergence.   Just as the oneness itself is an emerging from the different
Oneness of Being as Creator.

If this is so, *what is really real*?   Not primarily isolated and discrete
entities with their own historical facticity.   But primarily the emerging of

such entities from a background field that is never dissociated from them, even while it demands and engages their differentiation.   We are back again at *communion demanding differentiation*, as we were in chapter four.
To admit such a material matrix for all material beings, is a good analogy for sustaining that there is a *relationality prior to the emergence from it of relational terms*, as we have suggested in chapter two.

The upshot of all this is the establishment of a fulcrum on which to balance a mystical and a critical vision of being.   It is an attempt to see what it means to be in real time, and to flow in it as the unfolding of another kind of time where things are less disparate, and to see all that as a reflection of the eternally-different actuality that is Being itself.   If this is where physics is looking, philosophy would have no problem in standing and gazing in the same direction.

But how do we know it is there?   is it 'there'?   This takes us to our *third problem*, the *problem of anchoring our knowledge of the real*.   In the realist tradition, there have been many attempts to anchor our sense of real being through our real contact with material realities of space and time, from which we then, in various degrees, abstract our idea of being itself. Objections have been raised that the term of such abstraction is not quite 'being', and that some kind of direct intuition of being is needed beyond that.   Different types of intuition have been suggested: from intuition directly into being as such, to intuition directly into the Divine Being, to intuition of being in the perception of interpersonhood (the latter would appear to be Clarke's position).   One would have to return then to the material domain and maintain the realness of real material beings in the strength of a conviction begotten elsewhere about personal being.

Perhaps it could be suggested that - along the lines of Clarke's approach, but extending it - what we really intuit in the intuition of personal being, is the mystery of *emergence from oneness* into differentiation.   And if that were so, would it not be possible to intuit something of a *similar emergence* in our deeper perceptions - in physics, for example - of material being? Could that intuition occur directly, and then be recognised as germane to the independent and direct intuition of personhood?

There would be *consequences* from this, for the idea of material reality, and for the idea of personhood.   Material being would be intuited as a discreteness-within-a-background, that is primarily holistically.   It would not be intuited first of all in its own separateness.   Personal beings would be intuited as inherently possessing a history and a time-space manifold as the arena and natural home of their interpersonal relationships, and not primarily as either self-possessing, and/or as spiritual beings that transcend materiality.   Personal beings whose life is intended to be conscious emergence towards another, are meant to do so in a material and temporal context whose own intrinsic meaning is a similar, but not conscious, emergence.   There would be an integration of person and cosmos.

Our *fourth problem* is the problem of *'inclusive language'*.   Despite our insights, our language is hardened and tends to express the isolated adequacy of what appears to be separated and uncontexted.   A more congruent language would not lose the sense of differentiation so strongly emphasised here, but would situate it in the largeness from which it is originating, so that the mystery of its being could come through more as one of emergence than one of self-standing.   I do not know of the development of such a philosophical language.   Without it, we risk a basic ambiguity.

Finally, let us look at the *problem of styles of (re-) cognition of the real*. If this is reality, what is the quality of our knowledge of it?   How, and in what manner do we 'know'?

It may be helpful to think of *'knowing'* as entering consciously into the process of emergence that constitutes reality.   Our minds, that are geared to do this, have already emerged and differentiated from a mysterious communion and oneness.   They are, so to say, possessed natively of too strong a sense of their own differentiation, and too vague a sense of the ambience from which they have come, and are still bonded with.   They can indulge in a kind of knowing that it would be wise to ponder as *illusory*, when they project on to other things their own sense of too strong differentiation and too vague a sense of common bonding.   When they really *'know'* *'reality'*, they let go of all that, and enter participatively into the process of emergence that has always been going on, unbeknown to our minds, in and around us.   Real knowing is always a knowing of how bonded we are, and how we are emerging within the bondedness and how our differentiation enhances it, and it enhances our differentiation.   The moment of really knowing that, is a moment of appreciation and entering-into the flow of the mystery.   A sort of dying to staticism and a sort of birth into the dynamics of it all.   Our regret is that our minds have not been properly educated into their own proper activity, but have been technologised into the misrecognition of various reifications as 'reality'.

One can wonder if various cognitions sometimes called 'abnormal' are actually ways of penetrating behind the wall of 'normal' reifications into the process that is really going on.   I am thinking of various forms of telepathy, etc.   Is there a kind of *protopathy* with the flowing real that is in us all if we could only let go and use it?

Let us come back to the recurring subtheme of death and dying.   Our present philosophy of dying stresses the *letting go* of the *boundaries*, even of space and time, in which we now exist.   That is why dying is a radical act: we let go precisely of the boundaries that seem integral to our differentiation, and seemingly we let go of that too.   And yet, dying is not presented as the acquisition of alternative 'boundary conditions' or of a different differentiation.   It seems rather to be an entry into and a communion in a different order of reality, which of itself does not possess such boundary differences, but which can take into it our very own in its own way, since that is where they came from in the first place.   There is no succession there, and in comparison with our experienced world, all is still.   And yet, *every moment* of our experienced world is through the mystery of the final letting go subsumed and present with its full actuality in the new horizon of integration.   It is retained fully, but without our clinging to it.   I am not just saying that its moral value is still to be found there, but that it itself - a moment of time conditioned by space - is somehow 'there' without becoming a 'then' of the past.   That may be the first time that we really know the real, and know ourselves as knowers of the real in the same act.   Is this the final context of the beauty that we are, as it has always been its primordial context?

THEOLOGY

Theology has two reactions to the kind of thinking we have outlined: a hesitation, because it feels a need to defend the reality of God's saving acts in time; and a fascination, because it always feels a haunting sense of mystery that is beyond time.   Theology does not deal with a collection of myths whose referent point is in the unconscious.   It deals with real facts of real human history, identifiable in space and time.   But these time-bound realities are the surfacing of the eternal.

The eternal is mostly about the divine life communicating itself, realising itself, unfolding itself in the time and space of our real world.   The eternal that does this, is the mystery of Christ.   God's eternal life is unfolded in the life, death and resurrection of Jesus.   The paschal mystery of Jesus is the revelation in time of the eternal mystery of God.

The *moment of the dying of Jesus* is the point in time where things eternal and things human meet.   It could be said that the entire mystical sense of Christianity is focussed in that moment.

In that one moment, Jesus lets go definitively, and enters into the new and definitive bond with the living God that is the root of resurrection and of the imparting of the Spirit to those still in this world who believe in him. In a mystical sense, Paul celebrates the wonder of that moment when we says that we are all 'in' Christ, and we live 'with' his life, and die in his death and are enlivened in his resurrection.   It is possible that some theologians might make use of the thinking we have presented in physics and philosophy, to dare the suggestion that there is *an eternal perduring of the very instant* of Jesus' passing to the Father.   The thought is already there in germ in the intuition of F.X. Durrwell: the very act of dying-passing-over is eternally sealed into the personality of Jesus, and eternally actual.   It is there in the sacramental MysterienGegenwart theories of O.Casel and G.Sohngen: there is a mystic presence of the very act of dying-rising that we access in the celebration of the eucharistic liturgy, especially in the paschal vigil.   But there is an intuitiveness and a poetry about this rhetoric.   What the thinking we have tentatively presented would add to it, is some kind of validation that there is *more than rhetoric* here.   It may be in very truth the reality of what happens.   Perhaps we are always at the foot of the cross of Jesus, always in our dying involved not simply in his death (as past) but in the 'eternalised' *actuality* of the moment and act of his dying-rising?   If theology pursued this line of thinking, it could develop interesting perspectives on sacramentalism, on mysticism, and Christian ethic now.[13]   There has always been, in the popular theology of folk Christianity, some vague and ambiguous use of the idea of time when there is talk of what 'happens' beyond death. It is often insisted that whatever time occurs then, it is not like ours. Perhaps it is not 'another' time, but a communing of all moments of all time, and a holding in its embrace of the moments of our time that have most unfolded the mystery in our midst? There is very little of this that anyone could ever prove. But there is an interesting convergence of speculation from the metaphors of physics, philosophy and theology. The flow of the mystery is indeed an aesthetics of the beauty of every moment of all time.

§ § §

NOTES

1.   W.Drees, A Case against Temporal Critical Realism? Consequences of Quantum Cosmology for Theology, in *Quantum Cosmology and the Laws of Nature*, eds., R.Russell, N.Murphy, C.Isham, Vatican Observatory Publications, 1993, pp.331-366.

2.   Drees (n.1 above) names among them: Barbour, McMullin, Peacocke, Peters, Polkinghorne, Soskice,Torrance, Pannenberg.

3.   C.J.Isham and J.C.Polkinghorne, The Debate over the Block Universe, in Quantum *Cosmology and the Laws of Nature*, eds., R.Russell, N.Murphy, C.Isham, Vatican Observatory Publications, 1993, pp.135-144.

4.   J.A.Wheeler, *Time Today*, Princeton University Press, 1993.

5.   Cf. note 3.

6.   Cf. note 1.

7.   E.Laszlo, *The Creative Cosmos*, a unified science of matter, life and mind, Floris Publications, 1993.

8.   H.Stapp, *Mind, Matter and Quantum Mechanics*, Berlin, Springer-Verlag, 1993.

9.   D.Bohm, B.Hiley, *The Undivided Universe*, London, Routledge, 1993.

10. M.Lokajicek, Extended quantum - mechanical mathematical model, contribution presented to III Wigner Symposium (Oxford, September 5-11, 1993).

11. W.Pannenberg, *Towards a Theology of Nature*, Westminster, 1993.

12. G.McCool, review of W.N.Clarke, *Person and Being, International Philosophical Quarterly*, 1994, 121-123.

13. F.X.Durrwell, *L'Esprit du Père et du Fils*, Médiaspaul, Montreal, 1989.

CHAPTER 7

WHO IS GOD, REALLY?

Including the Includer
Personalising the Matrix

It is time to give the word to theology, and to ask what kind of God belongs to the kind of cosmos and the kind of person we are coming to know. Theology happens best when real questions are forced back to the God question. Theology is implicitly happening in today's physics and philosophy, because they are looking for a new language in which to speak of God. As we turn to theology to assist with the formulation of that language, we do so in the constant conviction that the language must be personal. Not, what is God, but who is God, really?

Let us look at *cultural, biblical, speculative,* and *spiritual* approaches to a theology of God.

CULTURAL APPROACHES

I would like to begin by sketching a three-point outline of avenues to God that may be found in thinking people today. They are: *modern, pre-modern,* and *post-modern.*[1]

The term *'modern'* here is intended to refer to much of the thinking that comes from Enlightenment philosophy and to the spirit of modernity which it inaugurated. It also includes a good deal of scholastic theology in 'modern' times, and much theology that would be broadly identified as standard and traditional.

A modern approach to God deals with issues of being, of existence, of the substantiality of God. It is resolutely monotheist - it believes in one only God. Its language is uncritically masculine in speaking of that God. For it, God is a Person, in the sense of Father, Source, Font of Son and Spirit. It is egoic: God has or is an ego or self in our sense of that term. It is onto-theological and logo-centric. When it ponders the Exodus axiom, 'I am who am', it puts the emphasis on the 'I'.   The classic proofs of the existence of God apply most naturally to this model of God.   It inculcates critical acceptance of the reality of this God, and the need for dutiful awareness and submission to the Infinite.

This post-Enlightenment understanding of God is culturally patriarchal, and Eurocentric.   It could be tracked back to medieval times, and even to understandings of God in Israel.   It has a high pedigree in traditionally classic sources of theology.

A *pre-modern* approach does not intend to convey data about an approach to God that existed before the modern one was developed.   The term 'pre-modern' rather suggests that it works with psychic processes that are prior to the formalised analytic processes characteristic of the 'modern' approach.   It is significant that it has emerged in our own times, and challenges the modern way.

A pre-modern approach to God deals with a sense, a hunch, an intimation about God.   Its God is polymorphic, and even polytheistic.   Its language is consciously feminine in speaking of God.   For it, God is a Person, in the sense of Mother.   It is richly symbolic, mythic, oneiric.   It is a theo-poetic approach.   It works with hints half understood, and prefers to remain uncentred, and unworded.   When it ponders the Exodus axiom, 'I am who am', it puts the emphasis on the 'am'.   Its attitude is intuitive, aesthetic, nurturing, fulfilling.   It believes in a God that changes in relationship with us.   It is a spirituality and an attitude to life.   It feeds on mystical writing.

The pre-modern shares with the modern approach to God an implicit conviction that God is an identifiable reality, separate from us, linked to us, and describable by us.

The word *'postmodern'* is a word that has often become vague by ambiguous use, but is used here to designate something that is neither modern nor premodern in the above senses.   It is the fruit of identifying and questioning their assumptions.   It is looking for a God that is beyond clear identifiability and description, a God that is neither resolutely one (monotheism) nor professedly manifold (polytheism).

The post-modern approach to God would wish to be 'participative'. It would want to share the experience of a sharing God. It comes from critical reflection, and much intuition, about a different kind of world than the one assumed by the two previous approaches. Its language is relational. For it, God can be said to be a Person, but it is in a new sense of personhood, and the adjective 'transpersonal' is used as much as the adjective 'personal'. It sees God as a communicativity, indeed, as a communion. It uses images like a 'ground state of enablement' for all reality, or an 'active matrix' of all relationship. When it ponders the Exodus axiom, 'I am who am', it reads the phrase in the sense of 'I am with you' and puts the emphasis on the 'with'. It feeds off an experience of something more than substantive words can convey, something that is accessed and approached and never fully grasped. This 'More' that is 'With' has always been 'there'. There is a conviction about the positivity of this 'With' that absolves from the need for accurate language and expression. Although God is described as a 'Someone', the accent falls on the 'Withness' of the someone with us and with all reality, rather than on any substantiveness of the God in a Godself in isolation.

In the context of our overall study, it is this third approach to God that we need to look at *more closely*.

We can look for the quiet presence of this sort of God in *modern science*, in *depth psychology*, and in *world religions*.

Jean Staune has spoken of a re-enchanted science as one sensitive to symptoms of meaning beyond the meanings its own methodologies can determine and articulate. He sees science of this kind, from quantum physics to neurology, sensing a pre-existent elusive Meaning towards which the human should be tender, since the Meaning (or Mystery) is tender to the human. Science gropes, at times without comprehension, towards a mysterious connection with this *Tenderness* and perceives that it is our destiny. We are not foreigners in a strange place with it. It is our home as persons, as it is the place where the cosmos is true.[2]

Thomas Moore has written of a renewed depth psychology that it has discovered simultaneously the positivity of the unconscious, and the positivity of the everyday. The profundities and the ordinarynesses are with each other, and they are both with a mysterious *Integrity* that is beyond us and yet in us.   It is another witness to the 'Withness' that is God.[3]

The Great Traditions of world religion, especially Asian traditions of Hinduism, Buddhism, and Taoism, concur; as do the little traditions of tribal people everywhere.   Perhaps the more ancient these peoples are, the closer they are to the mysterious 'With'.

The genius of the Judeo-Christian tradition seems to have been, in its best moments, to have grasped this sense of 'With' and integrated with it a sense of authentic personalism: *the 'With' is a Person*, amongst us. Perhaps this 'genius' is the fruit of faith in the person of Jesus.

Recent studies on the functioning of various parts of the *human brain* tend to illustrate the distinctiveness of this new approach to a 'With-God'.[4]

The left hemisphere of the neomammalian cortex is held to be the responsible site for perceptions of the Individual, the Hero, the Ego, the Patriarch...and the modern approach to God.

The right hemisphere of the same cortex is held to be responsible for perceptions of holism, of group and matrix, and Mother.   The reptilian brain is the site of quiet, peace and slumber.   Together, both give rise to the pre-modern approach to God.

Recent work on the frontal lobes, the corpus callosum, the fissure of Rolando, and the central sulcus suggest that they give rise to a different sort of consciousness, that is more than interpersonal in the usual sense.   There are suggestions that they are the originating site of androgynous love, and of various contemplative experiences known in Asian religion, such as Advaita, Tantra, Kundalini, etc.   It is perhaps from such sources that the post-modern approach to God as With is coming.

This would, in all, suggest that *a new sense of Godness* is arising in our cultural consciousness.   Assertions about the femininity of God, and of change in God, are only steps along the way to a massive paradigm change about God, in which we are using our brains differently.   We are on the threshold of a new understanding of contemplation itself.

Its *price* is a changing notion of person, and a changing notion of cosmos.

A *person* can truly be described as self-possessive, self-communicative and self-transcendent.   I believe that as recently as two decades ago, while all three adjectives would have been used, the emphasis would have fallen on the first of the three.

I do not think that is any longer the case.   The emphasis has been shifting from a primacy of self-standing autonomy, to a primacy of relational communication, participation, and solidarity.   It is intriguing to see a parallel in the understandings of God: from a primacy of the Absolute Transcendent to a primacy of the Relational Tenderness.

Cosmos, as we see it now, is the wholeness of the universe, but I think we are envisaging wholeness anew.   It is no longer seen as a collection of separate and adequately defined entities that hold their meaning outside the integration.   The vision is more holistic, and the 'parts' are not seen as 'parts' but as aspects of the whole that are meaningless outside the wholeness.   It is again intriguing to see a parallel in the understandings of God: from a God adequately defined in Godself separately from us, to a God in whose very definition the Withness with us must be included as a primary trait.

The price of all these shifts is a critique of the *narcissism* of our intellectual efforts.   We need to realise the primacy of connectedness, not the primacy of separate terms that are afterwards connected.

This change of paradigm demands a massive *educational* process. Tenderness and courtesy as divine attributes have not been highlighted in our recent past.   We are invited to a new understanding of intimacy itself. Prayer itself would change its felt meaning.

One may reasonably ask, *who carries the paradigm* of this new attitude to God?   The standard language of institutional Christianity - and in particular its classic theology - would do so with some difficulty.   That they should do so is clear, since these insights are central to their primary sources of revelation.   But the accretion of human baggage from different cultural sources, in the historical past, has been large.   Meantime, the scientific and philosophical communities are reaching out for a sense of mystery that is a sense of reconciling and healing intimacy - a mystery of the 'With' that is interpersonal.

BIBLICAL APPROACHES

I would like here to elaborate an understanding of God that comes from scripture, and that is fundamentally *a personal God of cosmic reconciliation*. To do so, *first*, I shall develop the difference between testament and covenant; *secondly*, I shall apply the results of that distinction to three test cases - sin and forgiveness, images of God, and the concept of history and biography; and *finally*, I shall present a God so personal that God is thereby a God of cosmic reconciliation and inclusion.

First, the difference between *testament and covenant*. It is true that these two conceptions are frequently equated, and the cultural mutation from the Hebrew berith (covenant) to the Greek diatheke (testament) is not sufficiently appreciated. This obfuscation seems to come from the losses sustained by the early church as a result of its passing from a Jewish to a Greek-Roman culture.

'Testament' is the more familiar, to us, of the two ideas. We speak today of one's last will and testament. It is literally a 'will' - voluntary, arbitrary, legal and changeable at 'will'. The testator of a testament can at any time annul, replace, or change his will, at least before his death. When God is said to be a testament God in regard to his people, God is conceived as a testator. In fact, God is so conceived 'twice': first, when God gives the Torah, or 'Old Testament' to his people; and secondly, when he gives Christ(ianity) to his people in the 'New Testament'.

This represents a change of will on God's part. The God of the first testament is as it were 'dead' and his first will is cancelled out: all this is dramatised, vicariously, in the death of Jesus. The God of the second testament communicates a resoluteness never to change his will again: its permanence is dramatised, vicariously, in the resurrection of Jesus, who is the mediator of the new testament, its first beneficiary, and its internal administrator through church and sacraments. This is known as a 'supersessionist' model of salvific history: Israel has been superseded by the Church. There is an inherent need on the part of the Christian people to be afraid, lest the God of their testament change his mind, or his will, as he did with the people of the first testament.   He has said that he will not, but the potential insecurity is not fully removed by the assertion. It may well be conditional, without at present a full revelation of the conditions.

'Covenant' is the less understood term, and is almost the polar opposite of testament.   It is a revelation, not of an arbitrary will, but of an eternal reality.   It is a profound accord, a radical compatibility between God and his people, that is forever, because it is the nature of the case.   What covenant conveys is beyond any 'arrangement' between negotiating parties, beyond oaths taken, promises made, and obligations assumed.   It is a mystery of solidarity for which there are hardly any analogies - that of the blood bond was perhaps the most available in the culture of the ancient writers.   The solidarity is that between the Unnameable One (God) and the nameless little people - in a mystery beyond our rationality, they belong.   They belong as it were by native right, and one cannot exist authentically without the other.   They are bonded together - in a 'covenant' relationship - so that their oneness can be expressed as a way of life, a Torah for the two who belong.

This means that God demands, by right, full participation in the history of the nameless little people, as one of them, on equal terms;   and the nameless little people can demand, by native right, full participation in the atmosphere, ambience, and horizon of enablement that is God's by definition.   In effect, once the covenant is revealed, they are no longer a nameless little people, since they have been called by the divine name, and they belong to God, as his, as God is called by their name, and he belongs to them, as theirs.   "I will be your God, and you will be my people".   A covenant, once declared and given, is forever, and there can only be one covenant.   It must include all the nameless ones, all Israel, indeed all creation.

When Jesus in his turn renews the one and eternal covenant and makes manifest its ever-freshness, he is not setting up a new 'testament' over against an old one: he is reaffirming the eternalness of the one and only covenant.   In you like, covenant is a Hebrew word for the eternal unboundariedness that is the stamp of authenticity of God's real attitude to us.   Such a covenant God cannot be feared: he will not change his 'mind'.

Let us *familiarise* ourselves with this idea of a covenant God, by seeing the difference the distinction between testament and covenant makes in some key areas: sin and forgiveness, images of God, and history and biography.

If we think in terms of *testament*, we conceive sin as a final and indeed 'mortal' severance of relationship with God: it breaks the testament relationship.   The 'book' is closed, and sealed, beyond repair, addition or interpretation.   It is literally all over.   *Forgiveness* is not even conceivable within the terms of reference of the testament.   If it were to be granted, it would be a further, unexpected, undeserved, act of graciousness on God's part: in fact, it would be positively heroic on God's part, and beyond the noblesse oblige of the situation.   And it would require of us, sinners against the testament, an almost equally heroic commitment to undergo cleansing from what we had done, and begin 'again' in a new relationship with an arbitrarily gracious God of supererogatory forgiveness.   The classic term for this cleansing in Greek, is katharsis: a purging, an elimination of the past, in a total rupture with it, as if it were something dead.   The 'new start' is not a sublimation of the L past, but a 'conversion', a meta-noia, where the hyphen between meta and noia is indeed a heroic one, both for the repentant sinner and for the forgiving God.

But if we think in terms of *covenant, sin* can never be quite as final as that. It is a major breach of covenant living, and a deadening to the enlivening gift of the Torah, but the Covenant, and the Torah, remain.   The 'book' is open: open to a reinterpretation, a revision, a change of meaning, a reinclusion of what has sadly happened.   The horizon of covenant is so large that a new perspective is always possible.   The classic Hebrew word for doing this is *Teshuba,* from the root Shub, which means 'return', 'come back', 'retrieve'.   When Israel returned and came back from exile, it was not given a new place to live that it had never known before: it retrieved the one and only Land.   The contretemps between the covenant God and the covenant people was real, but it was less important than the abidingness of the covenant.   It was not looked at by God as a one-on-one problem, but as something that the largeness of covenant could encompass. What the whole occasion brings out is not a new arbitrariness of God, but the incredible continuity of covenant, that includes even what seems not capable of being included.

It can be noted that the whole practice of scapegoating is a fruit of testament thinking, not covenant thinking: it is a ritual of cleansing elimination. Christian people, sadly and paradoxically, have often done this to the Jewish people, both theologically and even militarily. The Holocaust is a reminder of it.

We can pursue the differences between testament and covenant by looking at the *images of God* that fit each pattern of thinking. In a testament approach, God comes through as primarily offended, and almost furious at the injury and insult he has received. It is a case of personal injury and outraged dignity. The language of this theology is characteristically masculine! The undeserved gift of forgiveness from this kind of God includes a 'forgetting' of the past, in the 'starting again'. To 'forgive and forget' is only one way of forgiving, and it seems to retain some sense of injury that is forgotten but not fully removed. That is why this God of this forgiveness is still feared, and there remains a sensed need for further repentance, even in the declared grace of the forgiveness.

The image of a *covenant* God is vastly different. There is indeed recognition that an objectively wrong situation has occurred, implying injustice, and estrangement from authenticity. There is a negative attitude on God's part to this situation, often called the 'anger' of God.

But, in a revealing twist of language, the scriptural writers do not say that God 'gets angry', and never make God the subject of a verb that means 'get angry'. They do this, to bring out that God's basic attitude looks less at the situation than at why and how the situation took place. It is an attitude of understanding the difficulty little people have in living covenant. It is an experience of a need, in God, for a more basic covenant compassion. It is a concern for the covenant member, not an offendedness personally that would express itself in hostility to a covenant member. Perhaps that kind of response would even be a breach of covenant love!

This concern-compassion-understanding lead to an effective pathos in God for his weaker partner in covenant. It is a case of a grieving God, who remembers the covenant. God laments, but the lamentation is for the covenant, and for the covenant people whose fragility the covenant seems to magnify.   The language seems naturally to become more feminine. From Hosea, we get the image of the mother of a very young child: she has taught the child to walk, lifted it to the breasts, bent down to nurse it, so how could she give it up?

Her rehem (a Hebrew word that stands at the same time for the heart of a father and the womb of a mother) recoils within her, and her rahamim (a Hebrew word for a physically felt inner compassion, like a melting of the entrails) grows warm and tender, when she thinks about it, for she is "God, not man", where the Hebrew word for 'man' is ish - the word for a male of the species.[5]

From Hosea again, we get a further image of God as a husband who has been divorced by his wife, but still remains really espoused to her: he will speak to her with words of rahamim, and allure her, and she will answer as in the day of her youth.

The profoundly covenantal images of God bond the feeling (pathos) of God and the longing (pothos) of his people into a healing (therapeia) that restores a covenant that never went away.   Forgiveness is not a miraculous new mercy but a fidelity to the ever-ancient and ever-new covenant. The fidelity itself is an act of justice of a special kind, justice to and within - the covenant.   Paul called it the justice of God (dikaiosune tou theou). Faith (emunah, pistis) is really an unhesitating trust that this is so.   The Torah of Covenant is not a nomos (law) of a testament.

All this difference between testament and covenant makes a large influence on the way we write our *history or biography*.   If we write our story in a *testamental* way, we write it from a very selective point of view. We highlight the 'cognitive dissonance' in the account: the difference between ideal and real, and the contrasts within the story.   We give priority to what we like, and downplay, or even eliminate what we do not like, or like less.   We tend to present only the part of the 'problem' that appeals to us.   We do not write the whole story.   Some parts are omitted, and censored, hermetically sealed off and closed to inspection.   We develop a style of dialectical antithesis: it was this way, then it was that way; we play with the contrasts and sublate them into new syntheses.   We avoid parts that appear to us as stigmas that should not have been. Most history and biography is testamental.

If we write our story in a *covenantal* way, we write it from a fully inclusive point of view.   We highlight the 'cognitive consonance' in the account: the vision that we have come to, often retrospectively, of the congruence and the fittingness of it all.   We let it all be there in its allness.   It is the whole truth.   It is essentially an act of rehabilitation of our history, which we accomplish by the writing.   We perceive the whole span of it.   It is hermeneutic, a striving to spell out the meaning that was always there, but not always seen so clearly.

The Jewish writers   practise this art of dialogical midrash: they see through the gaps and the apparent contradictions in the text, and find the core meaning which they then embellish.   There is no reticence about the Tikkun, or paradox in it all: the Torah, as lived by us, has truly been a Torah of seventy faces - the fullness of number.   No stigma avoidance is needed, for in this perspective no stigma was ever there.   Forgiveness is not a forgetting.   It is a realisation that there never was any need for that kind of forgiveness.[6]

After this introduction, let us try to present a covenant *God of cosmic reconciliation and inclusion*, through the covenant personality that is his.

There are two approaches to *reconciliation*, testamental and covenantal. In a *testamental* approach, an arbitrary gift of restoration has 'reconciled' someone who was culpably estranged and alienated, and cut-off from the testament.   In a *covenantal* approach, a bond deeper than blood demands the vindication of the ever-remaining covenant, and when that vindication is made expressively, we are overwhelmed by the largeness of the love. It had never been withdrawn.   There is a realisation and a conscious awaring that covenant love is always all-including.

We could say that in *testament* thinking, there is always a dichotomy between inclusion and exclusion;   while in covenant thinking, there is only inclusion.   In the testament approach, God is an extrinsic determiner of who is included and who is excluded.   In the covenant approach, God is intrinsically the one who includes and does not exclude.   To move from testament to covenant, is to include the Includer!

Paul has grasped this sense of inclusion that is constantly being revealed to us in the ongoing history of covenant.   He has a word for this ongoing inclusion: *katallassein*, and we are used to translating it as *'reconciliation'*. Unfortunately in English at least, the word reconciliation carries too many of the undertones of testament for us to hear its richness.   In *2 Cor 5, 17-21*, Paul develops his thought about it.

God was in Christ, says Paul, progressively including us into himself, in a mystery in which the archaic is always becoming original.   God was in Christ, says Paul, progressively including the cosmos itself into himself, doing this because God is not a God who counts trespasses against people, but who brings to an awareness of bondedness even those who thought they were no longer bonded.   God has given us the ministry (diakonia) of including like this (katallassein: reconciling).   God has entrusted us with the understood-sense (logos) of this including and coming together (katallassein).   In this we are the ambassadors of Christ, and God is effectively exhorting the cosmos into this inclusion through our message. We beseech you then, says Paul, 'be included into God'.   We make this appeal on behalf of Christ, the sinless one who became a sin-offering so that in Him we might become the covenant-fidelity of God to the mystery of ongoing inclusion.   Perhaps the word *'togethering'* might stand equally well for 'being included', and capture some of the sense of Paul's idea of 'reconciliation'.

It is not necessary to say that this biblical notion of a covenant God sits well with the idea of God as a living personal 'With'.   There is an *energy* in it that takes the God question away from the limiting arena of guilt and places it in the moving horizon of cosmic integration.

This energy has not always been translated into liturgies of reconciliation. But there is one good example in which it has.   It is the liturgy of the *Easter Vigil*, as practised in the Catholic Church between 1956 and 1969. (Changes in the Roman Missal in 1970 put an end to it).   I am referring to the ceremony at the *baptismal font*, but I need to recreate the context.[7]

At the spring equinox, outside, in the open air, at midnight, a new fire is struck from a rock of flint.   A tall candle is lit from the fire, and adorned with symbols of the past and future, indeed of all time.   All those present take a new flame from the candle and shout and sing: Lumen Christi (The Light of the Christ).

The candle is set up in green boughs and flowers and other fertility signs. The 'Exultet' is sung: a solemn chant of creation myths and of the names of the holy ones of the past.   It is then that a great bath of water is prepared.   It is the baptismal font - as it were the womb of mother church.   It will be fertilised by the entry of the Holy Spirit, in the phallic form of a lighted candle entering the waters.   There are clear nuances of the primeval waters of chaos and the bringing to birth of the cosmos.

A priest lowers the lighted candle into the waters, in three stages, penetrating more deeply each time.   He then blows three times on the surface of the water in the form of Psi (is it the cross? or psychology? or a wave function??) singing on a higher note each time, 'Descendat in hanc plenitudinem fontis, virtus Spiritus Sancti' (let there descend into the fullness of this font, the energy of the Holy Spirit), and 'totamque huius aquae substantiam regenerandi fecundet effectu' (and let it fecundate the whole substance of this water with an effective power of regenerating (those who pass through it).   It is then that all who have passed through the water commence a sacred banquet, in which they share from the Risen Christ the power of including and togethering and reconciling the cosmos.

It is this kind of God who sits well with persons in the cosmos.

SPECULATIVE APPROACHES

The task of a Christian speculative theology is to make interpretative sense of the closeness of God with all creation, and to probe into that closeness and see, if possible, what is happening for God in the closeness.   I would like to *introduce* the endeavour by reflecting on the link between the study of God and the study of guilt;   and then to present *three* significant manoeuvres in the interpretation and the probe - those of *E.H.Wéber*, concerning the incarnation, of *F.X.Durrwell* concerning the procession of the Holy Spirit, and of *W.N.Clarke* concerning God the Father as Person.

There have been two great theological traditions concerning the Christian God: one in the east, the other in the *west*.   In the east, the focus has

been on the resplendent *glory* of God.   In the west, it has been on the
absolute *infinity* of God.   Both could be combined into a tradition of *'awe'*
about God, that soon leads to a sense of *'guilt'* in the presence of God.
All traditions about God are really secondary to traditions about justification from guilt: they spell out a meaning for a God who is offended, a
God who sends his Son who alone can satisfy for the offence, and a God
who as Spirit is given only to the justified-by-the-Son for offence-against-
the-Father.   The 'I am who am' of Exodus is taken as the symbol of the
infinite difference and distance between God and whatever (culpably?) is
not God.   God as Being is pure and integral; everything finite is so
ontologically ruptured that it can never coincide with its own being.
There is assumed then that there is an irremovable opposition between the
innate ontological integrity of God and the infinite impossibility of
ontological integrity in every finite being.   When humans become
conscious of this, they enter into a state, of what could be called permanent ontological schizophrenia condemned by the nearness of an integral
God.   God's closeness would then be a living condemnation of our very
finitude itself.

While allowing our existence, metaphysically, he interdicts our very being,
psychologically.   God's first message to us would be a 'no' to the roots of
our being.   No wonder that we then offend God in our actions.   So all
have sinned, and need the glory of God...   The metaphysical study of God
of this kind functions as a kind of *inverse-soteriology* of universal culpabil-
ity.   No need to say that this God is not a covenant God!   The task of
speculative theology is to get away from these impressions and clarify the
primary and positive relationship between God and persons in the cosmos.

E.H.Wéber has given us a historical reconstruction of the work of Aquinas
in this regard.[8]

There is a phrase in the writings of Aquinas that should stand at the head
of any discussion of his thought about the Incarnation: *'the descent of the
divine fullness into human nature'*.   Aquinas penned it, after he had had
access to Latin translations of the acts of the council of Chalcedon.   They
had not been available to him in Paris, and he found them in the archives
of Orvieto, Viterbo, and Rome, where he worked in the 1260's.   They
made him realise the difference between all forms of God's presence, as

philosophers and theologians had envisaged it, and the marvellous dynamic 'identity' of the divine and human in Jesus.

There had been truly a 'descent of the divine fullness into human nature'. It was the beginning of a change in his understanding not only of human nature, but especially of God.   He realised that God was a *dynamic God*, mysteriously revealing himself as God in the 'descent' into human nature. And once he had refined his idea of God, he began to see this kind of 'descending' God not just in Jesus Christ, but, in different ways, every-where.   The first philosophical tool he found to help him articulate this dynamism, was the notion of *'second act'* - which he learned neither from Augustine nor from Aristotle, but from Pseudo-Denis, and increasingly from Bonaventure.   The idea of 'second act' is that no being can be fully what it is unless it is in a state of *dynamic expressivity*: being cannot be being 'at rest' but only 'in act'.   This allowed Aquinas to think of God as always in 'second act' in our regard: indeed, he then conceived God as Being and not being, precisely because in God alone there is an absolute identification between first and second act.   This is vastly different from the static, aloof, distant God we have criticised above.

This took Aquinas into new ponderings about *intellectual activity*. He had already grasped that intellection was a mental oneness of knower and known.   Now he went on to see that the core of the understanding process was in the dynamic quality of that oneness.   The identity between knower and known dynamically 'expresses' itself in the human mind.   The mind has to be in its own 'second act', and is so in the expression of a 'verbum'.   The verbum is not the representation of an object, a presence of an object, a substitute for an object.   It is not a signifier.   It is not there to function for something else.   It is the fruit of the dynamism of the compenetration of the spirit and reality, a new dynamically expressed dynamic identity of the two as one, a richly new density of knower and known together that flowers in a richly new kind of mental creation.

Aquinas then applied this new idea of mental knowing to God, in the second act of *God's own knowing* (especially, may I suggest, in the scientia visionis).   God too expresses a Verbum.   So Aquinas comes to the realisation that there can be no act of intellectual understanding in anyone, finite or infinite, without the expression of a verbum.   Therefore, when our finite minds express their finite verbum, God's infinite mind is expressing God's infinite Verbum.   One is enfolded in the other.   Within every human process of knowing, there is a divine one, in act.   There is a divine noetic enclosed in every human noetic.   There is a divine Verbum in the hidden recesses of every human verbum.   The one *interpenetrates* the other.

Aquinas' God is then a dynamically self-communicating God through the divine Verbum, expressed by God within the human expression of a human verbum.   The very existence of anything finite is the index of the divine expression of the Verbum, indeed, it is the fruit of that divine act.

Aquinas attempts to use this kind of thinking when he considers the mystery of the *incarnation*, the 'descent of the divine fullness into human nature'.   There must be an incredible non-incompatibility between anything created according to the exemplar of the Verbum, and the Verbum itself.   This is so true, that we might be able to believe a mysterious identity between one and the other, if it were revealed to us. It would be something like an almost infinite increase of density between one and the other, at the very point at which humanity is constituted in being.   It would literally be a 'descent' of the fullness into the emptiness. In terms of such a descent, the Verbum who is Jesus could say, *'Moi, en tant qu'homme'*: I, in so far as I am man.   Aquinas was well aware that he did not know how this could happen: no one does, except the Fontal Thinker of the Verbum.

The incarnation is then for Aquinas a *divine mission*: the 'sending' of the Verbum (descent-wise) into the human nature of Jesus.   This perspective opens up the possibility, indeed demands the possibility of envisaging, at lesser levels of compenetrative density, an analogous mission of the Verbum into all creation, so that *all creation* is the result of that mission. The divine mission is the secret of all reality.   Aquinas then constructed the architecture of the Summa around this idea.

It is not difficult for us, at this point, to grasp the notion of the Fontal Thinker of the Verbum as majestically and generously self-communicative, and so creative of the entire cosmos.   It is an easy step for us to use the word "Person" to designate this Originator.   Aquinas does so, but needs a more developed philosophical notion of person than was available to him at the time.   The tradition was too linked to a Boethian definition of person.   His thought has theologically broken the boundaries of the tradition, and philosophically broken the boundaries of the current definitions, without explicitating the differences at all points.   But Aquinas has opened a real way *for a personal understanding of the nearness of a dynamic God to a cosmos that is the fruit of his personal presence.*   He has theologised the 'withness' and the 'covenant'.   The result is a trinitarian vision, both of God, and of creation.

F.X.Durrwell has given us the possibility of integrating an idea of the Spirit into this perspective.[9]

Durrwell has spent his life overwhelmed by the mystery of the *resurrection*. His language is always biblical, never metaphysical.   His favoured biblical image is that of the Father and the Son.   (Aquinas favoured the image of Thinker and Verbum, as metaphysically more suggestive than the explicit image of the scriptures).   For Durrwell, Jesus is Son of the Father in resurrection.   The Father is Father of Jesus in raising him from the dead. The resurrection is a mystery of the engendering of Jesus by the Father. This is the central mystery.   There is very little difference here from the theology of Aquinas, except in the chosen register of language, and the strong historicisation of the mystery in the event of resurrection.

Durrwell's concern is to integrate the mystery of the *Holy Spirit* into this perspective.   A long theological tradition has seen two processions within God: first, that of the Verbum/Son from the Thinker/Father, and secondly, that of the Spirit, as Love, from the Father and Son.   Durrwell senses that this dichotomy of processions is not well founded in scripture. He believes there is *only one procession*, and that we must find the presence of the Spirit intrinsically within that one procession.   For him, that procession is clearest in the resurrection, and he meditates on the role of the Spirit in the resurrection, to help him understand the role of the Spirit with the other divine persons.

He sees the Spirit as the mysterious factor that amounts to the *'engendering'* of the 'engendered' by the 'engenderer'.   That is, the Spirit enables the Son to be the Son of the Father, and enables the Father to be the actually engendering Father of the Son of his love.   What Durrwell is pointing to is relationship.

The Spirit is the mystery that enables the Father to be the relationally opened-out fontal person, in regard to the personal being of the Son. The Spirit, is equally and simultaneously, the mystery that enables the Son to be the relationally opened-up originating person from the Father, in relation to the personal being of the Father. The Spirit is a kind of *'élan'* of the Father towards the Son, and the Spirit is also a kind of *'accueil'* of the Father by the Son. It is concretised and enfleshed in Jesus, in the sending of Jesus by the Father, and in Jesus' consent and obedience to his mission. Durrwell is able to use the biblical term *'agape'*, love, to express the sense of oneness between the two integrated relationalities here. The Spirit is love: the loving relationality of the Father towards the Son, and the loving relationality of the Son towards the Father. They are one. The best way to suggest and express that oneness is to use the term 'Spirit'. Thus for Durrwell, it is the Spirit that makes the Engenderer and the Engendered *'We'*, that is, it is the Spirit that personalises them together. He does not see the Spirit as an *'I'* face to face in its own self-standingness with the Father, and with the Son. The Spirit is rather interior to both of them, 'in' person in them, a person in a unique way because personalising their mutual personhood.

Durrwell is strong in maintaining the unicity of procession within God. He conceives radically only one procession, and integrates the Spirit into it. The Spirit-ed Engenderer Spirit-engenders an InSpirited Son. He tends to speak of this one procession as generation, but I do not see why it should not also be described as spiration. Both expressions unfold the dynamic 'élan' of God. They do so as a revelation of how the 'élan' of Being is *interiorly relationalised and personalised*, with a sense of relation and a sense of personhood that are not those that we would normally have assumed from a more superficial reflection on finite things.

I do not think we are going to get metaphysical precision on these matters from an intuitive biblical scholar like Durrwell. But his whole vision does sit well with, and even adds to, that of Aquinas. The dynamic descent of the divine into the human and the cosmic, is only the visible manifestation of an inner 'élan' and 'accueil' that makes the Fontal Origin an open one, and the Verbum a truly intrinsic wording of that openness: and the ultimate mystery, so to say, in it all, is a Spirit that enables the opened font and the expressed openness of the font to relate as 'We'. The dynamic descent and mission that Aquinas has made central to his thought, somehow encapsulate these dynamics. For we ourselves are a verbum in the divine Verbum: we ourselves are the expressed openness of the divine Fontal Thinker: and the same Spirit that secretly made the Font an Opened One in regard to the Verbum, makes the Font an Opened One in regard to us: our existence, our very metaphysical being, is evidence of the inSpiriting of the Father, and of the Son, and of us, as a 'We'. Persons in cosmos.

It is from *Norris Clarke* that we get fresh philosophical precision about the meaning of being, and of person, that can serve this theology.[10]

His is a natively alive approach to reality, and his back-ground inspiration is that of the intensiveness of real being, of the dynamic élan of all being towards its infinite source, and the energy of action as the self-revelation of being. He has merged these insights into a highly personal philosophy, and used a participationist framework to give it a home.

His own primary move is to propose that what is participated in finite being, is nothing less than Being, or Esse itself, in the intensive, dynamic, active sense. He has refused to see 'essence' as an actual perfection in itself, really distinct from esse. He insists on seeing essence as a limiting mode of ESSE, composed with the esse that results from that limiting. In the end, he candidly confesses that no one can know the how of the limiting and the composing: they are not actual being, and are ungrasp-able. As a result, there is a realisation that the divine Being or Esse is never actually removed or separated from any finite or created esse, although they are really 'distinct'. No finite thing can ever be considered in isolation from God. And God can never be considered in isolation from creation. The connection between God and the creature is dynamically expressive and compenetrative.

This means that there is an *integrity* at the heart of created being that mirrors the integrity at the heart of Uncreated Being. There is no ontological rupture, as it were between essence and existence, in the finite realm. Such a thing is an impossibility! On the contrary, there is a composition into integrity of the limiting principle (essence) and the dynamic act resulting from the limiting (its own finite esse). This composition allows the reflection of infinite actuality in God to manifest it and unfold itself integrally in our world. There is then an intactness, a wholeness, a healthiness in the creation in its own right, as there is in God in God's own right, and the two very much go together.

This means, initially, that the presence of the divine Being can never be opposed to the being of the creature.   The creature is happy to be finite, somewhat as a reflection of the way the Creator is happy to be the Creator.   The Creator is there precisely to inculcate this kind of *happiness* in the creature, and they are both very content together.   The creature does not exist primarily to attempt to remove its own creatureliness and try to become God.   God does not exist primarily to interdict the creature from trying to do that.   God is happy being God, and the creature is happy being a creature, and in a way they reinforce each other's happiness.

It is fascinating to reflect on the processes by which a human mind recognises the reality/actuality of a creator God in the act of being finite. I do not think it is totally a conclusion of purely rational proof.   It must contain an element of awakenedness, a gasp of *delight* in the joyfulness of the non-finite, self-giving, authoring of the finite that makes it be there in the first place.   It is a certitude that is indeed freeing, from every hesitation about its inner coherence and the congruence of its place in a cosmos filled with the reality and presence of the Creator.   If God IS, it is good for anything to be!

This sense of *integrity-happiness-delight* could be called the *joy of being*. It is so written into the reality of being that is ontological, not psychological.   Our psychology is permanently trying to catch up with it.   I suggest that it is ontological evidence of the presence of the *Spirit* in us, opening us up to the opened up Being of the divine persons, in the bondedness of a reality that is divine-personal.

It is at this point that we can attempt to bring together the three trajectories we have presented.   They all seem to be pointing to a different vision of personhood and relationship.   It is not possible to define personhood without 'opened-up-ness'.   It is not possible to define relationship without 'élan' and 'accueil' together.   It is not possible to speak of personal relatedness, or of relational personhood, without 'joy'. The secret of the 'opened-up-ness', the 'élan', the 'accueil', the 'joy', the enablement of the 'We', in a different sense, in it all, is the Spirit.   We are able to glimpse an *ontological demand for a pneumatic understanding of person and relationship.*   Without this, the cosmos as cosmos could not be.

In a real sense, there is a kind of primacy, at least in our understanding, of the Holy Spirit.   The one who is not person in the same sense as the others, the one who is not relationship but whose whole existence is relational, is the secret source of the different personalisation of the others, and of the different sort of relationship they have with each other.   Not only anthropology and cosmology, but metaphysics itself is a function of *Pneumatology*!

In this book, I have introduced the idea of communion, of relationship and person, of a relationality and an interpersonhood deeper than the terms and persons involved, of a communion that demands and creates differentiation, of a music of and in it all, of a flowing force-field of the real.   I have suggested that the dynamics of the material cosmos are analogous to those of the personal world, and that both together can be put to use as a phenomenology of metaphysical being.   It has not been hard to describe a God that fits this vision.   In doing so, I have, implicitly at least, been suggesting that all these things are the tangibility of the inner life of God.   We cannot understand open persons in an open cosmos, without understanding the opening of the Source towards a Verbum that expresses the opened-out-ness of the Source.   It is the Spirit that makes them both speak as 'WE' to an inSpirited world.[11]

SPIRITUAL APPROACHES

Let us return to the three-point outline with which we began our cultural analysis: *modern, pre-modern*, and post-modern.   *David Tracy* has used this outline to suggest variations in the perception of God.[12]   In the *modern* approach, he sees various forms of panentheism: everything is in God.   Here, history, cosmic and personal, are constitutive of our understanding of God, and God is intrinsically relational in them and to us in them.   The cosmos affects God, and God suffers in its suffering and rejoices in its joy.

In the *pre-modern* approach, he sees an attempt at the retrieval of something of the great romantic tradition.   He sees its advocates as marvelling at the revelation of the hiddenness of God, and wondering at the comprehension of the incomprehensibleness of God.

In the *post-modern* approach, he sees a deconstruction of concepts like presence, language, consciousness, selfhood, person, relationship, and even cosmos, and an accent on otherness and difference.   Despite the dominance of this deconstructive mood, and its inherent enmity to most of the drift of this book, I believe, with Tracy, that it is also an attempt at a retrieval.   It is a retrieval of something about *love*.

For the moderns, love is relationality, and for the pre-moderns, it is emanation.   But love is more than either or both of these mysteries.   It is also *excess*, an excess that is almost a transgression of the limits of both of these understandings.   Like all real excess, this excess-love defies description.   It goes back to experience, and to mysticism, and there it is more real than the 'realities' it exceeds.   Love as excess is also love as *darkness*, because it has gone beyond the frontiers of the light.   It is the preserve of mystics, and fools, of dissenters and visionaries.   It is the experience of those who are poor in language to contain the ineffable, and it makes their very weakness and vulnerability a *prophecy* of the more that can never be said.

This post-modern model of love as excess/darkness/prophecy seems to fit well with the pneumatology of the cosmos that we have developed.   The *Spirit* in the cosmos is always an excess, and its very excess is what opens out beings into personhoods together, and establishes a relationality larger than the terms of the relationship.

Perhaps the active presence of God in the cosmos is an influence *towards excess*, that is always taking the cosmos further than its own conceptions of itself, that is, further than the limiting versions of person, relation, and communion it works with, while surpassing them on its cosmic way.

NOTES

1.   R.Tarnas, *The Passions of the Western Mind* for an abundant use of the common division used here.   See also D.Tracy, The End of Theism and the Renaming of God, lecture given at American Academy of Religion annual convention, San Francisco, 1992.

2.   J.Staune, paper presented at European Conference for Science and Theology, The Nature of Nature, Fresing-Munich, 1994.

3.   Thomas Moore, *Care of the Soul*, Harper Collins, 1993 and *Soul-Mates*, Harper Collins, 1994.

4.   P.Moore, The New Sciences, in *Anima*, 1993, and *No Other Gods*, Chiron Publications, 1992.   S.Grof, *Beyond the Brain*, State University of New York Press, 1985.

5.   W.Harrington, *The Tears of the Crucified*, Dominican Publications, Tallagh, Ireland, 1993.

6.   M.Rotenberg, The 'Midrash' and Biographic Rehabilitation, *Journal for the Sc.Study of Religion*, 1986, 41-55.

7.   H.McCabe, *The Easter Vigil: the Mystery of New Life*, New Black-friars, 1992, 157-169.

8.   E.H.Wéber, La personne humaine au xiiie siecle, Paris, Vrin, (coll. "La bibliotheque thomiste" xlvi), 1991.   Cf. A.de Libera, Une Anthropo-logie de la Grace, sur 'La personne humaine au xiiie siecle d' E.H.Wéber, *Revue des sciences philosophiques et théologiques*, 1993, 241-254.

9.   Durrwell's life works on resurrection, the redeeming Christ, eucharist as paschal mystery, apostolate, Holy Spirit, the Father, and the Spirit of Father and Son.   Cf. an interpretation of Durrwell's thought, by R.Tremb-lay, *Studia Moralia*.

10.   See ample listings in bibliography.

11. It is interesting to compare and contrast the psychological insight of J.Faur, De-authorisation of the Law: Paul and the Oedipal model, in *Psychoanalysis and Religion*, eds. J.Smith and S.Handelman, pp.222-243.

12. Now published in *Journal of Religion*, 1994.

CHAPTER 8

PARTICIPATIVE KNOWING

An epistemology of information...
Words for beauty.

This chapter is an attempt to explicitate a theory of knowledge that lies beneath the preceding chapters. Science has come up with new understandings of *'information'* which depend very much on the new physics. Philosophy tries to work out the underlying drift, and phases, of the development of information. Theology sees here an invitation to how the whole of human knowledge strives to participate in the vision of God.

PHYSICS

Physics today creates a background understanding of *culture* and presents its grasp of the meaning of knowledge against it.

It is already a remarkable thing that a discipline like physics feels the need to create a sense of the historical flow of cultures in order to locate its precise interest in knowledge. Culture can be taken here to mean a whole way of living humanly, a worldview, an idea of the human, which is open to the inclusion of an idea of God. A *threefold outline* of the history of culture - in this sense - is often used as a working hypothesis. First, there was the *'Matter'* Age, which was agricultural and instrumental. Secondly, there was the *'Energy'* Age, which was industrial and technological. And thirdly, now, there is the *'Information'* Age, which is 'informational'.[1]

A slightly different way of presenting the same idea of the historical development of cultures in relation to knowledge, would come up with a *five-fold division*. First, there was the culture of *'hunting and gathering'*. Secondly, there was the culture of early *'farming'*. Thirdly, there was the culture of *'early urban civilisation'*. Fourthly, there was the culture of *'high energy civilisation'*. And fifthly, there is the present and coming culture of *'information'*.

These two outlines clearly overlap.   The Matter Age includes the hunter-gatherers, the farmers, and some of the early urbans;   the Energy Age takes in the more advanced urbans, and the high energy people, and the Information Age is terminology common to the two divisions.

This whole perspective assumes that certain attitudes to matter and energy, and certain attitudes to human knowledge, are correlative.   Indeed, it suggests that our ideas of what knowledge really is, are mysteriously dependent on our ideas of what matter and energy are.   There is in it an obvious implication, that at present we are moving to new understandings of matter and energy, and so are beginning to work out a new theory of knowledge.

In ancient and medieval times, *matter* (materia) was considered to have no form or structure (forma) of its own, and so was equated with whatever could be formed.   In the times of classical physics, matter was thought to be whatever endures in space and time, and thus was the substrate for the flux of events.   Newton developed the idea of mass as the measurable quantity of matter.   In the whole ancient period, there was a conviction about the conservation of matter - indeed it was an axiomatic law.   In more recent times this same attitude is expressed as the law of the conservation of mass-energy.

With the harnessing of *energy*, there came an Energy Age which is soon rightly described by the inflationary high use of energy.   Its culture is not one of survival, or even of well-being, but of the massive and increasing rate of use of material resources that can be converted into energy, and of that energy itself.   It is said that the world population has increased a thousand times since the introduction of farming;   while the total use of energy has increased ten thousand times since then.   There is said to be ten thousand times as much carbon dioxide in the atmosphere as when farming began.

The use of energy, already great in 1950, doubled in the next twenty years, and doubled again by the 1980's, and will keep on exponentially doubling. Seventy-five percent of this energy use is in 'developed' societies, that is, it is available to twenty-five percent of the world population.   The material standard of living of this small percentage of the population is doubling, and trebling, with its exclusive use of energy for its material well-being.

Critics of this situation say that it cannot continue for more than a few decades without irreparable damage to the resources of the planet and to the human future of its people.   Questions are being asked, whether the latest (technologically) and the most sumptuous (in terms of the use of energy) lifestyles are 'best'.   There are large implications for urban development.

It is exactly at this point in history that *a new culture* is being advocated based on neither the primacy of matter nor the primacy of energy.   The new 'idea' is information.   The functions that matter, and energy, had in the older thinking and in the older culture, would be taken over by information.

What is *'information'*?   It is assumed, in science and in the attitudes of people who think about their cultural life today, that there is a large arena of uncertainty concerning any potential set of events.   The desire is to limit and decrease that uncertainty.   This is done by a relevant selection of available input data.   This selection, and its consequent function, is called 'information'.   Information limits the seemingly unlimited and limitless horizon of possibilities.   Information concerns the probability of decreasing a priori uncertainty.   *"Events"* are the concrete realisations of sets of possibles: "information events" are the concrete reductions of sets of uncertainties.

It has dawned on the minds of scientists that very often there is *more* information in such events than has been realised.   They do more than reduce uncertainty.   There is always a surplus of information in any and every event, that leads us to become aware of sets of uncertainty which had been previously hidden to us.   This more, this surplus of information, this transcending previously set horizons, keeps on happening and develops in time.   The history of this information pattern demands that we get swept up into the 'stream' - the *'information stream'* - of it all.   It is this notion of such an information stream that more than anything else is calling for a new culture.

There is then a sense that events that happen cannot be adequately described in the manner to which we have become accustomed. They are not just measurable data in space and time. There is a more to them, an empirically undecidable manifold.   The awareness of this on a given occasion, in relation to given events, is known as *'experience'*. Experience has something to do with the sense of the more, as a stream of the more.

This sense can be described in considerably more detail.   It involves *perception, expectation, setting, intentionality*, and *language*.

Perception is the raw sensory cognisance of a physical event. It comes from bottom-up, environment-activated input signals.

Expectation is the work of a previously learned imaginal matrix in our responding minds. The system-sets we already have trigger a reaction to and with the perception.

Setting is the emergent consensus that comes through the competing and the matching/mismatching of the perception and the expectation. It is a read-out as a result of the interaction.   It could be called a 'true' perception, one that has found its world-view or horizon.

Intentionality occurs when the 'I' of the knower is taken along with the activities mentioned, in a direction that it did not originally set.   The 'I' goes out of itself, and includes the new, and comes back 'new'.   There is evidence of this in the brain itself: there is a chaotic, metastable behaviour, a chaotic recursive filtering, that mirrors and founds this moment of 'enlargement'.   All true knowing includes a loss, and a new finding.

Language, or the use of the word to capture the experience, is not a univocal or predictable thing, it is always polysemic, always a short-cut. Words are like nodes in a dynamic matrix, and while they are an essential part of it all, they are not all of it, and can never be.   When words are expanded through grammar into symbols and phrases and true language, the further they get down the track, the less they 'include' the core mystery of 'knowing'.

A *culture of information* is then very different from a computer file of 'data'. It is an invitation to live differently from the sureties of the past. It is a way of 'knowing' what is not knowable like that. It is a way of coming to 'know' there is a different and larger humanness in that.

When science tries to deal with this, it makes use of models and methods.

Its *models* are basically mathematical and metaphorical. The use of all these models is intuitive of the 'stream of the more'. The formal mathematical models are not employed simply to give pin-point accuracy, but to suggest the limits that cannot be expressed with such accuracy. The metaphorical models try to connect functional relations between more sophisticated models in contexts that are never fully known: the metaphors are attempts to associate ambivalent matrices without fully knowing the fundamentum of the association. That is why, increasingly, the formal and the metaphorical models are intertwined: one type depends on the other.

Scientific *method* in a world of such 'knowing' is far from the deduction of theorems from axioms. It is always moving beyond the world of *proof*, of *stability*, of *reducibility*.

In terms of *proof*, Gödel's theorem stands like an axiom of the new information culture: given a set of axioms, there will eventually be a sentence that can be proven to be both true and false. It is an invitation to get out of the literalness of linguistic symbols.

Determinism had always looked for *stabilities*. It demanded unique solutions to dynamic equations, once initial conditions had been assigned, with the minimum of uncertainty intrinsic to measurement. It translated objects into numbers, attempting to find rational numbers in linear dynamics. Most of the numbers have turned out to be irrational, and the dynamics non-linear, so that the predicted paths are anything but stable. Complexity - not naive simplicity - is the new name for reality.

This complexity is structural, and not simply dynamic. We are no longer talking about geometric 'points' but about small 'blobs' that are *irreducible* to the interplay of their component parts. New holistic properties of systems are appearing which are frustratingly intractable and defeat characterisation. (Computers would literally need a time longer than the age of the cosmos to compute them, if they could.)

Overall, *a new logic* seems to be at work, one that is not defined as analytic or as dynamic, but is reverent of a larger and more global mystery. The mystery is in the interconnectedness and the fruit of it is a sense of culture that was not present in the cultures of matter and energy.

One way of expressing the difference, would be to suggest that in the cultures of matter and energy, the texts that we studied, in manuscript or in print, were *fixed texts*, that had a classic, central, authoritative, 'canonical' meaning as identity-constructing literature once they were 'received'. They functioned as a kind of exteriorisation of the living memory of tradition. In contrast, in the culture of information, we are trying to read reality, or nature itself, as a *hypertext*, in which there is no beginning or end, centre or margin, inside or outside, or any form of binary opposition: such a text has 'closure' only by reader-determination, and is infinitely recenterable, and multi-centred.   There is really no distinction between reader and text, but a collaborative collegium of ongoing 'writing' and fluid 'readings'.   Our efforts to 'know' are swept up into the ongoing 'known': they are part of the integral network, so to say.   Reality is a webbing of cosmic texts and person-interpretations.[2]

This new understanding of knowledge is reflected in the direction of studies of the functioning of the *human brain*.[3] Specifically, these studies are focussing on the mystery of consciousness.   They try to say what is going on in the brain when consciousness occurs.   There are three types of approach: materialist, idealist, and moderate realist.   It is the third approach that coheres with the philosophy of this book and with the new idea of information.

A *materialist* approach to consciousness would equate it with awareness, and then equate awareness with a combination of attention and short-term memory.   The primary model for it is visual awareness.   This is studied in animals as well as in humans, and is reduced to the functioning of certain neural mechanisms in a 'neuroscience of consciousness'.   It is a reductive, deterministic approach, that reduces consciousness to certain electro-physical charges.   Some claim a kind of 'neural Darwinism' as the core of consciousness, where specified groups of neurons compete to create effective representation of the world.

In contrast, an *idealist* approach to consciousness would ask why the performance of any of these physical functions is accompanied by the subjective experience called 'consciousness'. It would see this experience as irreducible, and see its primary model as the consciousness of selfhood. Information in the brain would have two aspects, one physical, and the other 'phenomenal'. The latter term is roughly equivalent to 'experiential' and 'subjective'. One is not reduced to the other. Physical systems and conscious states are phenomena of two distinct orders: the mystery is that one has the other. But the other is quite distinct and never allows its own mystery to be explained elsewhere.   Effectively, science can never understand consciousness, which is the preserve of philosophy.

The mid-way position of *moderate realism* tends these days to apply certain theories of contemporary physics to the functioning of the human brain. It tries to describe, with some plausible consonance, a manner in which the brain functions which can suggestively convey 'how' consciousness takes place.   To do so, it has recourse to some of the *models of physics*, especially to Complexity Theory and to Quantum Theory.

Those who use *complexity theory* have noticed that complex systems allow for the emergence of unpredictable and irreducible properties.   They suggest that the brain is such a system and that consciousness is such an emergent property.   Consciousness comes through as a leap into the unknown and beyond.

Roger Penrose is one thinker who is investing in *Quantum Theory* to help understand consciousness.   He is convinced that no deterministic rule-based system can account for the mind's creative ability.   He is looking for a new theory that will bridge classic and quantum mechanics and go beyond computation.   In effect, he sees consciousness as an effect of quantum activity of this kind in the brain.   He specifically sees it in micro-tubules, minute tunnels of protein that serve as a kind of skeleton for cells, including neurons.   Each neuron is a network within a network, and the holistic system (not the mechanistic switching on of neurons) is responsible for the emergent self-organising arising of consciousness.

Brian Josephson speaks of a subtle quantum effect that comes from a unified field theory that accounts for consciousness experience.   Ian Marshall has applied Heisenberg's uncertainty principle to the brain as a holistic system, and concluded that thought stems from quantum effects. Dana Zohar has acccepted and adapted their approach.

Perhaps consciousness is a quantum leap into a quantum world of information that is around us all the time?

The upshot of all this, is that there is a new epistemology emerging from the disciplines of science, and in particular of physics.   The key idea of it, 'information', demands a kind of knowing that is fully *'participative'*: we are not neutral observers of the real, we are swept up into the real that we know, and the knowing is the awaring of the being swept up.   This raises good questions for philosophy.

PHILOSOPHY

Philosophy is alert to the different *'logic'* implied by the 'information' approach.   Its interest is to specify what that logic really is.

Rather than pick up isolated points in the description of information, philosophy pays attention to the *whole story* of information.   For there is a story in it, a process of evolution.   And the evolutionary process of information is the real core of the information itself.

Let us once again review *cosmic history*.   In the earliest stages - pre Planck time, and with the Big Bang and its immediate consequences - there is no information, because there is no structure: the primordial appearance of matter is as something not yet structured.   As cosmic development goes on, information appears for the first time when matter is structured.   At pre-molecular levels, information is not great, and structure also is minimal, and the two, information and structure, could be perceived as virtually the same thing.

At the molecular level, something new occurs: the structure, that is, the information, appears to be somewhat independent of the matter that it structures and informs.   This introduces in the cosmos, the idea of a 'carrier' of information (or structure) or kind of infra-structure of information. An idea of matter as distinct from information and in some way serving information is developing.

With still more development of the cosmos, various informed infrastructures (or carriers) are seen to become increasingly cooperative. When life forms appear, this cooperation becomes coordinated in a very special way: in the appearance of life, information appears to transcend its own carrier infrastructure.   When we come to the level of human life, we meet a being that knows that the information that makes it be transcends all of the carrier infrastructures, and requires no definite specification of such structures. In this sense, the information that makes the human a knower is 'spiritual'.   There is a reality (this information) that is able to be independently of specific and determinate structure.   The knower, the human, then also appears to itself to be spiritual, that is, to be a spiritual self, whose openness informationally is too large to be contained in the particularity of matter and structure.

There is, from this point of view, an *evolution of information* which could also be called the *spiritualisation of information*.   What information has been trying to do throughout the cosmic time of its appearing, has been to present itself as spiritual.   Now that we appear to be entering into the 'age of information', in contrast to that of matter and energy, are we also entering into the epoch in which information can rejoice in being more spiritual than it has ever been?

This can be put in more technical philosophical terms.   The Age of Matter is epitomised by the analytic reduction of all things, e.g. to particles.   It is in philosophical language, the primacy of *material causes*, of what 'makes up' things.   The Age of Energy is epitomised by the primacy of mechanics and technology, that is, its interest is in dynamics. In philosophical language, this is the primacy of *efficient causality*, that is, of what 'makes things be'.   It could be sustained that there is a shift going on at present, from a focus on these two kinds of causality, to a focus on two other kinds of causality, namely, formal and final causality.

Final causality is what draws and attracts things to their ultimate meaning and purpose.   If we reflect on the drift of the cosmic history of information, perhaps we could propose that information has been progressively moving to a spiritualisation whose real and final purpose is union with the Ultimate Spirit, that is, God.   Every iota of information that ever was, was there only because drawn from its very roots across evolutionary history, to God.   Information in God is called the Word of God.   Every 'word' has always sought the Word.

Formal causality is what spells out the intrinsic meaning of anything, its form, or pattern, or beauty.   Perhaps we could suggest that the real inner meaning of everything is to be a relfection or participation in the meaning enshrined eternally in the divine Word.

An epistemology of information is an understanding of how the real meaning of everything is found in God, and how it is thus drawn to God. Nothing holds up in meaning without reference to God.   *Participative knowing* is participation in the Information that God is.

THEOLOGY

Have we already been in theology here?   Yes, but let us make one significant addition.

Throughout this study, I have made reference to the divine missions of the divine persons.   I have mentioned my attraction for what I believe to be the view of Aquinas, that the Persons have been sent out, not to be principles of a return to a God who is at rest, but to be permanent principles of the ongoingness of it all.   When I say, of it all, I mean the cosmos, and all the persons in it, human and divine.

May I suggest here that the ultimate purpose and inner beauty of all information is allow us to *participate, knowingly*, in the ongoingness of the eternal in time, that is, to become personal communional companions of the divine persons in their cosmic journey?

NOTES

1.   *The Science and Theology of Information* (Proceedings of Third European Conference for Science and Theology) eds., C.Wassermann, R.Kirby, B.Rordoff, Geneva, 1992.   See especially the contributions of Van der Lubbe/Laurent, Wassermann, Arecchi, and Schmitz Moorman.

2.   R.Fowler, The Fate of the notion of Canon in an Electronic Age, *Westar Institute Proceedings*, March 1994.   Reference is there made to the work of Bolter, Nelson, Landow, and Lanham.

3.   J.Horgan, Can Science Explain Consciousness?, *Scientific American*, July, 1994, 72-78.   See especially reference made here to Crick and Koch, Chalmers, Penrose, Josephson and Marshall.

CHAPTER 9

WHAT DIFFERENCE CAN IT MAKE?

Social science implications
of the vision

Where there is a different approach to beginnings, endings and middlings; where there is a different understanding of the make-up of the world and the harmony of its movement; where there is a different perception of its underflow, and even of its God; where knowledge is seen as a different kind of contemplation and participation in all of this; then we have a *different 'world-view'*. It could be sustained that different world-views give rise to different *conceptions of social living*. In this final chapter, I would like to draw out some of the implications for social living that I believe to be implicit in the different world view contained in the preceding chapters.

My argument is not that social perspectives depend on physics. It is rather that contemporary physics is the surfacing of a philosophy and a larger attitude to the world and to life and relationship, and that this philosophy and this attitude (which I call a 'world view') do make a difference to our options in the social sciences. What difference can a different vision make to a social world?[1]

I would like to suggest some differences of this kind, by focussing on the issue of *leadership*. It is the touchstone of many other social issues. My interest is less in the practice of social leadership than in its *concept*. There have been many models of the practice of leadership, ranging from top-down or highly authoritarian models, to bottom-up or highly democratic models. In church circles, there have been models of command and models of service. Beneath them all, there are conceptions of what leadership is supposed to be. I suggest that these conceptions depend on *certain implied world-views*. I would like to work then with a deliberate contrast between two such world-views, and their consequent conceptions of leadership. The first, *world-view (A)*, I assume to be the standard assumption in many approaches to leadership. The second, *world-view (B)*, I present as the conclusion from this study. Let us contrast the two, in reference to the qualities that describe them; to the function of consciousness implied in them; to the role model of leadership that derives from them; to the God-image that goes along with that; and to the psychological qualities congruent with that understanding. (See schema)

The *qualities* that are natural to world-view (A), are: part-ial, located, timed, interventionist, static. The adjective *'part-ial'* is written with a hyphen: it indicates that the focus is on the parts of the system. The system looks at the parts rather than at the whole, indeed, the whole, in its understanding, is the sum of the parts. The mood is analytic, atomistic, reductive, exploratory of the minutiae of detail, in which it tends to become lost. It is a mechanistic mentality.

The adjective *'timed'* indicates that everyone and everything is expected to be 'on time' and to perform at set times. Time becomes something absolute that must be served; it is not an instrument for human use. There is an assumption of synchrony: everyone experiences time at the same rate. The mentality is rather 'Newtonian': not even special relativity has had much influence here. It is the empire of the clock and the bell!

The adjective *'located'* indicates that everyone and every thing should always be in their (right) place, and if not, they should be 'put in their place' and so 'know their place'. The assumption is that when the proprieties are observed, all is well, and operates as it should. A certain hierarchy of place is not only presumed, but also inculcated. Certain places are off limits to those low down on the hierarchical scale. The emphasis is on a pre-ordained pattern of things.

SCHEMA: World-views and Leadership Conceptions

	WORLD-VIEW A	WORLD-VIEW B
QUALITIES	part-ial located timed interventionist static	holoversic rheomodal autochronic autocatalytic morphogenic
FUNCTION OF CONSCIOUSNESS	Rational coordination of predeterminates	Specular/eidetic and euphoric
ROLE MODEL OF LEADERSHIP	Planner organiser executive specialist	Intrinsic visual rejoicer (IVR)
GOD IMAGE	Managerial master-planner	IVR of cosmos
PSYCHOLOGICAL QUALITIES	Directive evaluative executive supervisory responsible	Mutuality sense of 'we' enablement of vision joy shared

The role of the leader in this understanding of things is 'interventionist': that is, the leader has to make sure everything is as it should be, and if it is not, has to intervene to make it so.   Vigilance and rectifying action characterise the leadership.   It is a 'mission control', or 'monitoring' model.   Again, at root, it is a mechanical model, as the leader ensures that parts not working well are 'fixed up', primed and oiled, to ensure maximum efficiency of output.   The leader intervenes to run a well-oiled machine.   To change the metaphor, it is a tight ship!

The *qualities* that are natural to world-view (B) are deliberately expressed in unusual and strange words, to spell out the marked difference from the previous world-view.   They are: holoversic, rheomodal, autochronic, autocatalytic, and morphogenic.   The adjective *'holoversic'* is a compound of the Greek 'holistic' and the Latin 'universal'.   It indicates that we are not talking directly about parts, but about the whole.   It is William Blake's 'universe in a grain of sand'.   Everything is enfolded, implied in, folded into, everything else: it is David Bohm's implicate order.   All is in everything, and everything is in all.   In effect, someone who looks at a system in this way, does not see autonomous parts there at all.   No part is ever expected to be able to function outside the whole system.   The vision is different.

The adjective *'rheomodal'* comes from the Greek root, rheos, which means a current, or the flow of a river.   The adjective suggests an attitude that appreciates the flowingness of everything, the natural capacity of the whole system to be what it is, and to move in its own way.   You cannot impose some extrinsic model of life on a cell that is already in possession of its own life: you can pick up the sense and the pace of that life, and move and flow with it.   It is like 'flowing with mystery'.

The adjective *'autochronic'* suggests that each person has his or her own time frame.   Each subgroup does too.   It is a case of an individual sense of timing, rather than of 'time' in general.   It is like a biological or psychological clock, or rhythm.   We are not all time symmetrical, as the assumptions of world-view A would have it (and as Newton presumed). We all have our different internal (and at times external) age and pace. In this mentality, people are helped to move as they are able, and not made to move as they are unable.

The adjective *'autocatalytic'* is a deliberate contradiction in terms.   A catalyst prompts a reaction without becoming an ingredient in the reaction. Here a system is proposed as being a catalyst to itself, so that it enables its own action, of which it is also an agent.   The suggestion is that the system is something like a 'dissipative structure'.   It is not content with entropy, and quiet, balanced equilibrium.   It accepts chaos, wants to go along with it rather than against it, wants even to create the possibility of its increase.   There is a confidence that when the chaos gets to a certain level, the system will metabolise it, and convert it into positive and creative energy.   Of course, there is need for quite a deal of trust in waiting for that to happen.

'Morphogenic' means engendering pattern.   It is the capacity to create appropriate structure where none was thought possible or creatable.   It is like letting patterns spontaneously form and seeing where they take you. The contrast to this attitude is a kind of fundamentalism about structures - a 'morphological fundamentalism' - that assumes there is only one kind of structure namely the one that has always been.   It is a 'static' mentality. "Morphogenic' realism is prepared to watch the growth of a living thing, and be positively surprised at its capacity to engender a life pattern that is life giving for it.   System break-down is the obverse side of system break-through.   It is like swimming with a rip tide in the ocean, rather than fighting it, and being carried by it to shore at some other place than where you entered the water.

These descriptive qualities of the two world-views allow us to focus on the different *function of consciousness* in each approach.   Under this heading, I am really asking how a leader uses his/her intelligence in exercising leadership.   In the first *world-view (A)*, the leader's job is to be a rational coordinator of predeterminates.   That is, the leader tries to be rational, clear, and organised in controlling a whole series of predefined and predetermined factors.   This rational way is only one possible way of using intelligence, which is a larger thing than rationality.   In the second *world-view (B)*, the leader uses intelligence by becoming a facilitator, a catalyst, a recogniser and an appreciator of others' talents.   The leader becomes (intelligently) like a mirror, in order to allow the whole system to see itself, and to realise it is doing well and so to continue to do so. The leader allows the group to 'mirror' itself - the function is *'specular'*, after the Latin, speculum, mirror.   When this happens, the group gets excited, even euphoric, not about the qualities of the leader, but about its own qualities which it has recognised in the mirroring provided by this kind of leadership. The leader provides the *eidos*, the space in which the group can find and appreciate its own image, and the result is happiness and joy - *euphoria* - in the group. This is a long way from economic rationalism?

When we look at *role models* for the two approaches, we can name what is appropriate for the first *world-view (A)* without difficulty. We are familiar with the role of a planner, organiser, executive. Indeed, we naturally deduce that the more specialised skills a person has, the better will they handle the role. In *world-view (B)* it is different: as a model, we are looking for someone intrinsic to the group and not an expert outside it; for someone who sees things, and enables others to see things, rather than for someone who does things, and enables others to do things; for someone who is positive and rejoicing and so enabling of positive rejoicing in and by the group itself. The phrase I have chosen for such a role model is *'Intrinsic Visual Rejoicer' (IVR)*. It is enablement by joyful vision, rather than management by objectives and organisation. Such a leader has flair, in communicating group positivity. When dysfunction and conflict occur in the group, the leader as it were angles the mirror so that the group sees the underlying 'goodness' in the conflict: only a group that was already strong and had a sense of its own belonging, would risk certain levels of conflict. What emerges from the vision is the amount of real concern and care that is going on in the whole group, and that realisation triggers a new positivity.

The *God-image* that implicitly undergirds each role model, for each world-view, is very different. For *(A)*, God is the greatest organiser ever, a supreme manager, who specialises in cosmos ! For *(B)*, God is a quiet mystery in which the cosmos can see itself (rather than see God), and in so doing catches the delight of God in a cosmos delighting in itself. Creation is a glimmer of the rejoicing happiness of God. There is, in Hopkins' phrase, the 'dearest freshness deep down things'. God looks at the cosmos, smiles at it, and communicates to it both God's own, and the cosmos' own, euphoria, because they are one and the same. Ecstatic enabling comes out of the excitement of God. God is the *supreme IVR!* This is close to the core of covenant thinking, as we have explored it.

The *Trinity* can be seen in this light.   The first person is the Rejoicer;   the second person is the image, or living mirror of the Rejoicer;   and the third person is the excitement, the euphoria between the two.   The Trinity is the source and origination of the excitement in the cosmos, and the cosmos vibrates with God's enjoyment.

The difference between the two world-views come out clearly here as one between *power and beauty*.   In world-view (A), God is an organiser, with power.   In world-view (B), God is a rejoicing person, with the passion of a person.

The *psychological qualities* that fit the two models are by now easy enough to estimate.   The one is directive, evaluative, executive, supervisory and responsible;   the other is nurturing, enabling, energising, visionary.   The one is full of individual responsibility and hierarchical accountability;   the other is an open mutuality, where 'we' work, happily, together.

It is possible to undertake *a loss-gain analysis* of the two models of leadership, (A) and (B).   In many ways, what one model gains, the other loses, and vice-versa.

The *gains of model (A)*:   you get better extrinsic management and more pattern and predictability;   the group members better internalise the stated group goals and targets;   there is a larger capacity for corporate action on an organised task;   the logic of the group is clear, and the criteria are in place for evaluating its performance.   The *losses of model (A)*:   there is a certain real loss of creativity, novelty, and associated relationship and ego functioning.   Persons are not enticed into being more personal in a group like this.   Its regimentation is not conducive to spontaneous problem solving, and positively developmental thinking.   When the members are often told, and wish to be told, what to do and what to think: and the result is that very often they lose the capacity to do much, or to think constructively.

The *gains of model (B)*:   you get an enlargement of life, a larger scope for personal creativity and participation;   there is more *personal* ownership of the groups' personally conceived tasks, in contrast to structural identification with the group's way of doing 'things'.   There is an invocation of life into the whole group.   In one way, the members are enjoying themselves and don't seem to be doing much; in another, paradoxical, way, they actually do more! *The losses of model (B)*: command and control are not strong, stability is not strong, superego functions are not strong. It is possible that the group may at times be perceived to be achieving less, depending on the criteria of the assessment. The group appears more chaotic and 'messy' than model (A), and less 'neat'.

Is it possible to have the *best of both worlds*? We would all like to. *Nature* itself seems to have done so, when, as it were, it has operated along the lines of model (B) at quantal level, and then made the transition to classical physics and used model (A). If this analogy is true, then nature has not used model (A) except on the foundation of a profound respect for and use of model (B). Is nature inviting us, through the perceptions of world-view that are emergent now, to imitate it in this?

What could a leader do, in practice, to function along such lines? I will hazard a suggestion, of *ten non-commandments* for such leadership.

1. *Be around*. There is a wonderful metaphor there: 'around'. Not isolated in predetermined places, nor inaccessible except at stated hours. To parody Heisenberg's Uncertainty Principle, if the group knows the position of the leader at all times, the leader will be perceived as having no momentum!

2. *Person* (in cosmos) is always a more profound value than worker (in institution). This suggests a deep appreciation of the values that are properly personal, those of mutuality and enlargement (communion and differentiation). A leader ought not demand technozoic things at the price of ecozoic things!

3. *Possibilities* are more interesting than predeterminates. What is predetermined is really a fossilised form of past possibility. The system is open, not closed. Entropy is overcome by self-organisation.

4. *Articulation* is important: especially of the processes that are going on in the group, much more than of the ideals of the group, or of assessment of group performance.

5. *Don't play off* one dimension of the group against another, especially, for example, the micro against the macro, or vice-versa.   Such activity is a form of killing.

6. *'Surprises'* are a better thing to look for, and stay with, than 'unresolvables'.   When things look unresolvable, expect a surprise!

7. *Rules* are rules, but that is all they are.   In practice, they are expressions of what it means to behave politely in this group.   They are a good idea, but not the be-all and end-all of the group.   They serve life, not vice-versa.

8. *Informal* things are often much more important than formal things.

9. In spelling out to the group what is going on in it, make sure that the group *sees its beautifulness* in a new way.

10. Develop a *catholic, or holistic, imagination* in the group.   Einstein once said that imagination was more important than knowledge.   Did he mean that model (B) was more important than model (A)?

The underlying real issue, in the application of the new world-view to leadership, and to community in the social sense, is the *attitude* people form to that *world-view itself*.   Some as yet do not know it.   Increasingly, many do.   Those who do have to take a position in regard to it, a position which challenges positions perhaps already taken in regard to *inherited world-views*, for example, those of the official church.   Without being judgmental, we could schematise *four basic attitudes* here: see schema.

This schema is *a logical square*, constructed by the juxtaposition of two contradictory opposites.   The first opposition is that between those who regard the 'new world-view' as good and those who regard it as bad: some take a positive and others a negative, attitude to it.   The second opposition is that between those who regard their inherited culture as good, and those who regard it as bad: some take a positive, others a negative, attitude to it.   It is agreed that at times the taking of one position affects the taking of the other.   That is why the two sets are juxtaposed.

This arrangement allows us to create four basic points of view. *First*, let us look at genuine *conservatives*, who think positively in regard to the inherited culture (eg. church), and negatively in regard to their perception of the new world-view.   They do so because they believe there is something worth conserving which they perceive as challenged.

SCHEMA

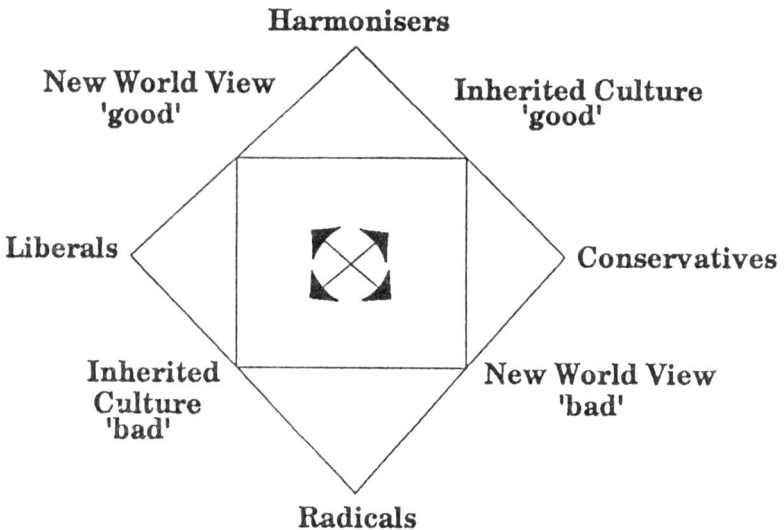

Harmonisers

New World View
'good'

Inherited Culture
'good'

Liberals

Conservatives

Inherited
Culture
'bad'

New World View
'bad'

Radicals

A *second* point of view is that of the *liberals*, who think positively in regard to the new world-view, and negatively in regard to the inherited culture (eg church) as they perceive it.   They do so because they perceive a freedom and a possibility for personal life in the former, which they perceive to be threatened by the latter.

A *third* point of view is that of the *harmonisers*, who attempt to take a positive position in regard to both the new world-view, and the inherited culture (eg church), as they perceive them both.   They do so to avoid any false opposition between the two, and much more so, because they believe that both are worth conserving, and both lead to a freedom and person hood that are worth achieving.

A *fourth* and final point of view is that of the *radicals*, who think negatively about both terms of reference, because neither satisfies their aspirations, and they are disenchanted with both.

One advantage of this schematic arrangement is that it avoids reducing problems to single and simple binary opposition.   Most real issues are a combination of more than one such opposition!   Of course, the model could be expanded by increasing the intersecting binary oppositions, but for our purposes, it would be too cumbersome to do that.

Our *question* might be: what would a *leader* who wished to function as an *Intrinsic Visual Rejoicer* do in a situation like this?   The oppositions seem unresolvable.

One response, from a scientific point of view, might be that the oppositions indicated are *unresolvable only on one plane*, that is, on the plane of the paper on which they are drawn.   Imagine attaching a string to each of the points of the square.   The strings could then be drawn together at some point which is not on the plane on which the oppositions are unresolvable!

Perhaps our whole attempt to draw metaphors of meaning from physics, philosophy, and theology, has been not unlike that.   Rather than harmonise what is not directly harmonisable, we have tried to suggest a plane of thinking on which all could find common ground for their irremovable differences.   A new communion, leading to a new and further differentiation?

§ § §

NOTES

1.   Perspectives parallel to those developed here may be found in D.O'Murchu, *Our World in Transition: making sense of a changing world*, Temple House Books, Sussex, 1992.

CONCLUSION

Seeing Differently

Words to say it: that is the title of a book by Marie Cardenal. It is her attempt, as an analysand, to put words on her own experience in psychoanalysis. It is her way of 'saying' that the human problem is always that of finding the 'words' to 'say' 'it'.

Modern physics has discovered a new 'it', and is always looking for new words to 'say' it.

Some of the older words are being dropped.

There was a time when we looked for the *'centre'* of everything, and thought it was earth, or our sun, or our solar system, or at least our galaxy. At least we thought it was somehow *'us'* - that we were the real centre of the universe! Physics is now telling us that the universe does not have 'a' centre at all: we just tell ourselves there is one, from whatever point of view we are taking. (Bad luck for 'centering' prayer?)

There was a time when we wanted to organise things, by making them move in straight lines as quickly as possible. Management by objectives! Physics is telling us that the universe is not constructed as a set of straight lines at all.... The apple may have fallen in a straight line on to Newton's head, but the particles that are the real stuff of the universe do not travel as directly as that.   The best way from A to B is not a straight line.

There was a time when we thought *time* was something absolute, and bowed to it, indeed almost worshipped it.   We took it to be 'there', outside of us, controlling us.   Physics is telling us that time is relative. Relative to the speed of light and the movement of the person trying to 'tell' the time.   If, in your imagination, you travelled by train at the speed of light, away from a clock you could still see, the clock would stand still.

No centres, no straight lines, no absolute time (there is no such thing as 'universal time').   What sort of world are we in?

A world of light.   Light is not something our eyes need to see 'reality'. Light is the reality.

We are not in a world of things, and spaces with centres, and straight line travel, and time that measures velocities.   We are in light.   Light that seems to play in its own way.   Light that makes its own different *patterns*.

What are they?   We look at a trampoline and the surface seems flat. Until we bounce on it.   Then the weight of our body changes its shape, and makes it *curved*.   You can imagine the universe like that.   A kind of trampoline, on which the mass of the matter in the universe 'bounces'. The 'lines' of the universe could not be straight, they curve and warp under the 'weight'.   The shortest distance between two points is a curve.

Imagine a universe of multiple and different curvatures. You could use the metaphor of a *'field'* (as long as it was not square or flat).   Call it a *matrix* if you like.   Physics calls it a *'system'*.   Ordinary mathematics can't handle it.   Bad luck for Euclid!   You have to develop a different mathematics for a different situation.

Light plays along the different 'lines' of this manifold curvature.

Physics has learned not to speak easily of this curved *'light-world'* as a 'space'.   And not to speak easily of the 'time' light would take to travel along these beautiful paths.   So it invents a new word, to say 'it': it calls it *'space-time'* and claims it is four dimensional.   As if height, and breadth, and depth, and time, were four dimensions of a new and wonderful 'arena', a *curved 'geometry'*, where the light moves in patterns of its own beauty.

Sometimes, at solar eclipses, scientists get excited when they actually see the light *'bend'*.

A universe like this is impossible to 'imagine'.   Our imaginations are geared to three dimensions of space.   We cannot even imagine time, we have to look at a clock.   We cannot form *'pictures'* of the universe physics is trying to disclose to us.   It is against our intuitions and our expectations. We can't 'picture' it.

One of the hardest things is to 'imagine' *'where'* the universe is.   There isn't any 'where' outside the universe, so it can't be 'anywhere' that isn't 'it'.   There is no *'container-space'* all round it.   It is just itself.

When physics thinks like this, it gets excited.   But its excitement stays humble, because at a few points its new principles don't hold up.

It is consistent with its principles to think that there might be some 'places' in the universe where the 'weight' of matter was so strong that it 'bent' the lines and curves inward so much that even mathematics couldn't 'say' what was going on.   There would be at least one dimension that could seem to be *'infinite'*.   Physics does not like infinities like this, and prefers to think its rules don't apply here.   In other words, we don't know what is going on: we have not found the 'words to say it'.   In such imagined situations, light would travel as it were 'inside' the tight warp and would never get 'out' to us.   It would be a 'black hole' and no information could ever get over the 'edge' or event-horizon.   All this is just saying that *we don't have a complete theory of the universe.*

This is where Quantum Theory helps - a little.   A quantum is a lump that jumps.   To say that it is a lump, is to say that the universe is ultimately made up of small 'packets' of matter and energy that are not continuous with one another, that is, they are 'discrete'.   And these packets, or lumps, change their energy levels jumping from one such level to another.   Now imagine that these jumping lumps are actually jumping lumps of light. This is what light is 'made up of', and this is how it 'plays'.

But there is more to it.   Physics likes to talk about particles, and waves. Are these little quanta, particles, or are they waves?   The best answer is - we are not sure.   Because if we set up experiments to see if they are particles, they turn out to be particles.   And if we set up experiments to see if they are waves, they turn out to be waves!   What the scientific observer does in measuring them, *determines* how they present themselves. There is no such thing as a neutral observer, detached and independent. The observer is part (participant) of the whole system.

It is not as though nature is trying to be facetious.   When physicists talk, sometimes they give the impression that before observation takes place, there are *neither* particles nor waves 'there';   and at other times, they give the impression that 'something' is 'there' - 'something' that has *integrated* whatever 'particle' means, and whatever 'wave' means: our problem is that when we pick up one side of it, we can never see the other.   The dimensions are *complementary*, but we stay *uncertain* about the ones we don't and can't contact.   True, we measure very accurately indeed the length, the mass, the density, etc. of the quanta (and as a result develop transistors, lasers, superconductors, etc.), but at root we don't and can't know 'what' they really are.   And every time we try, we bring ourselves into the act of observation, and never see what things are like, so to say, 'without' us.

At root, *we don't know*.   Nature has been called a Tao in a London fog. Space is a swarming in the eyes.   Time is a singing in the ears.   There *is* a dearest freshness deep down things.   Mystery everywhere.

I said that we can measure, accurately, but there are moments when we can't.   Measurement means mathematics, and mathematics means numbers.   Numbers have to refer to something real, or they mean nothing.   When the numbers hit what is called the *Planck Wall*, they have no real referent any more.   You can still use them, but they don't mean anything real.   It would be like talking about being one degree north of the North Pole.   Physics - Quantum physics - knows exactly in the micro world when the Planck limit is reached.   But beyond that?   Everything smears into uncertainty.

It is a strange world.   Lumps-jumps;   particles-waves;   complementaries-uncertainties;   observations-measurements;   real numbers - numbers without real referents;   Planck walls and limits... And its strangeness allows the presence of what any where else would be called *anomalies*, paradoxes, if not outright contradictions.   Such as: the instantaneous presence of events that would other wise seem distant in time, and the immediate influence of one thing on another, when they are not seemingly in the same 'locality'.

When mystery is invoked, there is *no complete theory* of the universe.

Does all this apply only to the very small, micro, levels of the universe? In Quantum Theory, yes, but there are other strange things that physics has become aware of at the *macro* level.

We speak, ordinarily, of things being 'as regular as clockwork'. A lot of things aren't.   Weather patterns.   Snow drifts.   Water turbulence. Insect populations.   The Red Spot in Jupiter.   Fluctuations on the stock market.   Many others.   What is happening here is the supersensitivity of the system to the initial conditions written into the system at its origins. If there are tiny variables in those conditions at the beginning, there can be major and even massive *fluctuations* in the behaviour of the system downtrack.   This means that it is hard, not to say impossible, to make accurate *predictions* about the behaviour of the system.   As Bonhoeffer said once in another context, we do not know what it will not do.

I have tried to sketch the kind of vision that physics has of the universe today.   It is a case of *'seeing differently'*.   Relativity, Quantum, and Complexity Theories combine to 'say' 'it' differently.   They teach us to see things as a whole ('holistically'), as they emerge ('historically'), in their situation ('contextually'), being alert to the way we are coming to know them ('epistemologically') and to the limits of our knowing ('humbly').

How does this vision of things sit with the tenets of a realist *philosophy and theology*?

Philosophy has some basic *principles* about which it is always very sensitive. Things are understandable;   there is always a sufficient reason for what happens;   every effect has a cause;   things have natures, and there are laws that tell us how nature works;   evolution is acceptable as long as there is a cause to explain the evolutionary jumps.   When realist philosophers reflect on the new world-view of physics, in the light of such principles, they come up with the verdict that there is no basic contradiction.

Realist philosophy is 'realist' mostly because of its conviction about *being*.

It is very hard to put words on the idea of being.   We all 'know' what it means.   We have a raw and immediate experience of the realness of it all, real be-ing.   It is not just the fact that we are 'around'.   We are more than just another instance of a lot of possibilities.   We are more than what can be described about us.   We *ARE*.   Physics can't measure it, mathematics can't number it, poets can't even name it, but it *IS*.   The sense of being is a precious thing: it gives us stability in the midst of changing descriptions of our world, and it gives us an invitation to ponder a reality that is deeper than change. It touches the MORE....

The philosophical tradition has often been quite sensitive about its insight into being.   It has refused to give it features, or allow it to be described.

At present, some philosophers are realising that being can be *described*, without losing any of its integrity.   Being at its best is Personal: the highest beings are *Persons*.   If we could spell out how Persons act as Persons, we could be spelling out, also, how being acts as being: we would be 'describing' being.

But not all beings are persons.   Only the higher ones.   What about the others, the lower ones, the *material beings* that are the principal interest of physics?

If we spell out how they function, it turns out that it is similar to the way persons function.   Something of what we see in persons is already there in 'nature'.   So we could use what we know from modern physics, in its descriptions of the universe, and put it to work to help us understand being itself.   We would come to see the parallels between the personal and non-personal worlds, and realise the way being operates everywhere.

This is what philosophy is starting to do.   To look at a personal world, and see what is happening;   to look at a material world, and see what is happening;   to realise that the two are *quite alike*;   to see how being expresses itself everywhere. It is a different way of doing philosophy.

Theology has to be involved in all of this.

There are three faith-traditions that come from Abraham: Israel, Christianity, Islam.   All three approach God as Creator.   Aquinas synthesised the intuitions of all three, when he grasped God, Being, as the Creator of all beings.   That means that God is so intimate to all beings that without God-Being, they cannot be at all.   Their being is a sharing in the Being of God.   God in that sense is an *'Insider'* within all being. Later theology changed this perspective.   It got so interested in the power of God, and what God could do, that it forgot God as Being and how God IS.   It made God an *outsider* to creation, and the presentation of both

God and creation lost out badly.   Theology is getting back to its real roots at present.

We are, overall, in a different way of seeing things.   In this different way, we can ask (differently from the past):

> *how did the universe begin?*
> *will it end?*
> *how does it work in the meantime?*
> *what sort of energy is in it?*
> *what is it made of?*
> *who is God?*
> *how do we know?*
> *can we live differently as a result?*

It is true that the different disciplines - physics, philosophy, and theology - speak in different languages, and that sometimes they are strange languages that make sense only inside a particular discipline.   It is possible to criticise each and all of them.   But it is also possible to benefit from them all, and hear what they are trying to say about an attitude to reality, to persons, and to the universe that may make sense today.

That is what we have tried to do here.

- - - - -

What is it that we thus see, differently?

We see Being, the Creator, as *Giver.* Giver of a Gift, that, received within our limits, makes us share in the unboundariedness of the Giver, and so become persons who go on giving to others.   We glimpse how the Giver 'sees into us' this gift of being, and constantly does so, as long as we are.

We see that in God, in the person, in the cosmos, there is always *'more'*, and that the 'more' is a Grace that is as permanent as being itself.   We see an ultimacy that is beyond images of beginnings and endings, an ultimacy whose real name is love.

We see life now, in the person, and in the cosmos, as an intouchness with the ebb and flow of communion and differentiation, so that, while there is *never absence*, there is *always novelty*.

We fumble for the words to say it.   We cannot find the words, and begin to hear the *music* of it all.   It seems to capture the movement, the underflow.

We are in *metaphor*.   Metaphors of communion, music, presence, emergence, and joy.   Avenues into the mystery of being.

We look for *a real God* at the core of this reality.   A God 'with' us, 'with' it all.   A God covenanted.   A God descending with all the divine fullness of Being into human and cosmic nature: a God joyful in what is not-God, in what is with-God.

We look for a God so personal that God's name is *Ongoingness* and *Outgoingness*: always.

We know we are from-God, with-God, and for the Ongoingness and Outgoingness that is God.   We know that we know reality only when we know, from the inside, the mystery of the involvement of ourselves and our cosmos, in the mystery of the Ongoing and Outgoing God.

We look for ways to *see it all joyfully, from the inside*, and so become persons in the cosmos of God.

In this way, we see the enigma of death, and see it as a letting go into living vision.   We call it a passing over, and see it as a share in the Christic and cosmic passover.   And we change the word, passover, into 'mission', to bring out the personal outreach that is beyond, and through, all boundaries.

- - - - -

This book has worked with *metaphors* for these mysteries.   It has, intentionally, been a footnote to the texts of those who have laboured at the limit point of disciplines that come near the mysteries in their different ways.

I have taken from Norris Clarke, an intuition that *personal metaphors* for being, are valid.   I have taken the liberty of extending those metaphors from person to *cosmos*, because I have learned to see in the cosmos reflections of what I have learned to see in persons.

I have taken from David Burrell, an intuition that Creator-Being *sees actively*, and the vision is creation.   I have taken the liberty of extending the adverb, 'actively', to the adverb, 'personally', because I have come to see that personal seeing is the only real seeing.   Creation mirrors personhood because it is a personal vision.

I have taken from contemporary physics (especially from those who work at the edges of relativity, quantum, complexity and self-organisation theories, and fused them together), an intuition that there is an *'aliveness'* in all reality.   I have taken the liberty, when physicists back away from their own metaphors and insist on 'hard' language, of staying with the metaphors, and putting them to work, to interpret a philosophy of being, and a theology of divine personhood.

In the end, it is perhaps best that physics remains physics, and philosophy remains philosophy, and theology remains theology.   But our journey has brought out something of their *convergence*.   While they do not, should not, and cannot speak in the same way or about the same things, they do, will, and must - at their limit points - *fumble with the same metaphors*.

Are we then left with metaphor?

I think not.   For a *metaphor* is an overture to something with which we are already in communion, something from which we are joyfully different yet never absent.

Presence.

BIBLIOGRAPHY

1. PHYSICS

A. General introduction.

E.R.Harrison, *Cosmology, the science of the universe*, Cambridge University Press, 1981.

W.Kaufmann, *Universe*, W.H.Freeman and Co., New York, 1991 (3rd edition).

T.Snow, *The Dynamic Universe*, West Publishing Co.,1991, (4th edition.

B. Historical introduction.

A.Lightman, R.Brawer, *Origins: the lives and worlds of modern cosmologists*, Harvard University Press, 1991.

D.Overbye, *Lonely Hearts of the Cosmos: the scientific quest for the secret of the universe*, Harper Collins, 1991.

C. Theoretical introduction.

P.Davies, ed., *The New Physics*, Cambridge University Press, 1990.
T.Hey, P.Walters, *The Quantum Universe*, Cambridge University Press, 1987.

N.Herbert, *Quantum Reality: beyond the new physics... an incursion into metaphysics and the meaning of reality,* Doubleday, 1985.

J.Polkinghorne, *The Quantum World*, Penguin, 1990.

D. Value-significant introduction.

J.Briggs, F.Peat, *Looking Glass Universe: the emerging science of wholeness*, Simon and Schuster, New York, 1984.

D.Bohm, F.Peat, *Science, Order, and Creativity: a dramatic new look at the creative roots of science and life,* Bantam Books, 1987.

E.   Popular introduction.

R.Weber, *Dialogues with Scientists and Sages, the search for unity,* Penguin, 1986.

F.Capra, *Uncommon Wisdom: conversations with remarkable people,* Bantam Books, 1989.

F.Capra, D.Steindl-Rast, T.Matus, *Belonging to the Universe, new thinking about God and nature,* Penguin, 1992.

D.O'Murchu, *Our World in Transition: making sense of a changing world,* Temple House Books, Sussex, 1992.

2.   PHYSICS AND RELIGIOUS STUDIES.

A.   Historical perspectives.

C.Kaiser, *Creation and the History of Science*, Marshall Pickering and Co., London, 1991.

J.Trusted, *Physics and Metaphysics: theories of space and time,* Routledge, Kegan, Paul, London, 1991.

J.Brooke, *Science and Religion: some historical perspectives,* Cambridge University Press, 1991.

B.   Speculative perspectives.

S.Toulmin, *The return to Cosmology: postmodern science and the theology of nature,* University of California Press, 1985.

A.Peacocke, *Creation and the World of Science* (The Bamptom Lectures), Clarendon Press, Oxford, 1979.

J.Polkinghorne, *Reason and Reality: the relationship between science and theology,* SPCK, London, 1991.

P.Clayton, *Explanation from Physics to Theology: an essay in rationality and religion,* Yale University Press, 1989.

P.Mar Gregorios, *The Human Presence: ecological spirituality and the age of the Spirit,* Amity House, New York, 1987.

K.Schmitz Moorman, *Evolution in a Roman Catholic Perspective, in Evolution and Creation: a European Perspective,* eds., S.Andersen, A.Peacocke, Aarhus University Press, 1987.

3.   COSMIC HISTORY.

A.   Descriptive studies.

B.Parker, *Creation: the story of the origin and evolution of the universe,* Plenum Press, London, 1988.

D.Darling, *Deep Time: the journey of a single subatomic particle from the moment of creation to the death of the universe and beyond,* Doubleday, 1989.

P.Coveney, R.Highfield, *The Arrow of Time: a voyage through time to solve science's greatest mystery,* Fawcett Columbine, New York, 1990.

S.Weinberg, *The First Three Minutes: a modern view of the origin of the universe,* Basic Books, 1977.

G.Smoot, *Wrinkles in Time,* Doubleday, 1993.

T.Berry, *The Dream of the Earth,* Sierra Book Club, San Francisco, 1990.

T.Berry, B.Swimme, *The Universe Story,* Harper, San Francisco, 1992.

D.Reanney, *The Death of Forever, a new future for human conscious-ness,* Longman Cheshire, London, 1991.

B.   Theoretical studies.

S.Hawking, *A Brief History of Time, from the Big Bang to Black Holes*, Bantam Books, 1988.

P.Davies, *God and the New Physics,* Simon and Schuster, New York, 1983.

P.Davies, *The Cosmic Blueprint: new discoveries in nature's ability to order the universe,* Simon and Schuster, New York, 1988.

P.Davies, J.Gribbin, *The Matter Myth: towards 21st century science,* Viking, 1991.

P.Davies, *The Mind of God: science and the search for ultimate meaning,* Simon and Schuster, New York, 1992.

W.Drees, *Beyond the Big Bang,* 1992.

W.Drees, Quantum Cosmologies and the 'Beginning', *Zygon* 1991, 373-396.

M.Reordan, D.Schramm, *The Shadows of Creation, dark matter and the structure of the universe,* W.H.Freeman and Co., New York, 1991.

J.Gribbin, M.Rees, *Cosmic Coincidences: dark matter mankind, and anthropic cosmology,* Black Swan, 1991.

S.Saunders, H.Brown, *The Philosophy of Vacuum,* Clarendon Press, Oxford, 1991.

A.Vilenkin, *Quantum Cosmology and the Initial State of the Universe,* Physical Review, 1988.

4.   COSMOLOGY AND PHILOSOPHICAL THEOLOGY: SYMPOSIA.

A.   Vatican Observatory Series.

The Galileo Affair: A Meeting of Faith and Science, eds., G.Coyne, M.Heller, J.Zycinski, Libreria Editrice Vaticana, 1985.

Newton and the New Direction in Science, eds., G.Coyne, M.Heller, J.Zycinski, Libreria Editrice Vaticana, 1988.

Physics, Philosophy, and Theology, eds., R.Russell, W.Stoeger, G.Coyne, University of Notre Dame Press, 1988.

Quantum Cosmology and the Laws of Nature, scientific perspectives on divine action, eds., R.Russell, N.Murphy, C.Isham, Vatican Observatory Publications, 1993.

B.   European Series (European Society for the Study of Science and Theology).

Evolution and Creation, a European Perspective, eds., S.Andersen, A.Peacocke, Aarhus University Press, 1987.

Science and Religion - One World, changing perspectives on reality, eds., J.Fennema, I.Paul, University of Twente Press, 1990.

The Science and Theology of Information, eds., C.Wassermann, R.Kirby, B.Rordorf, Geneva, Labor et Fides, 1992.

Origins, time and complexity, eds., G.Coyne, K.Schmitz Moorman, C.Wassermann, Geneva, Labor et Fides, 1993-4.

5.   THEORETICAL PHYSICS - ATTEMPTS AT SYNTHESIS.

A.   Overall horizons.

P.Davis, R.Hirsh, *The Mathematical Experience,* Penguin, 1986.

D.Hofstadtter, *Metamagical Themas: questing for the essence of mind and pattern,* Penguin, 1987.

R.Penrose, *The Emperor's New Mind, concerning computers, minds, and the laws of physics,* Oxford University Press, 1989.

M.Kafatos, R.Nadeau, *The conscious universe: part and whole in modern physical theory,* Springer Verlag, 1990.

J.Barrow, *Theories of Everything: the quest for ultimate explanation,* Clarendon Press, Oxford, 1991.

S.Weinberg, *The Dream of a Final Theory,* Simon and Schuster, New York, 1993.

B.   Self-organisation theories.

J.Gleick, *Chaos,* Viking Press, 1989.

M.Waldrop, *Complexity*, Viking Press, 1993.

R.Lewin, *Complexity,* J.M.Dent, 1993.

I.Prigogine, *From Being to Becoming: Time and Complexity in physical sciences,* W.H.Freeman and Co., New York, 1980.

I.Prigogine, I.Stengers, *Order out of Chaos: man's new dialogue with nature,* Bantam Books, Toronto, 1988.

R.Sheldrake, *A new science of life: the hypothesis of formative causation,* Collins, 1987.

R.Sheldrake, *The rebirth of nature: the greening of science and God,* Century, 1990.

E.Jaentsch, *The Self-Organising Universe: scientific and human implications of the emerging paradigms of evolution,* Oxford University Press, 1980.

D.Bohm, *Wholeness and the Implicate Order,* Routledge, Kegan, Paul, London, 1980.

D.Bohm, *Unfolding Meaning,* Ark Paperbacks, London, 1987.

D.Bohm, B.Hiley, *Quantum theory, an ontological interpretation,* London, 1993.

P.Davies, J.Brown, *Superstrings, a theory of everything,* Cambridge University Press, 1988.

E.Laszlo, *The Creative Cosmos,* a unified science of matter, life, and mind, Floris publications, 1993.

6.   PHILOSOPHY.   CONTEMPORARY REALIST TRADITION.

A.   Realism, retrieved and expanded.

Q.Lauer, *The Nature of Philosophical Inquiry, Aquinas Lecture,* Marquette University Press, 1989.

G.McCool, *Nineteenth Century Scholasticism, the search for a unitary method,* Fordham University Press, 1989.

G.McCool, *From Unity to Pluralism, the internal evolution of Thomism,* Fordham University Press, 1989.

G.McCool, The tradition of St.Thomas since Vatican II, *Theology Digest,* 1993, 324-335.

G.McCool, Why St. Thomas stays alive, *International Philosophical Quarterly,* 1990, 275-287.

G.McCool, The tradition of St.Thomas in North America: at 50 years, *The Modern Schoolman,* 1988, 185-206.

G.McCool, An alert and independent Thomist: William Norris Clarke,SJ, *International Philosophical Quarterly,* 1991, 2-22.

G.McCool, *The Universe as Journey: conversations with William Norris Clarke*, Fordham University Press, 1992.

W.Norris Clarke, To be is to be self-communicative, St.Thomas' view of personal being, *Theology Digest*, 1986, 441-454.

W.Norris Clarke, Person and Being in St.Thomas, *Communio,* 1991.

W.Norris Clarke, The 'We Are' of interpersonal dialogue as the starting point of metaphysics, *The Modern Schoolman*, 1992, 357-368.

W.Norris Clarke, To be is to be substance-in-relation, in *Metaphysics as Foundation: essays in honour of Ivor Leclerc,* eds. P.Bogaard, G.Treash, State University of New York Press, Albany, 1993.

W.Norris Clarke, Is natural theology still viable today? in *Prospects for a natural theology,* ed. E.Long, Catholic University of America Press, 1992.

W.Norris Clarke, Thomism and Contemporary Philosophical Pluralism, in *The Future of Thomism*, ed. D.Hudson, D.Moran, University of Notre Dame Press, 1992.

W.Norris Clarke, Fifty Years of Metaphysical Reflection, Suarez Lecture, Fordham University, in G.McCool, *The Universe as Journey,* Fordham University Press, 1992.

W.Norris Clarke, *Person and Being, Aquinas Lecture,* Marquette University Press, 1993.

Reviewed by G.McCool, *International Philosophical Quarterly,* 1993, 121-123.

Reviewed by J.M.McDermott, *Gregorianum,* 1994, 382-383.
Reviewed by D.Schindler, *Communio,* 1993, 580-592 (Norris Clarke on Person, Being, and St.Thomas) with response from Clarke, 593-598.

Reviewed by S.Long, *Communio*, 1994 151-161 (Divine and creaturely 'receptivity': the search for a middle term) and G.Blair, *Communio*, 1994, 162-164, with responses by Clarke (165-169) and Schindler, (The person: philosophy, theology, and receptivity), *Communio*, 1994, 172-190.

D.Burrell, *Aquinas: God and Action.* London, Routledge, 1979.

D.Burrell, *Knowing the Unknown God*, University of Notre Dame Press, 1986.

D.Burrell, B.McGinn, eds., *God and Creation*, University of Notre Dame Press, 1990.

D.Burrell, *Faith and Creation in Three Traditions*, University of Notre Dame Press, 1993.

D.Burrell, God's knowledge of future contingents, a reply to William Lane Craig, *Thomist,* 1993, 317-322.

R.McKinney, Towards the resolution of paradigm conflicts: holism vs. postmodernism, *Philosophy Today,* 1988, 299-311.

B.   Philosophy in dialogue with theoretical physics.

P.Heelen, Nature and its transformations, *Theological Studies*, 1972, 486-502.

S.Jaki, *God and the Cosmologists*, Washington, Gateway,1989.

S.Jaki, Thomas and the Universe, *Thomist*, 1989, 545-572.

J.Courcier, Chronique de philosophie des sciences: la signification des mathematiques et des langages formels selon Jean Dieudonne, Jules Vuillemin et Dominique Dubarle, *Revue des sciences philosophiques et théologiques*, 1989, 281-313.

J.Courcier, Bulletin de philosophie des sciences, *RSPT* 1990, 259-292.

A.Arnould, R.Bergeret, J.Fantino, R.Klaine, J.M.Maldamé, D.Renouard, Bulletin de théologie, théologie de la creation, *RSPT*, 1994, 95-124.

J.M.Maldamé, Quelle connaissance scientifique de l'au-de-la? *Lumière et Vie*, 1989, 15-28.

J.M.Maldamé, Place de l'homme dans l'universe, *Revue Thomiste*, 1990, 109-131.

J.M.Maldamé, *Le Christ et le cosmos, incidence de la cosmologie moderne sur la théologie*, Paris, Desclèe, 1993.

7. THEOLOGICAL TENTATIVES.

W.Pannenberg, Theology and the Philosophy of Science, Philadelphia, Westminster Press, 1976.

W.Pannenberg, *Metaphysics and the Idea of God*, Grand Rapids, W.Erdmans, 1990.

T.Peters, *God as Trinity: Relationality and Temporality in Divine Life*, Jn.Knox Press, 1993.

A.Gesché, J.Demaret, P.Gibert, R.Braque, P.Gisel, *Création et Salut*, Bruxelles, Facultés universitaires Saint-Louis, 1989.

J.Polkinghorne, *One World*, SPCK, London, 1986.

J.Polkinghorne, *Science and Creation*, SPCK, London, 1988.

J.Polkinghorne, *Science and Providence*, SPCK, London, 1989.

J.Polkinghorne, *Reason and Reality*, SPCK, London, 1991.

M.Balmary, *La Divine Origine: Dieu n'a pas créé l'homme*, Grasset, Paris, 1993.

A.Ganoczy, *Suche nach Gott auf den Wegen der Natur, Theologie, Mystik Naturwissenschaften, Ein kritischer Versuch.*   Dusseldorf, Patmos Verlag, 1992.

8.   CULTURAL AND SPIRITUAL REFLECTIONS.

D.Zohar, *The Quantum Self*, 1990.

D.Zohar, I.Marshall, *Quantum Society*, 1993.

D.Toolan, 'Nature is a Heraclitean Fire', reflections on cosmology in an ecological age, *Studies in the Spirituality of the Jesuits*, St.Louis, 1991.

D.O'Murchu, *Our World in Transition, making sense of a changing world*, Temple House Books, Sussex, 1992.

M.Wheatley, *Leadership and the New Science*, Beerett Publications, 1993.

ABOUT THE AUTHOR

Kevin F. O'Shea is an Australian philosopher-theologian and a Redemptorist priest. He has lectured for many years at Fordham University, the University of Notre Dame, and St. Norbert College. His academic work centers on the dialogue between the philosophy of Aquinas and contemporary cosmology, psychology, and history. His previous publications include *The Human Activity of the Word* (Thomist), *The Way of Tenderness* (Paulist), and *A Human Apostolate* (Liguori).